WHERE THE OLD ROADS GO

Driving the
First Federal Highways
of the Northeast

George Cantor

PERENNIAL LIBRARY

HARPER & ROW, PUBLISHERS, New York
Grand Rapids, Philadelphia, St. Louis, San Francisco
London, Singapore, Sydney, Tokyo, Toronto

FIRST EDITION

Designed by Cassandra J. Pappas

Library of Congress Cataloging-in-Publication Data

Cantor, George, 1941–
    Where the old roads go : driving the first federal highways of the northeast /
George Cantor. — 1st ed.
        p.   cm.
    ISBN 0-06-096508-8
      1. New England—Description and travel—1981– —Guide-Books.
    2. Automobiles—Road guides—New England.   3. New York
(State)— Descriptions and travel—1981– —Guide books.   4. Automobiles—
Road guides—New York (State)   5. Historic sites—New England—Guide-
books.   6. Historic sites—New York (State)—Guide-books.   I. Title.
    F2.3.C36   1990
    917.404'43—dc20   89-46079

---

90 91 92 93 94 CC/MPC 10 9 8 7 6 5 4 3 2 1

For my father,
who first took me
along the old roads.

Contents

Introduction

Sometime in the 1980s, U.S. 66 disappeared. Its passing was observed with genuine regret and an outpouring of television and newspaper features recalling sentimental journeys along its length. It was acknowledged that an important part of America's motoring past had somehow been allowed to slip away.

This had been the main road to California, the highway that called to John Steinbeck's Okies of the Dust Bowl years and to generations of travelers pursuing the western dream, either for a brief vacation or a new life. It had been celebrated in Bobby Troup's popular song of the 1940s, which catalogued the towns through which it ran on its way from Chicago to L.A. A television series was based on the adventures its heroes encountered on the road. Route 66 was engrained in American folklore, a contemporary version of the Oregon and Santa Fe trails. Now it was gone, swallowed whole by an Interstate system that had confiscated its route, obliterated its number and homogenized its experience.

This is a book about the old roads, like U.S. 66: where they go, how they got there, what remains of their past. They were created by the Federal Highway Act of 1921, which provided both for the expansion of a national highway system and for an orderly plan to number it. The act was the culmination of many years of lobbying by several local groups, most prominently the Lincoln

Highway Association. They sensed the enormous possibilities for commerce and tourism that would result from a federally planned system of routes. With the coming of the motor car, most states had built roads on the basis of local need, with no thought of linking them to the roads of adjacent states. They were indifferently maintained and confusingly marked, making trips of any length a trial by ordeal for motorized trailblazers.

But new sets of engineering standards set down by the Highway Act and, just as important, a plan for marking the roads in a continuous and logical manner changed the course of highway travel. Instead of a nightmare, the road became a romance, and Americans who had seldom traveled more than 20 miles from their birthplace were called to explore their native land.

Out of the welter of Lincoln Highways and Dixie Highways, these travelers learned to sort out a road by its number, illustrated by a distinctive, shield-shaped sign. Soon the numbers took on personalities of their own. U.S. 1—the East Coast Highway. U.S. 30 and U.S. 40—the great transcontinental routes through the heartland. U.S. 61—the River Road along the Mississippi. U.S. 101—the Pacific Coast Highway.

Many of them were built along the paths of far older roads. In the Northeast, they ran along Indian trails that were old when the Pilgrims landed. In the Midwest, they paralleled rivers, the first highways to the great western beyond. In the West, they followed the railroad tracks that had opened the country to settlement barely half a century before. As the roads were built, the country continued to grow along their paths, developing an automotive culture that soon became a familiar part of the American landscape: the tourist cabin and motel, the drive-in and gas station, the diner and billboard.

Then it all ended. Limited access highways were developed in the East in the 1930s, as an attempt to ease the already congested conditions on roads such as U.S. 1. These roads were called parkways and stressed aesthetics as well as convenience. By the start of World War II, the Pennsylvania Turnpike had been completed and dramatically sliced travel time across that mountainous state.

After the war, many parts of America embarked on projects to ease congestion along the older highways. Eastern states built toll roads bypassing the largest cities and linking major towns in a high-speed travel network. These roads were soon incorporated into the new Interstate system, which President Dwight D. Eisenhower signed into law thirty-five years after the first Highway Act.

By 1960, the Interstates had made nonstop travel of 1,000 miles and more a reality in the East. By the end of the decade, it was possible to travel from coast to coast without ever seeing a stoplight. Or a town. Or a country inn. National franchises for lodging and food grew right along with the Interstates. As land prices at the interchanges shot upwards, it was usually national franchisers who had the resources to buy and develop the property there. People in a hurry found it more convenient to reserve a room or eat a quick meal within a standardized format. The romance of the road had settled into a routine, and for many people it soon became an exercise in the humdrum.

The Interstates were a blessing for those with a load to haul or a meeting to make or bad weather to cope with or a night to drive through. For travelers in search of their country, however, Interstates led the wrong way. Instead of retracing the path of history, Interstates cut across its grain. They followed a route for which there was no other reason than ease of engineering. A sense of disconnection developed between traveler and environment. As William Least Heat Moon put it in his best-selling *Blue Highways,* "Life doesn't happen along the Interstates; it's against the law."

But the old roads are still there, and in many cases better than ever. If there is an adjacent Interstate, it drains off the heavy trucks and the long-haul drivers. The old roads are left with light, local traffic. More important, they retain the variety of a roadside that has been developing for two hundred years instead of twenty-five. They have a sense of character, a sense of place, which is the very thing the Interstates try to overcome.

After a couple of generations in the fast lane, many American drivers seem inclined to slow down and see what's out there. They're looking for something different. Call it roots or identity or merely nostalgia, but it has become a fast-growing portion of the travel industry. Country inns and bed and breakfasts have mushroomed. Restaurant owners have seen the possibilities of converting historic structures into eating places with a taste of the past. Many towns have taken the effort to dig into their heritage and develop attractions and festivals that explore it.

Old Roads is meant for this kind of traveler. It is by no means intended as a comprehensive guide. Instead, it takes each of the northeastern roads enumerated by the 1921 Highway Act, describes where it goes and mentions some of the more interesting things to see along the way. Some of the old roads are congested or urban or all but swallowed up by a parallel Interstate. I'll skim over these or try to locate side trips that bypass the crowds. The old roads we want are those far from the tentacles of urban sprawl, away from the Interstate system, where franchises seldom follow.

Every road is tracked from start to finish. Longer roads are divided into segments, each covering a separate region. Scenic drives and side trips are highlighted, as well as unusual local festivals and historical figures whose lives were entwined with the course of the roads. Many towns along the roads are printed in boldface type. The points of interest discussed in these places are listed at the end of each chapter in a segment called Visiting Hours, which gives the times and dates they are open. This information is accurate as of publication time, but it's a good idea to check by phone in advance.

No time frame is given for these drives. That is entirely up to the driver and passengers. These are essentially journeys of discovery, and the best parts are the unexpected: the odd sign, the unusual building, the people. You can't put a clock on trips like these. You won't find such things on the Interstates. But they are the lifeblood of the old roads.

There is no more U.S. 66. But an amazing thing occurred along its former path in the late 1980s. A few merchants, struck by the growing number of travelers who wandered by in search of the old route, formed an Original Route 66 Association. It highlighted many of the old roadside attractions. And more and more drivers began finding their way off the Interstate to see them.

Two of the old roads, U.S. 20 and 30, still make it clear across the country, from sea to shining sea. And there is still, thankfully, a U.S. 62. It runs from Niagara Falls, New York, to El Paso, Texas, across an America that remains astonishing in its diversity, thrilling in its scenery and inspiring in its ties to the past. There are plenty of highways like it. They meander far from the freeway. Strangers wave as you pass. This is where the old roads go.

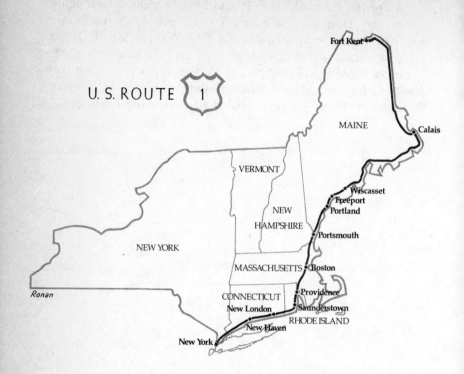

U. S. ROUTE 1

Fort Kent

MAINE

Calais

VERMONT

Wiscasset
Freeport
Portland

NEW
HAMPSHIRE

Portsmouth

NEW YORK

MASSACHUSETTS • Boston

Providence

CONNECTICUT

New London
Saunderstown

New Haven
RHODE ISLAND

New York

Ronan

The East's Main Street

U.S.1

It may not be the longest or the most scenic or even the most inviting of the old roads, but U.S. 1 is easily the most celebrated. It has been the subject of network television specials, countless magazine and newspaper articles and several guidebooks. It is, after all, Number One, and by that very digit attains a certain primacy. More than that, like a strong and slender thread it seems to bind its varied regions along a route that reflects the historical continuity of the eastern seaboard.

Still, for much of its run, U.S. 1 is a cluttered, congested, extremely unpleasant route. Between New York City and Washington, D.C., it is as nerve-grating and mind-deadening as a road can get. That very stretch of highway, in fact, was a major impetus for planning the first American expressways more than half a century ago, the initial turn away from the old roads. Nevertheless, in the northern portion of its route, along the Maine coast, through the sea-washed towns north of Boston and down the old Boston Post Road through southern Connecticut, U.S. 1 sometimes matches its own reputation.

THE ROCKBOUND COAST OF MAINE

Fort Kent to Bath, Maine
* 444 miles

This road leads through the heart of what most Americans have in mind when they visualize "the stern, rock-bound coast of Maine." Waves battering against tall cliffs. Huge boulders half hidden by the surf. Cozy villages clinging to the hillsides. Islands glimpsed across sun-dappled waters. Lobster fresh from a steaming kettle. This is the Maine of the travel posters. Especially in the 45 miles between Bucksport and Rockland, down the western edge of Penobscot Bay, the drive will enthrall and delight any traveler.

If you can, try to avoid the peak months of July and August. The little towns south of Belfast quickly lose their charm in the roar of weekend traffic. U.S. 1 is also such a winding road, following each indentation of the coast, that it is almost impossible to pass slow-moving vehicles. But why rush? The whole idea of traveling the old roads is taking it slow and seeing what's there.

* MILEPOSTS *

The drive begins at **Fort Kent**, a town famous for no other reason than being the start of U.S. 1. But this northernmost corner of Maine, the Aroostook, did have its brief, cranky moment in history. The border between Maine and the British colonies to the north was vaguely defined. Throughout the 1830s lumbermen from New Brunswick crossed over to cut rich stands of Maine timber. In the winter of 1839, Governor Edward Kent could bear no more. He sent the militia to fortify this frigid frontier and repel the invading tree-trimmers. A blockhouse was quickly erected at the St. John River and called Fort Kent to show that Maine meant business. By spring the so-called Aroostook War had cooled down without any casualties. Within three years, the Webster-Ashburton Treaty was signed, fixing the border permanently and saving Maine's forests for domestic lumbermen to ravage. The old blockhouse, off Main Street, is now a State Historic Site.

The lumbermen did such an efficient job once they secured exclusive rights that by the end of the nineteenth century logging had declined as the leading economic force in the area. You can still see remnants of it, though, in the huge Fraser Paper Mill in **Madawaska**.

This is Acadian country along the banks of the St. John River. Although the Canadian province on the opposite shore is New Brunswick, not Quebec, you are just as likely to hear French as English being spoken in the border towns. The French-speaking Acadians were forcibly removed from their homes in Canada by the British after 1755. Many were transported to the distant French colony of Louisiana where they became known as Cajuns and have kept alive their distinct language and culture to this day. Others simply made their way to the sparsely settled forests of the Aroostook and took up life much as they had known it in their old homes nearby. A marker at the rear of the church in St. David commemorates their first landing here in the 1780s. Many villages in this area, particularly Grand Isle, with its towering twin-spired church, preserve the look of old French Canada. These cultural roots are recalled at Acadian Village, north of **Van Buren**, which maintains several historic structures built by French-speaking settlers.

Large-scale logging activity continues in the state's interior, but in the Aroostook an alternative source of income had to be found. It came in the form of the potato. The short growing season of northern Maine was long enough for this crop and the soil was hospitable. By 1894, the Bangor and Aroostook Railroad had reached the area, along the route followed by U.S. 1, opening it to large-scale agriculture. Only the states of Idaho and Washington now grow more potatoes annually than Maine, and 90 percent of Maine's crop comes from the Aroostook. Huge warehouses line the road in Caribou. The University of Maine maintains an agricultural experiment station in **Presque Isle**, which is the commercial center of the county. Aroostook Farm, 2 miles south of Presque Isle, is involved in ongoing research to improve the strain. Free tours, but bring your own sour cream and chives.

Many farmers in this area are of Swedish descent. Their ancestors were brought here by contract arrangement in the 1870s. The Swedish influence is obvious in local names: you pass Stockholm Mountain north of Caribou, and just west of that town is the village of New Sweden, which still observes the traditional Midsummer Day festival.

As you pass through Mars Hill, you cross what the British contended was the border between Maine and Canada in the 1830s. No wonder the Aroostook went to war.

In Houlton everything stops when the potato crop comes in, including school. Children are traditionally dismissed from classes during that period to help bring in the harvest. Houlton's Potato Feast, held late in August, is the nation's biggest spud spectacular.

There are good views west from North Amity toward Mount Katahdin, the highest mountain in the state at 5,268 feet. In Weston, the views are toward the east to Grand Lake on the New Brunswick border. Between there and Princeton, the highway passes through an area of forests and lakes, well known to deer hunters and fishermen.

Despite past unpleasantness, the international border is quite amicable today. Nowhere is it friendlier than in Calais. The town shares police and library facilities with St. Stephen, its Canadian neighbor across the St. Croix River, and fire trucks respond to calls in both communities. Because New Brunswick's time is an hour earlier, Canadian tipplers traditionally take their last call on the Eastern Standard clock in Maine.

A few miles down the river is St. Croix Island (also known as Dochet Island) Historic Site. It marks the first European attempt to establish a permanent colony north of Florida on the American coast. Pierre du Guast, the Sieur de Monts, was given the French charter to the territory. Assisted by Samuel de Champlain and a force of seventy-five men, he established a base on this island in 1604 to scout out likely areas of settlement. They went up and down the Maine coast for two years, then decided they liked Nova Scotia better and left. Talk about hard to please. There is no public access to the island.

The highway reaches the 45th parallel and the Atlantic Ocean at Perry. This is the Bay of Fundy, noted for the extreme variations of its tides. At high tide, the powerful surge of water from the ocean causes coastal rivers to reverse direction and form fast-flowing waterfalls. If you happen to be passing through West Pembroke at this time of day, watch for the signs to Reversing Falls Park at Mahar's Point.

At Whiting, look for the turnoff to Maine 189. It is a short detour well worth taking, for both historic and geographic reasons. The bridge to **Campobello Island** starts at Lubec. Franklin D. Roosevelt spent many of his summers in the family cottage on this island. During one of these vacations, in 1921, he came down with the polio that left him unable to walk without leg braces for the rest of his life. The episode was dramatized in the Broadway success *Sunrise at Campobello,* which gave the island star quality in name recognition. Campobello actually belongs to the Canadian province of New Brunswick, and the Roosevelt home is part of an international park.

Continue from Lubec on the marked back road to South Lubec and Quoddy Head State Park. Sunrise at Quoddy Head may not have the same ring, but this is where you get to see it first—it is the easternmost point on the U.S. mainland. You can return to U.S. 1 by retracing your route from Whiting.

The deep indentations of the Maine coast make it a haven for sailing and photography. At the start of the eighteenth century, the same geography made this part of the coast preferred territory for pirates. Samuel Bellamy was the best known. He fancied himself a sort of Robin Hood of the Jolly Roger and he must have been persuasive about it—he frequently talked the crews of merchant vessels into joining his band of marauders. Since the alternative was too sad to contemplate, this did not require a great gift of rhetoric.

By the time Joe Burnham built his tavern in **Machias** in 1770, the renegade tradition of the coast was well established. Burnham Tavern became a favorite meeting place for colonial sympathizers. In the spring of 1775 they learned that the schooner *Margaretta* had been sent from Boston by the British to secure a timber supply, and they decided to act. Under Capt. Jeremiah O'Brien, they sailed out of Machiasport on June 12 and surprised the *Margaretta,* mortally wounding the British captain in the battle and capturing the vessel. This is regarded as the opening naval engagement of the Revolutionary War, and it helped win permanent funding of a navy by the Continental Congress. Burnham Tavern is on Main Street, just off U.S. 1.

Ninety percent of the country's blueberry production takes place in the area west of Machias. You'll pass through miles of "barrens," the local term for the treeless scrub in which the fruit thrives. (Oddly enough, one of the dictionary definitions for barren is "fruitless." Figure that out.) Machias holds a Blueberry Festival each August, and the University of Maine gives free tours of its Blueberry Hill farm, west of **Columbia Falls**.

After the Revolutionary War, this became a prosperous shipbuilding and trading area, and many of the towns along the route have preserved the fine homes built then. Watch especially for the Ruggles House in Columbia Falls, built in 1818 and famed for its spectacular flying staircase, and the Black House in **Ellsworth**, dating from the 1820s. Just east of Ellsworth, in Hancock, there are magnificent views south from the road toward Frenchman Bay, Mount Desert Island and Acadia National Park. Maine 3 heads south to Bar Harbor and the park from Ellsworth.

At **Bucksport**, U.S. 1 crosses the Penobscot River on the graceful Waldo-Hancock Bridge, a fit beginning to the most scenic portion of this drive. Four U.S. presidents have signed the register of the Jed Prouty Tavern, which opened its doors on Main Street, just off U.S. 1, in 1798. You can look it up, and also observe some of the terrible things one constituent had to say about John Tyler's executive capabilities. The Accursed Tombstone is in Buck Cemetery on Main Street and it shows what comes of hanging witches. The stone on the grave of the town's founder, Jonathan Buck, has the imprint of a woman's leg upon it, supposedly placed there by the dying curse of a witch Buck had ordered hanged. It's a bit hard to see what that was supposed to accomplish, but you know how witches are.

Just across the Penobscot bridge is Fort Knox, and the only curse upon it was that of sloth. It was planned as a defensive outpost during the Aroostook War, but Maine didn't get started on it until five years after the hostilities ended. No matter. The work dragged on for twenty years more, stopped only by the Civil War and more urgent business elsewhere. It is now a state park with fine views over the head of the bay.

Searsport was renowned as the cradle of captains during the age of sail, when men from this village circumnavigated the globe. Two vestiges of that era remain: Searsport is the leading antique shop stop in Maine, as bounty from those old voyages goes up for sale. And the Penobscot Marine Museum incorporates seven buildings in the heart of town to relate its nautical history in the great sailing days, with particular emphasis on the China trade.

The mountains come right down to the sea along the western shore of Penobscot Bay. The views are spectacular, and the best of all are south of Lincolnville in Camden Hills State Park. A road from U.S. 1 leads to the summit of Mount Battie and magnificent overlooks of the bay, its islands and the harbor in the pretty village of Camden far below. The scenery doesn't get any better than this.

Edna St. Vincent Millay, whose poetry won the 1923 Pulitzer Prize, was born in nearby Rockland. As a young woman, she recited her work during afternoon tea at the Whitehall Inn, in Camden. One of her wealthy listeners was so impressed that she arranged a college scholarship for the poet. The old inn, a captain's home built in 1834, is still there, the views from its broad porch sweeping unencumbered to the sea. Although tea is still served, poetry readings have been discontinued.

The dock area is especially atmospheric in **Rockland**, which is the largest fishing port in Maine. Its Lobster Festival, on the first weekend in August, is the biggest in New England and packs the town. The Farnsworth Museum, on Elm Street, which intersects U.S. 1, contains a fine collection of Maine-based artists, including Andrew Wyeth. He drew inspiration for some of his most popular works, including *Her Room,* while vacationing in the Rockland area. That painting is part of the Farnsworth collection.

Henry Knox served with George Washington through the Revolutionary War, succeeded him as commander in chief of the army, and was the nation's first secretary of war. After this active public career, he retired to Maine in 1795 and promptly lost most of his fortune in bad business deals. The reconstruction of his home, Montpelier, is located between Rockland and **Thomaston** and contains many of his possessions.

The Old German Meeting House in Waldoboro dates from 1772, and its charming, graceful interior is worth seeing. You get a glimpse of what the original settlers thought about the New World from a gravestone in the nearby cemetery, which reads "This town was settled in 1748 by Germans who immigrated to this place with the promise and expectation of finding a prosperous city, instead of which they found nothing but wilderness." The Maine Publicity Bureau does a better job today.

The Abnaki Indians came to the Damariscotta River for about two thousand years to harvest oysters. The shell heaps they left behind now cover 3 acres to a depth in some spots of 30 feet. This spot is one of the more unusual archaeological sites in the east. Watch for the signs leading to it as you approach the river from the east. The town celebrates an Oyster Festival in mid-July.

FOCUS

* * *

All the guidebooks call **Wiscasset** the prettiest town in Maine. The unanimity is amazing. Some of them don't even use a qualifier, as in "one of the prettiest towns in Maine." No halfway measures here. In a state liberally endowed with good-looking towns, such an accolade is both an invitation and a challenge to a traveler of old roads, provoking a combination of "Oh boy!" and "Oh yeah?"

It's a tiny place with fewer than 3,000 permanent residents, so the best idea is to leave the car somewhere on Main Street (U.S. 1) and strike out on foot to find out what makes it so wonderful.

Head back to the bridge across the Sheepscot River, and turn right on Water Street. In a few blocks you'll come upon an irresistible source of seacoast allure—a pair of scuttled ships. These two hulks, the *Luther Little* and the *Hesper,* have been delighting photographers since 1932 as they turn into picturesque ruins. The schooners were built when any practical commercial use for them was long past. New highways, such as U.S. 1, had penetrated this long-isolated area and supplanted vessels like these, delivering goods faster and cheaper. The owner soon repented of his folly and scuttled the two boats. Bad luck for him and a wonderful stroke of fortune for everyone who comes through Wiscasset with a camera. A sign at the pier urges tourists to contribute to a fund that will preserve the two vessels as wrecks. But it is their steady deterioration, the inexorable decay of the structures under the pounding of wave and weather, that is the fascination. They found a far greater fame in their ruin than they ever would have known in use.

Now turn back to Main and walk toward the middle of town. Wiscasset was home to a good many sea captains in the nineteenth century. Artists now make up the leading occupational group in residence. It is a natural progression. The previous century's rovers built fine, spacious homes with fortunes gathered from the sea. The combination of stately old homes and the ocean's proximity makes the setting perfect for those who seek visual inspiration in their roving.

The Nickels-Sortwell House on Main Street is open to visitors. Built in 1807 by Capt. William Nickels, it was locally admired for its graceful elliptical staircase, which rises to a third-floor skylight. Nickels only occupied this mansion for thirteen years. Afterward it became a hotel and was then purchased as a summer home by Alvin Sortwell, of Cambridge, Massachusetts. The furnishings now in the home belonged to the Sortwell family.

Behind this house, on Federal Street, is the Old Jail, built in 1811 and used for 102 years to cool off the troublesome. It is now a museum.

Now return to Main and continue up the hill to the Green, where the church and courthouse stand. At the crest, turn left on High Street. This is the loveliest of Wiscasset's streets, lined on either side with fine, white homes, their foundations in the sea. One of the houses has been turned into a museum of antique musical novelties and rare instruments. Called the Musical Wonder House, it gives you a chance to inspect the interior of one of these homes. At the end of the block, across Lee Street, is another Wiscasset showplace, Castle Tucker. Besides its view over the harbor, the Victorian mansion features fine period furnishings.

It wouldn't be right to leave town without a look at some of the local artistic output. Off Main, north of the Green, is the Old Academy, built in 1807, which now houses an art gallery of Wiscasset painters.

So, were the guidebooks wrong? Maybe only by the slimmest of adjectives. The praise may even have been restrained.

* * *

The Kennebec River is a traditional dividing line in Maine. It was the northern limit of the original Maine grant. South of here, the coast becomes regular, sandier, more accessible. It is also where U.S. 1 is joined by a spur of Interstate 95. All of which makes **Bath**, on the western bank of the Kennebec, a convenient place to end this drive. Famed as a shipbuilding center since colonial days, the Bath Iron Works still turns out vessels, albeit at a much reduced rate. Between 1862 and 1902, the town is credited with producing more than half the wooden sailing ships built in America. The Maine Maritime Center is a living history display on the site of former shipyards, recalling the heyday of this old port. There are old ships, views of construction in progress, rides along the Kennebec and land-based exhibits in a shipbuilder's mansion. The best of its kind in Maine.

VISITING HOURS

MAINE

Bath: Maine Maritime Center, (207) 443-1316. At 263 Washington St., south of U.S. 1, along the west bank of the Kennebec River. Daily, 10–5, mid-May–mid-October. Admission.

Bucksport: Jed Prouty Tavern, (207) 469-2371. At 52–54 Main St., off U.S. 1 on Maine 15. Daily, 8–8, all year. Free.
Fort Knox, (207) 469-7719. South on U.S. 1, across Penobscot River bridge. Daily, 9–dusk, May–October. Admission for adults.

Columbia Falls: Ruggles House, (207) 288-4939. On Main St., one-quarter mile off U.S. 1. Monday–Saturday, 9:30–4:30; Sunday, 11–4:30. June–mid-October. Donation.

Ellsworth: Black House, (207) 667-8671. On West Main St., off U.S. 1. Monday–Saturday, 10–5, June–mid-October. Admission.

Fort Kent: Historic Blockhouse, no phone. North edge of town, off U.S. 1. Daily, 9–9, Memorial Day–Labor Day. Free.

Lubec: Roosevelt Campobello International Park, (506) 752-2922. East on Maine 189, then across the FDR Bridge. Daily, 9–5, Memorial Day–mid-October. Free.

Machias: Burnham Tavern, (207) 255-4432. On Main St., off U.S. 1 on Maine 192. Monday–Friday, 11–4, late June–Labor Day. Admission.

Madawaska: Fraser Paper Mill, (207) 728-3321. Bridge St., north off U.S. 1. Monday–Friday, 9–11 and 1–3, all year. Free.

Presque Isle: Aroostook Farm, (207) 762-8281. South, on U.S. 1. Monday–Friday, 9–5, all year. Free.

Rockland: Farnsworth Museum, (207) 596-6457. At 19 Elm St., off U.S. 1. Monday–Saturday, 10–5; Sunday, 1–5, June–September. Tuesday–Sunday, at other times. Admission.

Searsport: Penobscot Maritime Museum, (207) 548-2529. On U.S. 1 at Church St. Monday–Saturday, 9:30–5; Sunday, 1–5, Memorial Day–mid-October. Admission.

Thomaston: Henry Knox Home, (207) 354-8062. North, on
U.S. 1. Daily, 9–5, Memorial Day–Labor Day. Admission.

Van Buren: Acadian Village, (207) 868-2691. North, on U.S. 1.
Daily, noon–5, mid-June–Labor Day. Admission.

Wiscasset: Nickels-Sortwell House, (207) 882-3956. U.S. 1 at
Federal St. Wednesday–Sunday, noon–5, June–September.
Admission.

Old Jail, (207) 882-6817. On Federal St., north of U.S. 1.
Tuesday–Sunday, 10–4, July–August. Admission.

Musical Wonder House, (207) 882-7163. At 18 High St.,
south of U.S. 1, from the Green. Daily, 10–5, Memorial
Day–Labor Day. Admission.

Castle Tucker, (207) 882-7364. High at Lee Sts., south of
U.S. 1, from the Green. Tuesday–Saturday, 11–4,
July–August. Admission.

NORTH OF BOSTON

Brunswick, Maine, to Boston, Mass.
* 133 miles

For much of its run down the Maine and New Hampshire shore
and through the northern suburbs of Boston, U.S. 1 is squeezed
tightly between the Interstate and the sea. I-95 assumes its role
as U.S. 1's constant companion here, a fast-lane alternate all the
way to Petersburg, Virginia. The two roads part ways there,
only to reunite in Jacksonville, Florida, and run in tandem all the
way to Miami. But that is far away in a warmer place. In this
part of New England, the old road makes its way through old
towns sustained by the sea. South of Portsmouth, New Hampshire, it retraces the route of the Stavers Flying Coach Line,
which began operating in 1761 as the first scheduled stage service in the colonies. It covered the trip to Boston in a mere three
days. Between Newburyport, Massachusetts, and Boston, the
straightness of the road made it a source of wonder to travelers
in an age accustomed to following trails blazed by cows.

* MILEPOSTS *

Once across the Kennebec River, you enter the original Maine land grant awarded to Sir Ferdinando Gorges and associates in 1620. Through the remainder of the seventeenth century, Maine was a battleground. An endless cycle of massacre and reprisal played itself out between the Indian occupants of the land and settlers venturing up from Massachusetts Bay. On this remote frontier, the colonial ambitions of England and France collided. King William's War, the first of the English-French conflicts that would last seventy-four years and come to be known collectively as the French and Indian Wars, began in 1689. In Europe, the English-French War was called the War of the Grand Alliance and was fought in set battles with professional armies. Here it raged murderously across the backwoods of southern Maine until 1697, leaving most of the pioneer settlements in ashes. At its close, the Indians' power had been destroyed and the process of colonization was truly under way.

The road skirts Brunswick. (For a description of this historic college town, see U.S. 201.) After linking up with I-95, U.S. 1 dips south and enters Freeport.

FOCUS

* * *

A few miles outside **Freeport** is a phenomenon known as the Desert of Maine. Here the topsoil wore away from a colonial farm and exposed a layer of sand below. With nothing to restrain it, the sand began to spread, slowly at first but steadily, until in the course of time it has turned the farm into a miniature Sahara.

Oddly enough, a similar thing has happened in Freeport. In 1912, local merchant Leon L. Bean opened a sporting goods store on Main Street, U.S. 1. From that single enterprise, a shopping empire has grown up to inundate the old town.

On summer weekends, tour buses stack up in smoky columns to disgorge batallions of eager shoppers. They flock through L. L. Bean's, now swollen into a huge sporting goods department store, and into the blocks of adjacent "factory outlet" stores. Most are operated by firms that don't have a factory within hundreds of miles of Freeport. But it's the thought—and the discount—that counts.

With all this clamorous commerce, you might assume the town was named for some sort of duty-free trade arrangement. Actually, its namesake was Sir Andrew Freeport, a fictional character who appeared in Joseph Addison's popular *Spectator* essays. The settlement of Freeport grew into a major crabbing center, and there are still several packing plants in the area. But it is Bean and friends who now dominate Freeport's life.

The Bean fortune was based on a better pair of boots. Old L. L. came up with the idea of sewing leather tops on rubber boots and marketing them as the Maine Hunting Shoe. When his first pairs literally came apart at the seams, Bean instituted his no-questions-asked, unconditional return policy. The next batch of boots was fine, satisfied customers spread the word, and the Beans were on their way. Over the years, they developed the famous mail order catalogue that spread their name and that of Freeport around the country. Mail order customers began dropping by in person on trips through New England, and that led to the store's other notable policy: it never closes. So if you suddenly develop an urgent need for mosquito netting at 3 A.M. on Christmas Day, you know where to find it.

With Bean's drawing all those shoppers, it didn't take long for other merchants to flock in and transform slow-paced Main Street into a Down East boulevard of fashion. On the six blocks between Mallett Drive and West Street, there are nearly a hundred outlet stores clustered on Main and the adjacent side streets. Name your brand—London Fog to Benetton to Laura Ashley to Polo—and you'll probably find it here.

Once you have shopped beyond all reason, leave town by way of Bow Street for some restorative scenery. The road leads to Mast Landing Sanctuary, operated by the Audubon Society, a 150-acre site with self-guiding trails. A few miles beyond that is the turnoff to Wolf's Neck Woods State Park. It is the perfect spot to rest your

aching feet and empty wallet with views of the calming waters of
Casco Bay.

*   *   *

The bounty of Casco Bay is varied. While Freeport has its crabs,
Yarmouth boosts its clams. Many hotels and restaurants here
feature summer clambakes that resemble scenes from a stock
company *Carousel.* The epiphany comes on the third weekend in
July, when the Clam Festival packs 'em into town ... well, as tight
as clams.

You enter the suburbs of Portland at Falmouth. This lovely
community has beautiful homes on the bay and provides a pleasant gateway to the state's premier city.

After many years of decline, **Portland** has suddenly emerged as
one of the most attractive smaller cities in the East. A dreary
warehouse district has been restored to its look at the height of
its nineteenth-century commercial power and so transformed into
the Old Port Exchange, a gentle, gaslit district of shops and entertainment. It typifies the sort of rediscovery that has softened the
face of Portland.

There is supposed to be one island for every day of the year in
Casco Bay, so they are called the Calendar Islands. Portland is
built on hills above these island-speckled waters. The best way
to get a view is to follow U.S. 1A (not the Baxter Boulevard
bypass) into town across the causeway. When you cross Congress
Street, you will be within blocks of the Observatory, an old naval
watchtower that provides a great lookout over both bay and
town. Turn left on Congress and you'll come to it.

Return to 1A and, once you reach Commercial Street, leave the
car and walk around the Old Port Exchange, which is to the
immediate north. In a few blocks, at the northern edge of this
district, you'll come back to Congress Street, the main thoroughfare in town. Henry Wadsworth Longfellow was born here in
1807, at 487 Congress, in the home built by his grandfather, Gen.
Peleg Wadsworth. Is there another American poet whose Famous
Lines spring so readily to the tongue? Drilled into us at school,
they pop into our minds like the phone numbers of old friends:

Under the spreading chestnut tree . . . Tell me not in mournful numbers life is but an empty dream . . . Listen, my children, and you shall hear . . . By the shores of Gitchee-Gummee. . . . The critics sneer, but Longfellow's sonorous phrases, uplifting sentiments and homely lessons of history still mark the earliest poetic awareness of most Americans. Longfellow even dashed off a few lines about Portland, "the beautiful town that is seated by the sea," which the Chamber of Commerce has put to good use. Longfellow left for Bowdoin College as a young man and spent most of his life in Cambridge, Massachusetts, but Portland was the start.

The road leaves town through the southern suburb of Scarborough, then comes to the twin cities of Saco and Biddeford. The economy of the two towns, divided by the Saco River, has been dominated for more than a century by the giant Pepperell Mills. Saco, in fact, was once known as Pepperellboro. The business was founded by descendants of Sir William Pepperell, of nearby Kittery. He commanded the New England forces during the siege of the French stronghold of Louisbourg in 1745 and the following year was named the first American-born baronet. Biddeford remains the more industrialized of the towns. It has a large French-Canadian population, and the annual Kermasse Festival in early July celebrates these ethnic roots.

The **Kennebunk** area enjoys a certain literary cachet. Kenneth Roberts, whose novels of the New England frontier were big sellers in the 1930s, was born in the middle of town. Booth Tarkington may have celebrated the Midwest in his books, but he spent his summers here. But these mere bits of fame were eclipsed with the election of George Bush, of adjacent Kennebunkport, to the presidency in 1988. The coming of the summer White House to Maine has ended the days of tranquillity for a while around Kennebunk. For a reminder of the old days, drop in on the Brick Store Museum, recreation of a typical Down East nineteenth-century commercial block, in the heart of town.

Wells is surrounded by a national wildlife refuge named for Rachel Carson, the writer who sparked the modern environmental movement with her 1962 book, *Silent Spring.* Just south of town, the Storer Garrison House recalls one of the most dramatic engagements of King William's War. Fifteen colonists inside withstood a siege by five hundred French and Indian soldiers for two days in 1692. The house still stands but is not open to the public.

The road now once more runs near the ocean through a very popular resort area. If you want to choose just one beach to visit on this drive, make it Ogunquit, a 3-mile-long strand that is the best in this part of New England. If you don't care to laze about, you can survey it from the heights as you walk the cliffs along the Marginal Way, with the breakers rolling in far below. Ogunquit is also the unofficial artsy-craftsy capital of Maine, with venerable colonies of art and theater folk.

Of all the early settlements in this area, **York Village** is the best preserved. It shows off several historic structures that date back nearly to the town's founding as Agamenticus. The name was given to the place by explorers from Plymouth, who had made it this far up the coast by 1624, only four years after landing in Massachusetts. It was named for nearby Mount Agamenticus. At 692 feet, it is not one of Maine's most prepossessing peaks. But rising so close to the sea in an otherwise level area, it became an early landmark for mariners and was also a place of religious pilgrimage for nearby Indian tribes.

York Village is just off the main highway on U.S. 1A. The Old Gaol dates from around 1720 and is believed to be the oldest English public building still standing in America. Other significant structures in this museumlike cluster are the Old School House (1755), Jefferd's Tavern (1759) and the Emerson-Wilcox House (1742).

History and ships may carry the name of the Portsmouth Naval Yard around the world, but the shipyard is actually located in **Kittery**, Maine, across the river from the New Hampshire city of Portsmouth. The shipyard was established along the Piscataqua River by the federal government in 1800. Still active, it is closed to the public. But the Kittery Historical and Naval Museum recaps the shipbuilding past of the place, all the way back to the Revolutionary War hero John Paul Jones. It is located on the Maine 236 rotary at U.S. 1.

It was at the shipyard that the Portsmouth Treaty was signed in 1905, ending the Russo-Japanese War. Nobody liked it. There was rioting in Tokyo when its terms were announced, and the Winter Revolution took place in St. Petersburg shortly afterward. Yet President Theodore Roosevelt was awarded the Nobel Peace Prize for arranging it. When the treaty was signed, says an old story, the traditional champagne toast was called for. But the shipyard was in Maine, which was then a dry state. So a courier had to be sent across to New Hampshire for a bit of the bubbly. He was permitted back across the border, no doubt, under diplomatic immunity.

As soon as you enter **Portsmouth**, the best strategy is to make your way to Market Square and ditch the car. This is another of the colonial towns whose secrets yield themselves only to the explorer on foot. (It is very compact, the important sites only a few blocks apart, so we're not talking about packing pith helmets and snakebite serum here.) Portsmouth has been conscientious about preserving its past. But in recent years, despite a spurt in population, the town has dedicated itself to becoming a full-fledged museum. The Strawberry Banke project aims at restoring the remnants of the original settlement on the river, named for the profusion of wild berries growing on its banks by those who landed here in 1630. Several homes, shops and other historic buildings (although use of the word *historic* is a bit redundant in Portsmouth) are included in the 10-acre tract. The most familiar name in the area is probably that of Thomas Bailey Aldrich. As devotees of children's literature know, his *Story of a Bad Boy*, published in 1870, was a classic of its kind well into this century. The home in which he grew up, built in 1790, is part of the restoration.

Apart from Strawberry Banke, the Portsmouth Trail winds its way to six historic houses near the downtown area. The most popular is called the John Paul Jones House, although the actual owner was Mrs. Gregory Purcell. The captain boarded there, at 43 Middle, while his first ship, the *Ranger*, was being built in Kittery in 1777. He apparently liked the amenities because he returned to Mrs. Purcell's in 1781 during construction of another vessel, the *America*. The house is now a museum of the Revolutionary era.

The house of Gov. John Langdon is at 143 Pleasant. Langdon, a wealthy merchant, pledged his household plate and 70 hogsheads of rum to the revolutionary cause. He reasoned that if the colonials won he stood a chance of being repaid, and if they lost, his goods would probably be confiscated anyhow. (A hogshead, by the way, is about 63 gallons, although in colonial times it could have ranged as high as 140 gallons. Which size did Langdon pledge? Your guess is as good as mine.) Finding himself on the right side at war's end, Langdon set out to build "the handsomest house in Portsmouth." His good friend George Washington, on a stay with him in 1789, declared he had succeeded. As the first president pro-tem of the U.S. Senate, Langdon administered the oaths of office to Washington and John Adams.

You can explore the old lanes of Portsmouth for several days, but the topic of this book is old roads. This short stay should give you some taste of the town's flavor. U.S. 1 continues down the narrow strip of New Hampshire's coastline, albeit at a 3-mile remove from the sea. A few miles south of Portsmouth, you'll notice a sign leading to Breakfast Hill on the west. The name commemorates an incident of King William's War. In 1696, Portsmouth was surprised by a dawn Indian raid. But while the raiders later dallied here over breakfast, they were caught by pursuers from Portsmouth. The Indians were killed and their captives set free. Brunch may have been a better choice that day.

In **Hampton**, the Tuck Museum on Meeting House Green recaps some local history, including exhibits on Goody Cole, the Witch of Hampton. She was imprisoned in 1673, charged with an entire casebook of local misfortunes. She was not put to death, however, the popular way of dealing with witches in nearby Salem.

The poet John Greenleaf Whittier was a frequent visitor to Hampton Falls, and it was a point of pride with him that he was descended from the town's founder, Stephen Bachiler. Whittier died here in 1892 in the family home, Elmfield.

Seabrook is a serene village set amid salt marshes and dunes. It was once best known for its gladioli displays, but that all changed in the 1970s. Since then it has become a familiar news dateline, scene of some of the most persistent and uproarious antinuclear protests in the country. Tours are offered through the power plant that caused all the commotion, along with nature walks through the adjoining marsh.

Whittier was well acquainted with Salisbury, the first town across the Massachusetts line. He made it the dramatic focus of his poem "How the Women Went from Dover." Persecution of Quakers was one of his major themes, and this poem recounts the sentence handed down to three Quaker women in 1662: they were to be carried in a cart from Dover, New Hampshire, along what is now U.S. 1 to Dedham, Massachusetts, and lashed in eleven towns along the way. Salisbury was the second stop on the route. The chief legal officer here was Justice Robert Pike, who took the court order, trampled it underfoot and said, according to Whittier, "Cut loose these poor ones and let them go;/ Come what will of it, all men shall know/ No warrant is good, though backed by the Crown,/ For whipping women in Salisbury town."

For a time, **Newburyport** was regarded as Boston's greatest commercial rival. This town near the mouth of the Merrimack River was the northernmost outpost of the Massachusetts Bay Colony and from its settlement in 1642 thrived on shipyards and sea-borne trade. But history turned bitter here after the Revolution. The Jefferson Embargo of 1807 cut off all trade with England, touching off secessionist sentiment throughout New England and crippling Newburyport's economy. Then the textile boom in the towns farther up the Merrimack finished the job, since a series of tariffs intended to protect these infant industries cut back the shipping trade still more. Newburyport enjoyed a brief revival when gold was discovered in California. Many of the clippers built here led the way around Cape Horn to the goldfields. Since then, the town has been best known as the residence of author John P. Marquand, whose novels delineating class and caste in Boston were great successes in the 1930s and 40s.

High Street in Newburyport is a display case of Federal architecture, among the most beautiful avenues of that era in existence. The Historical Society is based in the Cushing House, at 98 High, built in 1808 and owned by Caleb Cushing, first U.S. envoy to

China. The Coffin House dates from 1654. The Custom House Museum contains maritime exhibits and displays relating to the local creation of revenue patrols, which grew into the U.S. Coast Guard.

Parson Capen House in **Topsfield** is regarded by historians of architecture as the best-defined Elizabethan-era dwelling surviving in North America. The massive central chimney and surrounding overhang are its characteristic features.

As the road enters Danvers, it becomes a high-speed divided expressway, the Blue Star Memorial Highway. We are now approaching the congestion of Boston's northern suburbs. Before we enter the highway madness surrounding the Hub, there is one more stop to make. Watch for the **Saugus** exit and head east for about a mile. Saugus was the birthplace of the country's steel industry. Because of the deposits of bog ore and plentiful supplies of charcoal, it was chosen as the site for an ironworks, the first in the colonies, by John Winthrop, Jr., in 1645. Within a year, backed by English investors, it was turning out 8 to 10 tons a week. The enterprise lasted only nine years, until the ore ran out. But the Ironworks House, in which the mill director lived, remained standing through the centuries, marking the site. When researchers began digging into the adjacent ground, they uncovered a wealth of seventeenth-century industrial tools and products. Using what was unearthed here as the guide to accuracy, the entire mill has been restored and made a National Historic Site. Saugus Ironworks contains a furnace, forge and mill, as well as the old director's house, whose massive oak beams were sent by ship from England because the sponsors weren't sure if such trees would be available in the New World.

Returning to U.S. 1, you will soon find yourself on the Northeast Expressway, passing through the history-laden Charlestown area, which is now part of Boston. You can see the shaft of the Bunker Hill Monument rising to the west, and on the other side of the road is the Navy Yard, home of the U.S.S. *Constitution*, "Old Ironsides." The temptation will be strong to get off the road and see these places close up. Don't do it. Unless you plan an extended stay in Boston, the best plan is to drive right through, preferably under cover of darkness. There may be worse American cities to drive in than Boston, but if so, they have yet to be discovered. Boston delights in keeping a sense of mystery about its roads, and once you leave the expressway, chances are quite slim that you will ever find your way back again. Instead, you will drive around for hours on one-way streets that dead-end at bridge abutments. Remember the old song about poor Charlie, who went riding forever 'neath the streets of Boston on the MTA? He had it easy compared to the lost souls who must find their way around those streets on the surface.

Boston is a wonderful city. By all means, stay and see it at leisure. But trying to sightsee by car on a driving trip through town is the way to madness. Don't even think about it. Just cross the Charles River into the city and prepare for the third segment of this drive down U.S. 1.

VISITING HOURS

MAINE

Freeport: Desert of Maine, (207) 865-6962. West of U.S. 1 on Desert Road. Daily, 9–dusk, Memorial Day–mid-October. Admission.

Kennebunk: Brick Store Museum, (207) 985-4802. On U.S. 1, at 117 Main St. Tuesday–Saturday, 10–4, all year. Admission.

Kittery: Historical and Naval Museum, (207) 439-3080. North, off U.S. 1 at rotary, on Maine 236. Monday–Saturday, 10–4, Memorial Day–mid-October. Admission.

Portland: Observatory, (207) 774-5561. East of U.S. 1A, at 138 Congress St. Wednesday–Sunday, 1–5, July–August. Weekends only in June. Admission.

Wadsworth-Longfellow House, (207) 774-1822. West of U.S. 1A, at 487 Congress St. Tuesday–Saturday, 10–4, June–September. Admission.

Wells: Rachel Carson National Wildlife Refuge, (207) 646-9226. North, off U.S. 1. Daily, dawn to dusk. Free.

York: Old York Historic District, (207) 363-4974. East, on U.S. 1A (York St.). Daily, 10–5, mid-June–mid-October. Admission.

NEW HAMPSHIRE

Hampton: Tuck Museum, (603) 926-3287. On U.S. 1, at Meeting House Green. Daily, 10–4, July–August. Free.

Portsmouth: Strawberry Banke, (603) 433-1100. East of U.S. 1, on Marcy St., from the east end of the Piscataqua River bridge. Daily, 10–5, May–October. Admission to house tours.

Portsmouth Trail, (603) 436-1118. Headquarters for the walking tour of historic homes is in the Chamber of Commerce Building, at 500 Market St., off U.S. 1. Maps are available here.

John Paul Jones House, Middle and State Sts. Monday–Saturday, 10–4, mid-May–mid-October. Admission.

Governor John Langdon House, 143 Pleasant St. Wednesday–Sunday, noon–5, June–mid-October. Admission.

Seabrook: Nuclear Education Center, (603) 474-9521, ext. 2727. East, off U.S. 1. Tuesday–Friday, 1–4, all year. Free.

MASSACHUSETTS

Newburyport: Coffin House, (508) 227-3956. East of U.S. 1 on Massachusetts 1A, at 14–16 High St. Tuesday, Thursday, and weekends, noon–5, June–mid-October. Admission.

Customs House Museum, (508) 462-8681. Off Massachusetts 1A at the harbor, at 25 Water St. Monday–Saturday, 10–4:30; Sunday, 1–4, mid-March–December. Monday–Friday, at other times. Admission.

Saugus: Ironworks, (617) 233-0050. Saugus exit from U.S. 1 (Main St.), then north on Central St. Daily, 9–4, all year. Free.

Topsfield: Parson Capen House, (617) 887-9264. West from U.S. 1 on Haverhill St., at 1 Howlett St. Wednesday, Friday, Sunday, 1–4:30, mid-June–mid-September. Admission.

THE BOSTON POST ROAD

Boston, Mass., to New York, N.Y.
* 243 miles

This is the oldest highway in the country. The Boston Post Road was the lifeline between Boston and New York during the colonial era, through the string of tiny settlements that clung to the sea. Separated by distance and by deliberate British policy, the colonies had surprisingly little to do with each other. This road was one of their few means of contact. Mail started to move over the Post Road in 1673. Eighty years later, Benjamin Franklin supervised the placement of mileposts along its length. George Washington traveled the road to assume command of the Continental Army in 1774, and fourteen years later he returned in triumph after his inauguration as first president.

Variants of the Post Road eventually cut north through Hartford instead of hugging the coast. But in many towns along the way, U.S. 1 is still known as the Boston Post Road, so profound an influence did it have on the development of this area. Although it runs near the coast, this is not an especially scenic route. It weaves in and out with Interstate 95 and occasionally shows disturbing freeway tendencies. West of New Haven, it enters the congestion of suburban New York. But on this road there is almost one historic attraction for each of Franklin's mileposts.

* MILEPOSTS *

The highway takes its leave of Boston in a pleasant drive along the Charles River and the Back Bay Fens, mud flats that were reclaimed as parkland in the mid-nineteenth century. The road scoots by some of the city's best-known museums and schools as it skirts the Fens, but I repeat my earlier caution. Boston is a difficult city to drive in even when you know where you're going. Content yourself with a quick pass through unless you want to check in and explore the city further by means other than your car.

The road turns into Jamaica Way, running along Olmstead Park and past Jamaica Pond, through the city's necklace of parks, before widening into the VFW Parkway and entering the town of **Dedham**. This town was originally known as Contentment, but in more recent times it became a symbol of radical discontent. It was here that the notorious Sacco-Vanzetti trial was held in 1921. In this celebrated case, two men, both Italian immigrants with radical political views, were found guilty of armed robbery and murder in the holdup of a payroll truck. The verdict, in a trial marked by massive irregularities and judicial impropriety, was protested on an international level for the next six years. To no avail. The men were executed and the case lives on as perhaps the most controversial capital trial of the century. The courthouse where the trial was held still stands on High Street. Most visitors to Dedham will also want to see the Fairbanks House. Built in 1636, it is thought to be the oldest frame house in the country and was inhabited by several generations of the Fairbanks family. It is located on East Street east of U.S. 1 by way of High.

For the rest of its run through Massachusetts, U.S. 1 is a fairly fast, nondescript road that bypasses most towns and parallels Interstate 95. It crosses the Rhode Island line and enters **Pawtucket** as Broadway. Established in 1638, Pawtucket was given the Indian name for "place by the waterfall" because the Blackstone River tumbles across the fall line at this point to form the Seekonk. As early as 1671, industry had grown up around the falls, and this suburb of Providence became known for its sailing equipment. That industrial foundation would change the course of Pawtucket's development, and New England's, after the Revolutionary War.

Many of Rhode Island's great fortunes were built on trade. When the Revolution restricted commerce with traditional trading partners in other British colonies, many of these rich families sought other outlets for their capital. One outlet was to be furnished by Samuel Slater, an immigrant from Scotland. He knew that the British government jealously guarded the operating details of the cotton-spinning machine patented by Richard Arkwright in 1769, for it gave Britain worldwide dominance in the textile industry. Slater worked in one of Arkwright's mills and, in a prodigious feat of mental gymnastics, committed its details to memory. Working with neither minicamera nor duplicating machine, Slater was the prototype of the industrial spy. With this information tucked inside his skull, he emigrated to Rhode Island in 1790 and got in touch with Moses Brown, of Providence, who was looking for new investments. Within three years, a textile mill was built for Slater on the Blackstone. The Industrial Revolution had landed in America.

Over the next century, textiles would furnish the economic foundation of New England. Gigantic mill complexes, entire new cities financed by Boston money would rise. Eventually, control of the industry would pass to other places, but in the early years, Pawtucket's head start gave it an edge. When James Madison wore a suit of Pawtucket yarn at his inauguration in 1809, both the city and the domestic industry received a boost to what later generations would call their image. Slater Mill, across the Main Street bridge on Roosevelt Avenue, is now a historic site. The original mill and a later addition with power looms have been restored. There are ongoing demonstrations of what industry looked like at the dawn of the era.

U.S. 1 widens to become Main Street again as it enters **Providence**. During the last years of the Revolution, in the 1780s, French troops were billeted in the Providence area, and for generations afterwards tales of their adventures in the taverns along the Post Road were the stuff of local romance. The taverns are gone, but the Jeremiah Dexter House, at 957 North Main, was one of these quarters and remains open as a memorial to nights of Gallic gaiety.

U.S. 1 now passes North Burial Ground, with the graves of Roger Williams, the founder of Rhode Island, and several other Providence pioneers, and before starting its winding course through downtown, it circles the statehouse. You will have seen it coming from a good distance away. The unsupported marble dome is visible throughout the city, and the building occupies one of the highest points of land in Providence. Built in 1891, this was the first dome of its kind in America and remains the second largest in the world. Only that of St. Peter's basilica in Rome is larger. The statue on its top is called the *Independent Man.* Exhibited inside are the colony's parchment charter, granted by Charles II in 1663, and a full-length portrait of Washington by native son Gilbert Stuart, whose birthplace lies a few miles ahead of us.

U.S. 1 is not the most interesting route through this historic city. (The attractions of Providence are discussed more fully in the chapter on U.S. 44.) But the highway does pass the neo-Gothic Cathedral of St. Peter and St. Paul, built in 1838. It then turns into Elmwood Avenue and runs through a succession of city neighborhoods before reaching Roger Williams Park. There are 430 acres of woods and gardens here, a string of ten lakes and scenic drives that wind across the expanse, which marks the city's southern end. At the Elmwood entrance is the Betsy Williams cottage, owned by an eighteenth-century descendant of the park's namesake, with historical exhibits. Nearby are the museum of natural history and the park zoo, the only accredited zoo in New England.

Rhode Island was a colony based on the right to dissent, and Williams himself was the most sweet-tempered and reasonable of men. But even he couldn't stand Samuel Gorton. Gorton, known for his extreme individualism, rejected both state and church authority. He was tossed out of Massachusetts Bay and after a few years in Providence was asked to leave there too. Massachusetts Bay found him guilty of blasphemy upon his return and banished him permanently. But there was no getting rid of the man. Gorton was a cagey fellow; back in England, he obtained the support of the powerful Earl of Warwick. Returning to America under Warwick's protection in 1648, he founded a settlement of that name. The earl said he was touched and surprised. Apparently, Gorton must have found some accommodation between state and individual, because he lived on there, preaching his unorthodox views, for another twenty-nine years. The town of **Warwick** reflects his personality. More a collection of villages than a cohesive city, it has become the state's second-largest community. Its chief feature is the Theodore F. Green Airport, named for the oldest man —he was 93 when he retired— to sit in the U.S. Senate. It is the only state-owned airport in the country.

A man with a similar name also figured prominently in this part of the state. Gen. Nathanael Greene of Warwick was second in command to Washington by the end of the Revolution. He headed the southern armies, driving the British relentlessly before him during the Carolina campaign. At the battles of Cowpens and Guilford Court House, Greene inflicted heavy losses on the British under Cornwallis, pushing them back into the final trap at Yorktown. The general also helped to raise the Kentish Guards, a local militia chartered in 1774. Their armory is now a museum of local history. Greene was born a Quaker and was expelled from the church when he organized the Guards. After his wartime service, he was given land by several grateful southern states. While working on his Georgia grant in 1786 he died of sunstroke, a malady unknown in New England.

An even older Kentish Guards Armory stands in the neighboring town of **East Greenwich**, which U.S. 1 enters after a short run along Greenwich Bay. James A. Varnum was a first colonel of the company and later a brigadier in the American army, an associate of Greene's and a judge in the Northwest Territory. His home, on the same street as the armory, is a museum of the colonial period.

Richard Smith built a blockhouse south of here in 1636 to trade with the Indians in the wilderness. When it burned to the ground after thirty-eight years, the family decided to rebuild on a grander scale. The new version became known as Smith's Castle, the name it carries today. Over the centuries, this plantation house entertained many famous guests, but its chief historic importance is that it is the only surviving home in which Roger Williams is known to have preached. Williams died in 1683, five years after the castle was completed.

While some of Smith's descendants contented themselves with castles, others went out and planned entire towns. **Wickford** was laid out by his grandson, Lodowick Updike, in 1709. This is one of the loveliest, least spoiled seaside towns in New England. It lies just east of the highway. On Main Street, between the town center and the harbor, are twenty homes dating from before 1804, with twice that number on the adjoining streets. Old Narragansett Church, built in 1707, is one of the oldest Episcopal houses of worship in the country. This is a place to leave the car and wander on foot. You can drive this stretch of Main Street in about three minutes, but if you do it right it can take most of the day to walk.

From Wickford, continue south on Scenic Highway 1A.

FOCUS

* * *

He became rich and famous by painting portraits of the richest and most famous Americans of his time, but he said the only presence he ever felt awed by was George Washington's.

It is through his portraits of Washington that he is best remembered by history. It is indeed through Stuart's eyes that most of us picture the first president, most memorably and familiarly from the likeness on the dollar bill.

But it was by calculation and not by admiration that this son of a Rhode Island snuffmaker planned his career. He was fully aware, from his vantage point as an artist, in London, of the low state of portraiture in the American republic. Yet in the first pride of nationhood, Americans were eager to have their great figures memorialized in portraits, which were the ultimate measure of fame and respect in those days before photography. Stuart knew that a huge market for his services was forming there, and the quickest way to reach it was to build a reputation by painting the greatest American of all.

Simple economics was also at work here. Stuart's tastes out-stripped his income in London. He had studied with Joshua Rey-nolds and Benjamin West and was highly respected in England, but competition for wealthy clients was keen there. The age of the portraitist was in its fullest flower. Stuart had been commissioned to paint George III and the Prince of Wales, but he knew oppor-tunities would be even greater in his homeland.

The question for him was to what degree it was still home. His father had emigrated to the colonies to make snuff. The craze for pulverized tobacco was peaking in Europe, and he sensed that the main chance lay in America. He established a mill on a rural lane along the Mettatuxet River (just west of Scenic Highway 1A, on Snuff Mill Road) near **Saunderstown**, and in 1755 his son was born in the two-story house next door. By the time Gilbert was 6, the family had moved to the prosperous city of Newport, where the youngster grew up. The political situation was darkening throughout the 1760s, and the Stuarts had no doubts about where their sympathies lay—they were wholeheartedly Tory. So when Gilbert showed an aptitude for drawing, they decided to send him back to England. At the age of eighteen, one of his works, *The Skater*, was accepted by the British Academy. As the first shots of the Revolution were fired, he was becoming established in the salons of London.

Ten years after the war's end, Stuart's Loyalist family was living in Nova Scotia. But he was not without contacts in his homeland and in 1792 made the move to Philadelphia, the na-tional capital. He was soon granted permission to begin his first series of portraits of Washington. Best known is probably the Athenaeum head, so called because it was acquired by the Boston Athenaeum. This is the head and shoulders portrait with the remainder left unfinished. Stuart said this was deliberate. He was pleased with the composition just as it was.

Stuart would go on to paint the first six presidents and many of the first ladies, as well as most other prominent Americans of the time. At his death in 1828 he was virtually alone at the summit of American art.

Somehow the old snuff mill and Stuart homestead managed to

survive through the years, and by the end of the nineteenth century a movement to restore them was begun. The mill is operational today, even though the demand for snuff has dropped somewhat in the last two hundred years. The birthplace itself is filled with replicas of Stuart's best-known works, and a guide supplies helpful background on the pictures and the setting.

∗   ∗   ∗

Return on Snuff Mill Road to Scenic 1A, the Boston Neck Road. This is a more interesting alternative to high-speed, four-lane U.S. 1. Immediately after turning onto the highway, you'll come to Casey Farm. Settled in 1750 and in the hands of the same family for two hundred years, it is now a working museum of colonial farming. The Caseys, unlike their neighbors the Stuarts, were actively engaged in the Revolution on the colonial side and the farm was a hotbed of political activity. The massive barns are especially impressive.

The road reaches the ocean at the old resort town of **Narragansett**. The town preserves the name of the Indian tribe driven from the area in King Philip's War. This conflict raged across New England in 1675–76 and broke the last hold of the Indians on the southern part of the region. West of here and into Connecticut, the country is dotted with reminders of that bitter struggle.

Philip was the son of Massasoit, the early protector of the Plymouth settlement. As chief of the Wampanoas, he watched uneasily as the colonists, first with entreaties and then with forced concessions, wrenched the land away from its native occupants. When three members of his own tribe were executed in a land conflict, Philip unified the tribes of the area and declared war. The conflict raged for two years and ended, as all such conflicts did, in the annihilation of the tribes, the deaths of their leaders and the advance of the frontier. Because fear of a general uprising had always been in the back of the colonists' minds, the war was a temporary impetus to colonial unification in New England. But once the threat was smashed, unity would have to wait another hundred years.

Canochet was the sachem of the Narragansetts, and he's remembered with a limestone statue on Exchange Place. Canochet Farm is a 174-acre park in town, containing the South County Museum, with a regional historical collection. Narragansett was a fashionable resort in the late nineteenth century, with a smart casino designed by famed architect Stanford White. But all that's left is the towers, twin turrets bridged by an arch across the highway. The nearby pier was destroyed years ago by a hurricane.

Scenic 1A now becomes Ocean Road, and as it continues south it passes a succession of excellent state-run beaches, some of the best in New England. This road ends at Point Judith, with its lighthouse dating from 1816 and magnificent views across Rhode Island Sound. The last German sub sunk in World War II went down 2 miles off this point.

The road now loops north to rejoin U.S. 1. At Perryville, you pass the boyhood home of Oliver Hazard Perry, who defeated the British fleet on Lake Erie in the War of 1812, and his brother Matthew, who opened Japan to American commerce in 1853.

This part of Rhode Island is known as the South County. It is sparsely populated, with large portions given over to marshland, wildlife preserves and beach. In colonial times, the area supported several large plantations, with a greater use of black slaves than any other part of New England. Some historians have written that the name South County was more than a mere geographical description. The style of life here more nearly resembled the South than it did the rest of Rhode Island.

The road is four-lane and fast through this area. At **Charlestown**, the last of the Narragansett chiefs rests in the Royal Indian Burial Grounds. A few miles away, on R.I. 2, is an Indian church, which holds services each Sunday. In an adjoining long house, Narragansett rituals are reenacted annually. Kimball Wildlife Refuge on Watchaug Pond is among the best in New England, with an ongoing series of interpretive shows and displays and numerous trails.

Soon you'll come to **Westerly** whose name reflects a triumph of patience. It was part of a land grant known as the Misquamicut Tract. For three-quarters of a century, until the 1720s, Rhode Island and Connecticut battled over where their boundary line should be drawn through the town. Rhode Island won, though the town could just as easily have wound up on the other side of the border and be known as Easterly. Dr. Joshua Babcock was the town's first physician and a close friend of Benjamin Franklin, a frequent visitor to the house at 124 Granite. It is now a colonial museum. The street name is a nod to a subsequent owner, Orlando Smith, who discovered one of the area's largest deposits of granite on the property. Just south of town is Watch Hill, a charming Victorian resort on the ocean, named for lookouts posted there to watch for British marauders.

There may be no other part of the country where the traditions of the sea are as strong as in the southeastern corner of the Connecticut coast. In Stonington, Mystic, Groton and New London you pass through towns that have drawn their spirit and sustenance from the deep for centuries.

Stonington was known as the Nursery for Seamen. The first whaling franchise was granted to the town as early as 1647, but it really didn't start to develop until after King Philip's War. (One of the most effective of the tribal leaders, Canochet, whose statue we encountered back in Narragansett, was brought here for execution. "I like it well that I should die before my heart is softened and I say things unworthy of myself," he stated. The townsmen obliged him.) Stonington repulsed British naval attacks in both the Revolution and War of 1812. The latter was directed by Capt. Thomas Hardy, in whose arms Lord Nelson had died at Trafalgar. Stonington occupies a narrow neck of land dipping into Long Island Sound. At its end, on Water Street, is the Old Lighthouse Museum with a local collection of salty history.

On clear days, from the U.S. 1 bridge over Quambaug Cove, you can see Fisher's Island, which belongs to New York, out on the Sound.

Mystic is probably the best known of all New England's museum towns. The Seaport on the eastern bank of the Mystic River is a living reproduction of a nineteenth-century seaside town, with both seagoing and land-based exhibits. This was a shipbuilding center in the age of sail and the clipper trade. During the California gold rush, the *Andrew Jackson,* out of this port, made the run to San Francisco in the record time of 89 days and 4 hours. But that era was only a distant memory when the Mystic Museum began to organize a modest collection of figureheads and ship models in 1930. In 1942, the museum located the last of the wooden whalers, the *Charles W. Morgan,* languishing away in New Bedford, Massachusetts. Its owner, a son of the eccentric financier Hetty Green, wanted to exhibit it there but couldn't develop any interest in the ship. Mystic took it off his hands, and that seemed to act as a stimulus. The Seaport soon began to turn up other historic vessels, including the fishing schooner *L. A. Dunston* and the square-rigger *Joseph Conrad.* Eventually, the Seaport widened the scope of its displays to include not only the ships but a restoration of the port from which they sailed. Mystic Seaport now encompasses 17 acres, easily worth several days of your time. It has also developed several satellite attractions. The Marine Life Aquarium, just north of the Seaport and south of the Interstate 95 entrance at Conn. 27, is the best of these.

Capt. James Avery built his homestead east of **Groton** in 1656, and for the next 338 years "The Hive of the Averies" was occupied by members of that family. The memorial to the home and the remarkable family who lived there was financed by one of the captain's descendants, John D. Rockefeller.

Nine Averies fell at Groton on September 8, 1781, in the battle of Fort Griswold. This was one of the darkest episodes of the entire Revolutionary War. Succeeding generations tend to romanticize this conflict as a struggle fought at a high level of military etiquette. But on the Connecticut coast it was a brutal war of attrition. No part of the colonies was more savaged by the struggle. Cities were torched, homes destroyed, families uprooted and noncombatants killed as part of the routine. Losses were so great that tracts in the west, the Firelands and Western Reserve in Ohio, were specifically set aside for those who lost their property here. Even today, towns in those areas bear the names and the stamp of Connecticut.

The Battle of Fort Griswold began when Groton was attacked by two regiments of British regulars. All that could be mustered to defend it were 150 militia under Lt. Col. William Ledyard. The assault was directed from across the river in New London by the recent turncoat, Benedict Arnold. Ledyard's force held on determinedly and inflicted a large toll on their attackers, but sheer numbers made surrender inevitable. Ledyard handed his sword to the opposing commander in the traditional gesture of subjugation. In a moment of rage, the commander turned the sword on Ledyard and ran him through. This prompted a general massacre—and the word is perfectly apt—of the defenders. A total of 84 militiamen were killed, most of them after surrendering. A state park and museum now preserve the memory of this horrifying encounter, so surprisingly unknown outside this area.

In this century, Groton became known for its submarines. The first diesel sub was built here by General Dynamics in 1912. The world's first nuclear sub, the *Nautilus,* came from the same company forty-two years later and is now on permanent display at the entrance to the U.S. Submarine Base. The Submarine Force Museum traces the history of America's underwater warfare, which has been linked to this coast since its inception, as you will see in a few more miles. Also on exhibit is the U.S.S. *Croaker,* a submarine that saw repeated combat in World War II.

U.S. 1 and Interstate 95 cohabit the bridge to **New London**. This river was first called the Monhegan, but shortly after the town was settled in 1646, its residents were encouraged to think big. They named their community New London and felt the only appropriate designation for its river would be the Thames. John Winthrop, Jr., led that first settling party, and the mill he erected is still in operation, just south of the bridge.

In Revolutionary days this was a notorious base for privateers. They exacted an enormous toll on British shipping, which explains why New London was attacked with a special fury and burned along with Groton in 1781. It recovered, though, and soon became the chief rival to New Bedford for whaling predominance.

The most visible surviving links with maritime tradition are the annual Harvard-Yale Regatta each spring and the Coast Guard Academy, which is located on the river, just north of the Conn. 32 exit from U.S. 1. There is a visitors' pavilion containing a museum, and full reviews of the cadet corps take place each

Friday afternoon in April, May, September and October. Across from the entrance to the Academy is the Lyman Allen Museum, named for a whaling captain. It is a fine, small facility, which concentrates on colonial art and silver.

Backtrack a bit into New London from westbound U.S. 1 Pequot Street. It runs south from Bank Street, which is the main access road into the city from the west. At 325 Pequot is Monte Cristo Cottage, the boyhood home of playwright Eugene O'Neill. The set designs for two of his greatest works, *Long Day's Journey into Night* and the comedy *Ah, Wilderness!,* both based on his childhood experiences, were modeled on this home. The house itself was named for the greatest role of O'Neill's actor-father, the Count of Monte Cristo. The home has been restored to its appearance of the early twentieth century. The O'Neill Theatre Center, in **Waterford** to the west on U.S. 1, mounts productions of his works every summer.

Old Lyme is a premier example of a town that made the transition from port to paint. The town was named for the British port of Lyme Regis and its boast was that a sea captain lived in every house. By 1900, artists were moving in, and most of them piled into one house. Florence Griswold, a descendant of the town's founder, was a patron of the American Impressionist movement and to board at her Georgian mansion came Childe Hassam, Willard Metcalf and the other leaders of this school. They used the house in their paintings repeatedly, a more meaningful gesture than a simple rent payment, and it is now a museum of their works. Another favorite subject was the Congregational Church. This is an especially fine, high-steepled structure, dedicated in 1907 after the original burned down. Guest speaker at the ceremonies was Woodrow Wilson, who was then president of Princeton. The Lyme Academy of Fine Arts, a few doors down from the Griswold house, exhibits works by the current generation of artists who live here.

The Connecticut River empties into the Sound here, and in the early seventeenth century it was the frontier between the British colonies and the Dutch settlement centered on Manhattan. Even after England wrested the island from Holland, New Yorkers cast covetous eyes on **Old Saybrook**, the town on the river's western bank. A party under Gov. John Andros moved on it in 1675 only to be thwarted when defenders raised the British flag, on which the party dared not advance without risk of treason. Oliver Cromwell boarded ship in England to seek refuge here when it seemed his arrest by Charles I was imminent, but the ship was refused clearance and he remained in England, with unfortunate consequences for Charles.

Old Saybrook was the first home of Yale University, founded in 1701 as the Collegiate School. It moved down the road to New Haven fifteen years later. The submarine legacy, which came to fulfillment in Groton, also originated here. David Bushnell developed a one-man sub, which he called a turtle, in 1776 and tried to sink a British warship with it. He didn't, but it was a nice try. Bushnell was born in Old Saybrook and worked on his boat in nearby Westbrook. The most significant slice of history in Old Saybrook today is the General Hart House, on Main Street, built in 1767 and noted for its elaborate tilework and paneling.

We still have many miles of Connecticut to traverse, but the New Yorkers who wanted to annex this land years ago have worked a subtle revenge over time. The state starts to change in little ways once you get west of the Connecticut River. You see as many Yankee as Red Sox pennants in the stores. With each town westward, more people commute into New York or, more likely, to one of the suburbs that have become corporate centers. You have entered the furthest orbit of metropolitan New York. The gravitational pull is still slight, but it gets stronger every mile you go.

Past Clinton is the turnoff to Hammonassett Beach, the largest state park on the north shore of the Sound, with 921 acres and first-rate swimming facilities.

Members of the nautically innovative Bushnell clan also lived in **Madison**. Cornelius Scranton Bushnell was the chief sponsor of the Civil War ironclad, the *Monitor.* The Allis-Bushnell House features local history and some unusual corner fireplaces. The town's Green is also unusually well kept, with excellent visual unity, as the preservation experts like to say.

Guilford has lots of saltbox houses, thought of as the typical New England residence. Actually, the saltbox has been traced back to the East Anglia section of England. The steeply pitched design was mandated by the cramped conditions of medieval towns, when it was necessary to get the most living space out of a tiny plot. Such restrictions were no longer needed in the wide New World, but colonial architects were reluctant to abandon a traditional design that had come to be associated with people of substance, so even though a geographical anomaly, the saltbox became a symbol of New England. The Hyland House dates from 1660 and is one of the earliest surviving constructions. The Thomas Griswold House was built a century later and represents the saltbox style at its peak. Both homes are museums. So is the Henry Whitfield House, believed to be the oldest stone home in New England. Whitfield led a party of Puritans from Kent and Surrey that settled here in 1639, the same year the house was built.

Guilford made a few other contributions to national life. One of its early inhabitants was a keen participant in the democratic process. He was always running for one office or another. Eventually, his name became proverbial in the area to describe the physical act of running, and the expression "running like Sam Hill" caught on in the rest of the country. Granite quarries here also produced the stone for the foundations of the Statue of Liberty and Brooklyn Bridge.

From Guilford, a little side trip along Conn. 146 is worth your while. The road passes Sachem Head, named for the skull of an Indian leader slain in the Pequot War by Uncas, chief of the Mohegans. This conflict of 1676–77 was a Connecticut extension of King Philip's War. Uncas saw the advantage of allying his tribe with the colonists to destroy his old adversaries, the Pequot, which he did. (James Fenimore Cooper, who lived further along this road, in New York, borrowed the name of Uncas and moved his activities about eighty years forward in time to create the title character of his novel *The Last of the Mohicans.*) The road continues west for views over the Thimble Islands, a most scenic portion of this coastline. Short cruises to the two dozen or so tiny islands leave from the dock at **Stony Creek**. Romantic legends of buried treasure abound here, but no one has hit paydirt yet.

The old interurban trolley has vanished from the American scene, just as surely as the square-masted ships in Mystic Seaport. In **East Haven**, though, you'll find an excellent trolley museum, boasting everything from interurbans to city streetcars to subway and elevated cars. There are more than a hundred exhibits here, including a chunk of the oldest operating line in the country, which still runs about 3 miles. The complex is a National Historic Site and a fascinating stop for those who want to experience the countryside the way we saw it before the coming of even the old roads.

The story of **New Haven** is encapsulated in two Elis: Yale and Whitney. Between the two of them, the Puritan settlement, which once tried to run its affairs by the Laws of Moses, was transformed into a thriving educational and industrial center.

Elihu Yale was a Boston merchant and officer of the East India Company. In 1718, two years after the college moved to New Haven, he donated some books and merchandise worth 562 English pounds. Overwhelmed by this largesse, New Haven renamed the struggling Collegiate School in his honor. His father had been an original settler here, so it was probably a sentimental gesture on Elihu's part, an uncharacteristic act for a tough old codger. But it was great exposure.

Whitney, a member of Yale's class of 1792, went South to seek his fortune, but a battle over patent rights erupted when he finished his cotton gin. Disillusioned by his failure to make any money from the invention, he returned here to work on his production theory of interchangeable parts. Applying it to the manufacture of firearms, he developed the principles of mass production and division of labor, which led to the assembly line. An authentic genius, Whitney, in reality, invented modern times.

New Haven was named for a Sussex port, but it became a real haven for fleeing Puritans when Charles II was restored to the British throne in 1660. High on the new king's agenda was revenge upon those who had sat on the court that sentenced his father to death eleven years before. His agents followed these judges to the New World, where many had fled to seek refuge in the settlements of sympathetic coreligionists. New Haven was one of these. (It had, in fact, sought union with Connecticut because New York was royalist in its politics.) New Haven managed to hide three of the fleeing judges in the nearby hills and caves, now part of West Rock Ridge Park. The event is commemorated in tablets in the First Church of Christ (Center Church) on the Green.

The Green and the Yale campus are within blocks of each other at the core of the city. U.S. 1 skirts New Haven, but you can take Church Street and make your way easily to the heart of town. The first settlers, led by John Davenport, determined to make this the first planned town in America, with the Green at its center. Temple Street bisects this space today, and rising along Temple are three landmark churches. The oldest, Center Church, dates from 1814 and is noted for its Tiffany glass and spire, modeled on that of famed St. Martin's in the Field, London, which inspired the New England church style. United Church on the Green opened the following year and was a center of Abolitionist sentiment. Henry Ward Beecher's passionate sermons sent dozens of antislavery militants off to Bleeding Kansas to enter combat for the Lord. Trinity Episcopal was the third church in three years to be built here. An architectural sensation when it opened in 1816, it gave impetus to the Gothic Revival movement in this country.

Yale is one block northwest of the Green. For a fast overview, enter the Old Campus through the Phelps Gateway on College Street. Take a look at Connecticut Hall, dating from 1752, the oldest building at Yale. The Yale Art Gallery, at Chapel and York, is one of the finest university collections in existence. Finally, see the Memorial Quadrangle, built between 1917 and 1921. Enter from High and Elm and take a long look around. This is the scene that probably comes to mind when you hear the words *Ivy League.* These Gothic buildings with their air of permanence and solidity are the visual signature, not only of Yale, but of an entire educational tradition.

Retrace your route back to U.S. 1. West of New Haven, you are assuredly on New York turf. The pace and congestion on the road increase noticeably, though there is still the charm of **Stratford**, home since 1955 of the American Shakespeare Theatre. It seems to have taken a surprisingly long time for the connection to be made between the name of the Bard's hometown and this old shipbuilding port on the Housatonic. But Stratford has made up for lost time with a year-round offering of dance, music and drama, with special Elizabethan entertainments in the summer months.

The best-known resident of the next town, **Bridgeport**, seems appropriate to the world we are entering: P. T. Barnum, master showman, czar of the czany and grand duke of the dubious. The Connecticut-born Barnum first rose to fame in New York City by exhibiting an aged black woman as George Washington's nurse. Then a strange newspaper report brought him back to his home state at the age of twenty-seven. He read of a Bridgeport youth named Charles Stratton who had stopped growing at a height of 29 inches. Barnum just had to have a look at this. Seeing a veritable goldmine before his eyes, Barnum renamed him Tom Thumb and took him off to Europe, where he amassed a fortune and an international reputation. Barnum later settled down in Bridgeport, establishing winter quarters for his circus here for a while. He became quite a solid citizen and was even elected mayor. The Barnum Museum, expanded and remodeled in the late 1980s, contains mementos of his incredible career and all the semiunbelievable characters with whom he was associated. Both Barnum and Stratton are buried in North Park Cemetery, on U.S. 1 (North Avenue) near Dewey. Stratton's memorial statue there is life-sized. Bridgeport, by the way, is where the car named the Locomobile was manufactured. Sounds reasonable.

Now we have come to some of the most expensive real estate in America. The communities lining U.S. 1 in this area are home to some of the wealthiest individuals in the country. In surveys, the contentment factor here goes right off the charts. In recent years, as businesses have streamed out of Manhattan to flee rising costs and impossible congestion, this area has also been transformed into a major corporate center.

Westport, with its hills and secluded coves, has been favored for decades by writers and actors. This is home base to Peter DeVries, who writes extensively about the oddities of life in the tweedy exurbs. It's also home to actor Paul Newman and writer A. E. Hotchner, neighbors who went into the food business here and were then sued by a neighborhood deli-owner who accused them of swiping his recipes. It isn't easy trying to make a living in Westport.

The Great Swamp Fight was the culminating battle of the Pequot War in 1676, removing all hostile tribes from the area and making it safe for exclusive shops. A monument to the battle is located just west of Fairfield.

To an earlier generation, **Norwalk** meant only one thing: oysters. The town shipped three-quarters of the domestic supply between 1870 and 1890. It still celebrates an oyster festival on its waterfront each September. Part of the city's Maritime Center, which opened in 1988, is a restored oyster house, showing how the tasty little bivalves used to be prepared for consumption.

Norwalk was one of the towns most heavily damaged by British raids in the Revolutionary War, and its residents were among those for whom land was set aside in Ohio. It took a while for the settling party to get organized, though. In fact, it didn't leave until 1820, thirty-seven years after the war ended. But a town in the middle of the Firelands grant in Ohio still bears the name of Norwalk.

This was also the home of Civil War–era financier LeGrand Lockwood. He lost most of his fortune in the Black Friday debacle of 1869, but the year before he completed his fifty-room chateau on West Avenue. Famed for its inlaid woodwork and skylit rotunda, the Lockwood-Mathews House was restored in the 1980s.

No Connecticut community has felt the impact of the corporate exodus from Manhattan more than **Stamford**. This city of 100,000 is headquarters for almost 20 percent of the companies listed in the Fortune 500. One of them, Champion International, has donated part of its office center as a branch of the Whitney Museum of American Art. The First Presbyterian Church, built in 1958, was designed in the shape of a fish, the early symbol for Christianity. Ten years later, abstract stained glass made in Chartres was added. The church is at 1101 Bedford, north of U.S. 1 by way of Conn. 137.

On down U.S. 1 in **Cos Cob**, the Bush-Holley House is interesting in its own right and also for its associations with the history of art in America. Built in 1685, it is a good example of how an early saltbox grew and expanded over the generations. Earlier in this century, it was owned by Elmer Livingston MacRae, one of the artists who organized the sensational New York Armory show of 1913. This landmark exhibit is usually credited with altering the perception of modern art in this country.

The **Greenwich** area was supposedly purchased from the Indians for the price of 25 coats, or an energetic afternoon of shopping for one of its current residents. It was also the scene of one of the Revolution's great escapes. As the Connecticut-born general Israel Putnam stood shaving in his tavern room on the morning of February 26, 1779, he saw an alarming sight in the mirror: British troops were advancing on the place. Realizing that his own forces were unprepared for battle, he leaped from a window and scrambled down an adjacent ravine, hollering a warning as he fell. By that margin, the colonials managed to scatter, regroup and beat back the invaders on another day. The tavern is now the Putnam Cottage, a museum showing off local relics of that era.

Once you get across the New York line, there is a short detour that is well worth the time if you have any interest in cartoons, either the animated or static variety. The Cartoonists Museum and Hall of Fame is the only one of its kind in the country. It is also housed in a landmark of sorts: Wards Castle, built in 1876, was the first house constructed of reinforced concrete. There are ongoing exhibits and film programs. It is located in the village of **Rye Brook**, on Comly Avenue.

The Square House in **Rye** was once a famous tavern, the first major stop out of New York on the Post Road. Run by the Widow Haviland, it entertained many eighteenth-century notables, including the first two presidents and the Marquis de Lafayette. The house has been restored to its appearance of that era.

The old DeLancey house in Mamaroneck hasn't fared quite as well. It was once the residence of James Fenimore Cooper, but he didn't occupy it here. When he lived in the place, it sat on a bluff above Long Island Sound. It was there that he told his wife, Susan DeLancey, that he would respond to a British taunt of "Who reads an American book?" by writing one. He did. Several. But that didn't keep his former home from being moved to 404 West Post Road and becoming a gas station.

New Rochelle was the setting for one of the first theatrical productions to celebrate the move to suburbia. George M. Cohan's hit of 1906 was called *Forty-five Minutes from Broadway* and made a good deal of sport contrasting the show folk who had moved up from the big city with the local "rubens." Sometimes its current residents wish the commute were still just 45 minutes.

Before its suburban conversion, New Rochelle was known for its association with fiery pamphleteer Thomas Paine. He galvanized public opinion in the colonies in favor of revolution with *Common Sense,* and his later work *The Crisis* bucked up colonial spirits at a low ebb in the war ("These are the times that try men's souls . . ."). Afterward, Paine went, ill-advisedly it would seem, to England to defend the French Revolution there. This did not play at all and he was expelled to France, where he was thrown into prison for counterrevolutionary activities. (Remember the irascible Samuel Gorton way back in Warwick, Rhode Island? Sounds like a kindred spirit.) Paine completed the cycle by returning to America in 1802 and attacking the government for betraying the ideals of the Revolution. Ostracized for his views, he spent the last seven years of his life in a cottage here, mad at a world that generously returned the favor. His home is combined with a museum of the town's Huguenot settlers, who named the town after their former home in La Rochelle. They were forced out of France in 1688 when the Edict of Nantes, which had granted them tolerance, was revoked.

Another who sought religious freedom in this area was Anne Hutchinson. She was branded a heretic and banished from Massachusetts for her views on salvation by faith alone. She settled near here on the shores of Pelham Bay, where her family was massacred by Indians in 1643 (which was regarded as a providence back in Boston). The Hutchinson River, which U.S. 1 crosses near the **New York City** line, is named for this gentle dissenter.

WHERE THE OLD ROADS GO

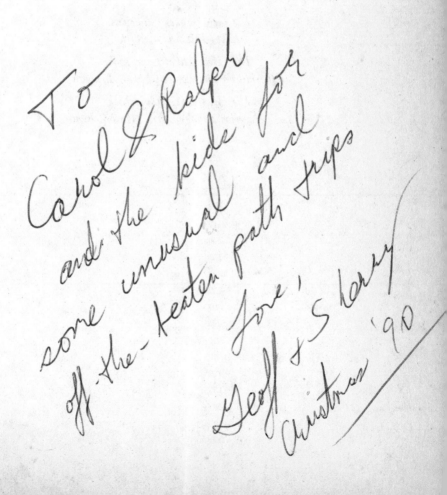

To
Carol & Ralph
and the kids for
some unusual and
off-the-beaten path trips

Love,
Geoff & Sherry
Christmas '90

The reputation of the Bronx is far from gentle. Named for Jonas Bronck, a settler of Swedish descent, this borough of New York has become a symbol of urban disintegration. (Have you ever wondered, incidentally, why it is called *the* Bronx rather than just plain Bronx? It isn't the Brooklyn or the Queens, after all. It's an odd locution, especially since it is named not after a place but a man.)

U.S. 1 passes through Bronx Park as Fordham Road. This enormous park contains two of the city's cultural gems, the New York Botanical Gardens and the Bronx Zoo. Both are easily accessible from the road and, since you're almost at the end of this drive, they make a good place to stop for a long visit. Beyond the park, the road passes the Gothic structures of Fordham University, then turns south to link up with Interstate 95 and cross into New Jersey as the George Washington Bridge. Walking through these gardens in New York is a suitable close to a drive that began in the gardens of Back Bay Fens in Boston.

VISITING HOURS

MASSACHUSETTS

Dedham: Fairbanks House, (617) 326-1170. East of U.S. 1 on Eastern Ave., at East St. Tuesday–Sunday, 9–noon and 1–5, May–October. Admission.

RHODE ISLAND

Charlestown: Royal Indian Burial Ground, no phone. East, then north from U.S. 1 on Narrow Lane. Daylight hours, all year. Free.

East Greenwich: Varnum House, (401) 884-4622. East of U.S. 1, at 57 Peirce St. Tuesday–Saturday, 1–4, Memorial Day–Labor Day. Admission.
   Independent Company of Kentish Guards Armory, (401) 884-1519. East of U.S. 1, at Peirce and Armory Sts. Open by appointment.

Narragansett: South County Museum, (401) 783-5400. North, on Boston Neck Road (Scenic Highway 1A). Wednesday–Sunday, 11–4, June–August; weekends, 11–4, April, May, September, October. Admission.

Pawtucket: Slater Mill, (401) 725-8638. North of U.S. 1 on Roosevelt Ave., from the west end of the Main St. bridge. Monday–Saturday, 10–5; Sunday, 1–5, Memorial Day–Labor Day. Weekends, 1–5, March–May, September–Christmas. Admission.

Providence: Jeremiah Dexter House, (401) 274-4564. On U.S. 1, at 957 North Main St. Open by appointment.
    State House, (401) 277-2300. On U.S. 1, at Smith St. Monday–Friday, 9–3:30, all year. Free.
    Betsy Williams Cottage, no phone. Off U.S. 1, at Elmwood Ave. entrance to Roger Williams Park. Sunday, 1–5, all year. Free.

Saunderstown: Gilbert Stuart Birthplace, (401) 294-3001. North on Scenic Highway 1A, and west on Snuff Mill Road. Saturday–Thursday, 11–5, April–mid-November. Admission.
    Casey Farm, (401) 294-9182. North on Scenic Highway 1A. Tuesday, Thursday, Sunday, 1–5, June–mid-October. Admission.

Warwick: Kentish Artillery Armory, (401) 737-0010. On U.S. 1, at 3259 Boston Post Road. Tuesday–Friday, 11–4; weekends, 1–4, all year. Closed Sunday, June–September. Donation.

Westerly: Babcock-Smith House, (401) 596-4424. At 124 Granite St., off U.S. 1. Wednesday and Sunday, 2–5, July–August. Sunday only, May, June, September, October. Admission.

Wickford: Smith's Castle, (401) 284-3521. North, on U.S. 1. Thursday–Saturday, 10–5; Sunday, 1–5, mid-April–mid-October. Admission.

CONNECTICUT

Bridgeport: Barnum Museum, (203) 331-1104. South of U.S. 1, at 820 Main St. Tuesday–Saturday, 10–4:30; Sunday, noon–4:30, all year. Admission.

Cos Cob: Bush-Holley House, (203) 869-6899. South from U.S. 1, at 39 Strickland Rd. Tuesday–Saturday, noon–4, all year. Admission.

East Haven: Shore Line Trolley Museum, (203) 467-6927. South of U.S. 1, at 17 River St. Daily, 11–5, Memorial Day–Labor Day. Weekends only, May, September, October. Sunday only, April and November. Admission.

Greenwich: Putnam Cottage, (203) 869-9697. On U.S. 1, at 243 East Putnam Ave. Monday, Wednesday, Friday, 10–noon and 2–4, all year. Admission.

Groton: Fort Griswold State Park, no phone. South of U.S. 1, on Monument St. Daily, 9–5, Memorial Day–Labor Day; weekends only, to mid-October. Free.

Nautilus Memorial and Submarine Force Museum, (203) 447-3174. North from U.S. 1 on Connecticut 12. Wednesday–Monday, 9–5, mid-April–September, mid-October–mid-January, February–March. Free.

USS *Croaker,* (203) 448-1616. Off U.S. 1, at east end of Thames River bridge. Daily, 9–5, mid-April–mid-October; 9–3, at other times. Free.

Guilford: Griswold House, (203) 453-3176. South of U.S. 1 and east from the Green, at 171 Boston St. Tuesday–Sunday, 11–4, mid-June–mid-September. Admission.

Hyland House, (203) 453-9477. South of U.S. 1 and east from the Green, at 84 Boston St. Tuesday–Sunday, 10–4:30, June–Labor Day, weekends, 10–4:30, to mid-October. Admission.

Henry Whitfield House, (203) 453-2457. South of U.S. 1, on Connecticut 77, at Whitfield St. Wednesday–Sunday, 10–4, all year. Admission.

Madison: Allis-Bushnell House, (203) 245-4567. On U.S. 1, at 853 Boston Post Road. Wednesday–Sunday, 1–4, Memorial Day–Labor Day. Free.

Mystic: Seaport, (203) 572-0711. North from U.S. 1, on Connecticut 27. Daily, 9–4, all year. Admission.

Marinelife Aquarium, (203) 536-3323. North from U.S. 1, on Connecticut 27, at Interstate 95. Daily, 9–5, all year. Admission.

New Haven: The Green and its churches, no phones. North from U.S. 1, on Chapel St. Trinity Church, Monday–Friday, 10–2; Saturday, 10–1; Sunday, 8–1:30. First Church of Christ, Tuesday–Friday, 9–noon and 1–4; Saturday, 9–noon. United Church on the Green, Tuesday–Thursday, 9:30–4:30. All are open all year. Donation.

Yale University and museums, (203) 432-2300. North from U.S. 1, on Chapel St. Call for museum hours.

New London: Ye Olde Towne Mill, (203) 444-2206. Exit U.S. 1 at southbound Connecticut 32 and follow signs. Daily, 1–4, June–mid-September. Free.

U.S. Coast Guard Academy, (203) 444-8270. North from U.S. 1 on Connecticut 32 (Mohegan Ave.). Daily, 10–5, May–October; Monday–Friday, 8–4, at other times. Free. Cadet Corps reviews are held at 4 P.M., Friday, April, May, September, and October.

Lyman Allen Museum, (203) 443-2545. North from U.S. 1 on Connecticut 32, to Williams St. Tuesday–Sunday, 1–5, all year. Free.

Monte Cristo Cottage, (203) 433-0051. East on Bank St. from U.S. 1 at the west edge of town, then south on Pequot Ave. Monday–Friday, 1–4, all year. Admission.

Norwalk: Lockwood-Mathews House, (203) 838-1434. Off U.S. 1, at 295 West Ave. Tuesday–Friday, 11–3; Sunday, 1–4, March–mid-December. Admission.

Maritime Center, (203) 838-1488. South of U.S. 1, at 10

N. Water, on the harbor. Daily, 11–6, all year. Admission to some attractions.

Old Lyme: Griswold Museum, (203) 434-5542. South of U.S. 1, at 96 Lyme St. Tuesday–Saturday, 10–5; Sunday, 1–5, June–October. Wednesday–Sunday, 1–5, at other times. Admission.

Lyme Art Gallery, (203) 434-7802. On U.S. 1, at Lyme St. Tuesday–Saturday, noon–5; Sunday, 1–5, May–October. Donation.

Old Saybrook: Hart House, (203) 388-0614. South of U.S. 1, on Connecticut 154, at 350 Main St. Friday–Sunday, 1–4, June–mid-September. Donation.

Stamford: Whitney Museum, (203) 358-7652. Off U.S. 1, on Atlantic St., at One Champion Plaza. Tuesday–Saturday, 11–5, all year. Free.

First Presbyterian Church, (203) 324-9522. North of U.S. 1 on Connecticut 137, at 1101 Bedford St. Monday–Friday, 9–5; weekends, 9–1, all year. Donation.

Stonington: Old Lighthouse Museum, (203) 535-1440. South of U.S. 1, at the end of Water St. Tuesday–Sunday, 11–4:30, May–October. Admission.

Stony Creek: Thimble Island Cruises, (203) 481-3345 or 481-4841. South from U.S. 1 at Guilford on Connecticut 146. Daily, Memorial Day–mid-October. Call for schedule.

Stratford: American Shakespeare Theatre, (203) 375-5000. South of U.S. 1, on Connecticut 113, at 1850 Elm St. Call for schedule of performances.

Waterford: Eugene O'Neill Theatre Center, (203) 443-5378. South of town, on Connecticut 213, at 305 Great Neck Rd.

NEW YORK

New Rochelle: Thomas Paine Cottage and Huguenot Historic Museum, (914) 632-5376. North of U.S. 1, on North Ave. at Sicard St. Wednesday–Sunday, 2–5, all year. Donation.

New York City: New York Botanical Gardens, (212) 220-8777. Off U.S. 1 in Bronx Park. Grounds open daily, 8–6. Conservatories, Tuesday–Sunday, 10–4, all year. Admission. New York Zoological Park, (212) 220-5100. South of U.S. 1 in Bronx Park. Daily, 10–4:30, all year. Admission.

Rye: The Square House, (914) 967-7588. On U.S. 1, at Purchase St. Tuesday–Friday and Sunday, 2:30–4:30, all year. Admission.

Rye Brook: Museum of Cartoon Art, (914) 939-0234. North of U.S. 1 from Port Chester on King St. to Comly Ave. Tuesday–Friday, 10–4; Sunday, 1–5, all year. Admission.

U. S. ROUTE  2

Houlton

MAINE

Bangor

VERMONT

Burlington

Montpelier Peacham Gorham

NEW
HAMPSHIRE

NEW YORK

MASSACHUSETTS

Ronan

CONNECTICUT

RHODE ISLAND

The Northern Forests

U.S. 2

Houlton, Maine, to Rouses Point, N.Y.
*   454 miles

This is the road across the roof, a drive along the northern tier of the United States. But it is an interrupted journey. For several hundred miles, between the shores of New York's Lake Champlain and Michigan's Straits of Mackinac, U.S. 2 disappears. It ends, to all appearances, at Rouses Point, New York, only to emerge, as if from a 500-mile tunnel, in St. Ignace, Michigan. No other old road has such an extensive gap in its route. In fact, it makes U.S. 2 two separate highways. The eastern portion, through New England, is complete unto itself. International geography is the culprit that cuts the road in twain. Along the St. Lawrence Valley and the eastern Great Lakes, the Canadian border dips to its southernmost point. If U.S. 2 continued straight on its course, it would cut right through the Province of Ontario. Canadians are constantly distressed over American cultural imperialism, and running a U.S. highway through their country is more than they could be expected to endure. However, when federal officials handed out route numbers for the national highway system, they wanted to maintain as much continuity as possible. So it was decided to ignore the interruption and make the most northern highway U.S. 2 all the way across the country.

In this segment, you will travel from the New Brunswick border of Maine across a region of forest, marsh and mountains. The road parallels the Penobscot River in the heart of Maine, and later the Androscoggin. Its dash across New Hampshire, just north of the towering Presidential Range, features some of New England's wildest mountain scenery. The road then crosses the Green Mountains of Vermont by way of the state capital, Montpelier, and its largest city, Burlington. Finally, it runs the length of the Hero Islands on the eastern shore of Lake Champlain.

* MILEPOSTS *

When Maine decided to declare war on border-jumping lumbermen from Canada, the federal government elected to sit it out. As Maine militia units made their way through Houlton in 1839 on their way to the bloodless Aroostook War on the disputed frontier, they were studiously ignored by regular army troops stationed at the Hancock Barracks. This caused some hard feelings between state and federal officials. But as the hostilities ended amicably, all was forgiven. The barracks, which were manned from 1828 to 1846, are maintained as a museum on Garrison Hill, 1 mile east of town. (The Houlton area and the war are more fully described in the chapter on U.S. 1.)

The highway now heads south and west across the County, as the Aroostook is called around here. This is a near wilderness, speckled with small lakes and streams. Near the town of Island Falls is Pleasant Lake, a favorite fishing hole of Theodore Roosevelt, who spent many summers in this part of the state. Near Golden Ridge, you'll catch some views of Mount Katahdin, the highest peak in Maine, rising to the west. The summit is 5,267 feet high and is the first point in America to be lit by the rising sun. Even the names sound remote in this part of the state, as you run through the Macwanoc woods by the side of Molunkus Stream. At Mattawamkeag, you reach the Penobscot River, which will run alongside U.S. 2 all the way into Bangor.

Lincoln has a population of only 3,500 souls, but it is a commercial giant in this area. The road crosses to the eastern bank of the Penobscot River there and then runs through a string of tiny resort towns. At Milford, you reach the northern terminus of the Bangor, Milford and Old Town Railroad, completed in 1835 and the second oldest in the country. U.S. 2 parallels its course between here and Bangor.

From a time beyond the reach of history, there has been a settlement on the big island in the broad Penobscot. Even the Abnaki, who occupied the land long before the Europeans came, cannot say how long their people have lived there. So it seemed natural to call the adjacent mainland settlement **Old Town**. The island today is home of the Penobscots, once the most powerful member of the Abnaki Confederacy. Gradually, their domain has shrunk to this island. Until the bridge opened in 1951 it was accessible only by boat. A few hundred native people still live on the island, and a museum of the Penobscot tribe is maintained there. Tribal ceremonies are also held throughout the year. On the mainland, the prime attraction is canoes. The Old Town Canoe Company claims it runs the last assembly line for traditional wood and canvas canoes in America. The company also uses more contemporary materials, but it is the old methods that draw the crowds to Maine's top manufacturing attraction.

Orono has been the home of the University of Maine's main campus since its opening as a land grant school in 1868. The school does not play bigtime football, but one of its traditional songs is probably more familiar than those of many institutions whose bands march on national television. That's because Rudy Vallee picked up his megaphone and belted the Maine Stein Song across the airwaves in the early 1930s. The story goes that a radio executive bet the new medium was so influential it could make a hit out of any song and directed Yale man Vallee to sing this one to prove his point. The exec was right on the money. But don't let the intoxicating lyrics fool you. Maine is a hard-working university, noted for its excellent College of Agriculture and its Cultural Center.

The state emblem is the pine tree, and it was in **Bangor**, in the mid-nineteenth century, that those trees came to symbolize Maine to the world. In the years before the Civil War, Bangor was the country's greatest lumber port, a title it relinquished to Chicago only in the 1870s. In its time, Bangor was a hell-raising town, with the sort of goings-on that made the Stein Song pretty sedate by comparison. Bangor today is trying to recapture the texture if not the license of those days with a downtown restoration program. The Union Street mansion of Isaac Farrar, one of the timber barons, has been returned to all its splendid excess. Right across the street is the Thomas A. Hill House, a more subdued Greek Revival home that is now the city's historical museum.

The most visible reminder of those lumbering days is the 31-foot-high statue of Paul Bunyan on Main Street. Most of the old timber states have such tributes to Paul, but this is the only one with a literary citation. It came murderously to life in the Stephen King novel *It*. King grew up in Bangor and makes his home nearby. Many of his horrific best-sellers employ area landmarks in their plot lines. But that isn't too unusual. This part of Maine has a history of harboring the odd and unsettling.

Hermon, the next town along the road, was the base of the Second Adventists, usually known as the Millerites after their founder, William Miller. An offshoot of this movement evolved into the current Seventh Day Adventists. Miller predicted the imminent end of the world in 1843 and gathered his followers, dressed in white and freed of all worldly possessions, atop Mount Hermon to await events. When it became apparent that his calculations were in error, an event referred to by the Adventists as "the great disappointment," the group dispersed. Mount Hermon is now a ski resort.

Carmel was the home of the Higginsites, a religious cult of slightly later vintage, which believed in faith healing and abstinence from pork. But child beating was also part of the program, reportedly, and the sect disbanded when local citizens tarred and feathered its leader.

Etna was a lively center for spiritualism. This odd movement, with its ongoing efforts to contact "the other side," enjoyed a certain vogue in the last quarter of the nineteenth century. It attracted a great many wealthy women to its teachings (including

Mary Vanderbilt, who handsomely endowed the center at Etna) and for a while was all tangled up with the women's suffrage movement. A succession of scandals involving free love, another favorite spiritualist teaching, ended that alliance and its brief fling with respectability.

Back in the material world, Newport is pleasantly situated on Sebasticook Lake. At Skowhegan, the highway reaches Maine's other great northern river, the Kennebec. As in the Old Town settlement on the Penobscot, the island in the Kennebec at Skowhegan was an Abnaki settlement. The name means "place to watch for fish," and the Abnaki found them here in abundance, as salmon clustered in the deep pools below the river's falls. A 62-foot-high sculpture by Maine artist Bernard Langlais near the center of town pays tribute to these ancient watchers.

Log drives down the Kennebec didn't end until 1976, and the town still observes Log Days, on the last weekend in August, to commemorate that final run.

Skowhegan was also the home of Sen. Margaret Chase Smith, who in 1964 became the first woman placed in nomination for the presidency by a major party. If you consider the Republicans a major party. A research library containing documents from her thirty years in Congress and the Senate is located here.

Once across the Franklin County line, the land begins to change perceptibly. You are nearing the Blue Mountains, Maine's more compact version of neighboring New Hampshire's towering White Mountains. The countryside rolls and the towns get prettier, more in the familiar New England style than like grown-up lumber camps. New Sharon and Farmington Falls are the first evidence of this change, pleasant farm towns set amid the hills.

There is a University of Maine branch in **Farmington**, and Franklin Hall on the campus contains several galleries devoted to state artists. North of town is the birthplace of Lillian Nordica, a young woman who came out of the Maine woods to win acclaim as a coloratura soprano in the late nineteenth century. Her birthplace contains mementoes of her career, providing a fascinating glimpse at this golden operatic age.

Wilton is the home base of the G. M. Bass Shoe Company, whose Wee-Juns have been a collegiate favorite since the era of the toga party. At Dixfield, the road joins the rushing Androscoggin River and begins a twisting run along its banks as it cuts its way through the mountains. The enormous Boise Cascade mill, one of the world's largest suppliers of book paper, dominates the entrance to Rumford. Penacook Falls in the heart of town furnishes power for this huge complex.

Just past Newry, watch for the turnoff to Sunday River ski area. A few miles along this access road is Sunday River covered bridge, in a lovely hill-rimmed setting.

Finally, at **Bethel**, you reach resort New England. This is a delightful old town, surrounded by the Oxford Hills, with the Androscoggin bubbling through its center. Earlier in the century it was noted as a health spa. Dr. John Gehring, a New York neurologist, operated a retreat here where his frazzled big-city patients could pull themselves together. It's still a good place for that. The middle of town has a number of pleasant inns and shops, with the Bethel Inn situated right on the Common. Moses Mason served two terms in Congress in the 1830s and his Federal-period home on Broad Street is now a museum, with some exceptional murals.

The great peaks of the Presidential Range loom to the south as soon as you cross into New Hampshire. Here is Mount Washington, rising 6,288 feet above sea level, the highest point in the Northeast. Flanking it are the other giants of this magnificent range, reading like a lesson plan for American History 101: Adams and Madison, Monroe and Jefferson, Pierce and Eisenhower. The names ring like chimes, joining the scenery to the solemn flow of history.

Just past Shelburne, the road plunges into a canopy of birches. White trunks line either side of the highway, illuminating the otherwise dark forest setting. Flickers of sunlight flash down through the branches. Just to the north of the road, the Androscoggin rushes past from its origin in the nearby hills. The birches were first celebrated in the watercolors of Dodge MacKnight, and the tract remains serenely undisturbed.

Gorham is a slightly busier version of Bethel. Two of the major roads through the White Mountains meet here, and in summer and foliage season, U.S. 2 is quite crowded as it passes through. Just to the west is Moose Brook State Park, with outstanding views of the mountains, hiking trails and picnic facilities. A few miles further, past the village of Randolph, a pullout to the south has the best look yet at the Presidential peaks. You are practically on the flank of mounts Madison and Adams here, the closest the road will come to these giants, and the view down their green and rockbound walls is awesome.

U.S. 2 bends to the north as it leaves the edge of White Mountains National Forest. Now it is Mount Starr King that closes the horizon dead ahead. Although not nearly as tall as the Presidential peaks, it dominates by its isolation. The mountain is named for Dr. Thomas Starr King, a Boston clergyman who was one of the first men to explore the mountain as a traveler rather than a settler or soldier. His newspaper writings about his journeys in the 1850s popularized the area throughout New England and began the tourist industry here. This was a mixed blessing, as some of the more obtrusive roadside attractions around the town of Jefferson demonstrate. But the old roads helped bring the masses to parts of the country where previously only the wealthy could travel. The benefits outweigh the shlock.

Soon the road links up with the Israel River, named for early settler Israel Glines. Western views open up toward the Connecticut River Valley and Vermont. Lancaster was the first town in northern New Hampshire, founded in 1764 by settlers making the rugged overland trek from Haverhill, New Hampshire. The settlement was pretty tenuous in the early stages. Discouraged by weather and Indian raids, all the original settlers abandoned the place. Except for Eamons Stockwell. He hung on alone through the winter, whence all but he had fled, and when his companions returned in the spring, Lancaster was established for keeps. A covered bridge dating from 1862 crosses the Israel River on Mechanic Street, just east of the highway.

The Connecticut is a narrow stream this far north, and after crossing it the road hugs the western bank for a time. It then cuts through the village of Lunenburg and joins the Moose River. That's appropriate, because in Vermont, U.S. 2 is named after the old Bull Moose himself and called the Theodore Roosevelt Highway.

Jean de Crèvecouer was one of many idealistic Frenchmen who grew intoxicated on American freedom in the late eighteenth century. The French consul in New York, Crèvecouer was no mere political theorist. He plunged right into the American soil, introducing many European crops to these shores. His *Letters from an American Farmer,* published under the pseudonym J. Hector St. Jean, became popular in Europe just as the Revolutionary War was ending, and no tourist brochure ever whipped up such enthusiasm for a foreign land as this book did. So when settlers of a new town on the Moose and Passumpsic rivers went to choose a name, they decided to honor this American farmer and called their town St. Johns, using the Anglicized version of his pseudonym. Crèvecouer insisted they add the *bury,* to distinguish it from all other St. Johnses, and they obliged. Crèvecouer is also remembered in the town of Crèvecouer in Illinois. That double-dip is unique in the field of American community nomenclature.

St. Johnsbury's greatest growth came after the invention of the platform scale by Thaddeus Fairbanks. Patented in 1831, the device took a load off everyone's mind and tripled the town's population with its manufacture. The civic-minded Fairbanks family endeavored to make it a culturally rich community for the benefit of their employees. They established the Athenaeum in 1873, now noted for its collection of paintings from the Hudson River School. Sixteen years later, a bit further down Main Street, they added the Fairbanks Museum, a science and natural history facility. The entire Main Street area, on a ridge above the valley, is now a historic district, and so is Railroad Street, which parallels Main on the valley floor. The scales are still made here by Colt Industries.

The town is also known for its maple sugar production. Just east of St. Johnsbury is the Maple Museum, with demonstrations of syrup and candy making. The enterprise got its start when George Cary had the brainstorm of flavoring chewing tobacco with maple sugar. This taste sensation led to an entire range of maple-flavored products, most of a less disgusting nature.

FOCUS

* * *

Anyone who has spent any amount of time in this state has a candidate for the most nearly perfect Vermont town, the one that best typifies Vermont's look and texture. There are so many of these places that a list of nominees could fill pages. Mine is Peacham.

Long after a trip is over, memory selects moments to burnish and replay. One day spent by chance in an unfamiliar place may be set apart forever from all the ordinary days around it. These accidental memories are among the best reasons to travel the old roads.

I first came to Peacham on a perfect October day in 1963 with my two closest college friends. We had finished school the previous year. Bob had already left town for a job in Chicago, and Tom was planning a January wedding. So this little trip would be the last time the three of us would be together in quite this way.

We drove into St. Johnsbury at lunchtime. The first game of the World Series was on the tube, and the three of us, bred-to-the-bone Yankee haters, watched in glee as Sandy Koufax whipped his way toward a new strikeout record. We got out some maps over coffee and decided where to go next. I noticed the town of Peacham nearby—just south of U.S. 2—and it raised a memory. When I was young, we had a book at home called something like *Scenic Wonders of America.* The chapter on Vermont carried a picture of a white church and autumnal hills that was labeled Peacham. I convinced the others we should go there.

Peacham is on an old military trail to Canada, the Hazen-Bayley Road, built during the Revolution. There is an academy there, founded in 1795, and the church, looking just as it did in the picture book, dated from 1806. We passed through town, then doubled back as I tried to figure out how to reach the vantage point from which the photograph had been taken. We tried the road behind the church. It started to ascend a hill and within a quarter mile or so I could look down and see the familiar view— the church, its spire and clock tower backed by miles of rolling hills, the hazy peaks of New Hampshire in dim outline on the horizon. We found a clearing on the ridge and sat down to take it all in.

We stayed for hours. We talked about college escapades, the dissatisfactions of our work, hopes for the future. Tom would write novels, Bob would win awards, and I would get the kind of jobs that would let me watch Sandy Koufax and also travel a lot. The hopes didn't seem unreasonable. Life had a good deal of certitude to it then. It may have been 1963, but we were still in the 1950s. Things were secure, predictable. In little more than a month, shots would be fired at a motorcade in Dallas and everything would start to come apart. But on this perfect October day in Peacham, time was suspended. We stayed on the hillside until the light began to fail, then got on with our trip and, eventually, out of each other's lives.

I went back to Peacham eleven years later as a travel writer. I tried to find our hillside, but nothing looked familiar. I drove back and forth for several minutes. Then it struck me that the place where we had sat was now occupied by a private home. The perfect view of Peacham was gone. Private property.

When I got back home I wrote a melancholy article about this for my newspaper. I received a letter in response from a reader who said my article seemed to describe the location of a friend's home. He said he would forward my article, but I never heard anything further.

I didn't get back to Peacham until I was researching this book, almost twenty-five years to the day after my first trip there. Once more I reacquainted myself with the village and, just out of curiosity, started the drive up the hill behind the church. I found the old vantage point easily enough. The house was still there. But this time there was a large sign on the maple out in front: PHOTOGRAPHERS WELCOME. On the lawn beside the house, travelers had set up their cameras and tripods and were busy snapping the perfect scene below.

I wondered if the article I had written years before had influenced the owners to permit seasonal intrusions on their property. But no one answered the doorbell when I rang. I thought of how Tom and Bob—one writing novels in Colorado, the other winning awards for journalism in Chicago—would have liked to hear about it. As I recall, Koufax was a pretty good interview for me too.

* * *

Back on the main road, the drive continues through West Oanville. Joe's Pond here was named for a famed Indian guide, and there is also a Molly's Pond, named for his wife. Just beyond that is the turnoff to **Cabot**. Besides maple sugar, the distinctive taste of Vermont is cheddar cheese. At the Cabot Farmers' Co-op Creamery Company, you can watch cheddar and other dairy products being made, then buy a chunk for a roadside snack. Thankfully, no one has yet come up with the idea of making a cheese-flavored chewing tobacco. We'll just stick to maple, thank you very much.

Plainfield is the home of Goddard College, a small, progressive liberal arts school. Several buildings on the campus were designed by students and built by the large number of Goddard-trained artisans who couldn't tear themselves away from the area.

Vermont is the most rural of all states. Its capital, **Montpelier**, has the smallest population of any state capital, and its largest city, Burlington, is the smallest largest city. (Alaska and Wyoming contain fewer people, but their cities are a bit bigger.) Many state capitals started off as wide spots in the road, chosen only for a central location or because opposing factions from larger cities could not agree. A bit of both resulted in Montpelier's selection in 1805. But while other capitals have swelled into large cities because of the constantly expanding apparatus of state government, Montpelier remains as it was, a small town with a big dome. The figure atop the capitol dome is Ceres, Roman goddess of agriculture. Inside the portico stands a statue of Ethan Allen, demanding the surrender of Fort Ticonderoga. His raid of 1775 is regarded as a milestone in the fight for independence from Britain. Allen, however, was a stalwart Vermonter who was just as concerned about fighting off a hostile takeover by New York. Territorial claimants from New York were regarded with as much enmity as the British, and for a time, Allen and his Green Mountain Boys were defending Vermont against all comers. The fact that Fort Ticonderoga was situated in New York must have doubled Allen's delight at taking it. The statehouse itself dates from 1859 and is the third on the site. A state historical museum is in the Pavilion Office Building next door.

The works of several state artists, especially Thomas W. Wood, are displayed at the Vermont College Art Center, on East State Street. Wood founded the gallery in 1895 to ensure permanent exhibition space for himself and his colleagues, who painted scenes of rural life.

Montpelier's other main industry is insurance. National Life was chartered here in 1848, and its landmark headquarters is on a hill opposite the statehouse. The son of the company founder was George Dewey, whose name is probably more familiar with Admiral in front of it. The hero of Manila Bay in the Spanish-American War was born here in 1837. A nice overview of the town is available in Hubbard Park, west on State from the State House, then north on Terrace Street. From a lookout tower on the hilltop, you can see the Winooski Valley stretching to the distance.

The Winooski River cuts through one of the major Green Mountain passes. Winooski means "onion" in English, and for a time, that's what the river was called. Upon reflection, however, Vermonters decided they liked Winooski a lot better, so they reverted to the Indian original. U.S. 2 follows its course and, west of Montpelier, also picks up Interstate 89. Only for a while, though.

You approach the crest of the mountains near Waterbury. The Bolton Valley and Smugglers Notch ski areas are just to the north. So is Mount Mansfield, the state's highest peak at 4,393 feet. More distinctively shaped is the twin-peaked mountain to the south. The French called it Sleeping Lion, but to the English-speaking settlers it more resembled a Camel's Hump, and that's the name that survives. It is Vermont's third highest, at 4,083 feet, and there are fine views of it west of Waterbury.

One of the oddest examples of the ecclesiastical spirit is in the town of **Richmond**. The Old Round Church actually is a 16-sided structure, built cooperatively by five different religious denominations so that each would have a separate area in which to conduct services. When the various groups broke away, the building became the town hall. There isn't much utility to a 16-sided town hall, though, and for a number of years the place was abandoned. Recently restored, it is regarded as a historic treasure and one of the state's most unusual buildings.

Williston is another delightful small town, the home of the state's first governor, Thomas Chittenden. It has a historic district that includes several blocks of nineteenth-century buildings.

Vermont is tiny in population, but it has undergone some sweeping demographic change in recent years. The state has become something of a haven and symbol for young urban professionals, who find in its serenity and unchanging charm the sort of stability they longed for in the city. Of course, many of their grandparents eagerly fled just such stability to find opportunity in the city. But instead of feeling stifled, their descendants find the same surroundings enriching. Once the most rock-ribbed of Republican states, Vermont now elects Democrats regularly to state office. **Burlington**, its largest city, is a surprisingly cosmopolitan sort of place.

The city descends to Lake Champlain in a series of terraces, and the University of Vermont occupies the uppermost. It was established in 1791, the same year Vermont became a state, with a bequest from Ira Allen, the brother of Ethan. He stipulated that no development was ever to intrude on the school Green, and that wish has been scrupulously respected. The Green continues to form the tranquil core of the school. Among the classroom buildings around it is the Old Mill, dedicated by General Lafayette on his farewell trip to America in 1825. A short distance away, on Colchester Avenue, is the Robert H. Fleming Museum, with excellent collections of Oriental and primitive art. This is the only state university in the country that enrolls more out-of-state than native-born students. Many stay on to live here after commencement. The university is north of U.S. 2, by way of Prospect Street, at the eastern edge of Burlington.

The next terrace contains the city's business district, its most interesting area located around the intersection of Church and Pearl, west of U.S. 2, along Pearl Street. The commercial structures on Church have been turned into a historic district and pedestrian mall.

Finally, at the level of the lake, at the western edge of the city, Battery Park offers spectacular views of sunsets over the water and the Adirondacks of New York. The area was fortified during the War of 1812, hence the name. The cannon actually did fire a few salvos at a menacing British fleet, but mostly it was commerce that came calling on the lake.

Ethan Allen retired to this area on a farm confiscated from a hastily departed Tory. Part of that 4,400-acre tract is now a park, with a viewing tower over the lake and mountains. It is located out North Avenue, west from U.S. 2 and the business district.

On the north side of the Winooski River is the town of the same name. For years a drab industrial suburb, Winooski was home of the American Woolen Mills and a variety of smaller industries built around the river's falls. Now the old mills have been converted to offices, shops and residences and the downtown has won several awards as a model for redevelopment.

The highway runs with U.S. 7 for a few miles north, before breaking to the west for its climactic run up to **Grand Isle**. This is another scenic summit for U.S. 2, as it makes its way up slender fingers of land with views of mountains opening out across Lake Champlain to either side—the Adirondacks to the west and the slightly smaller peaks of the Green Mountains to the east. Bridges connect the two largest islands, North and South Hero, which were named after the Allen brothers. (Actually, the Allens named them after themselves, but why quibble.) In spring, when the apple orchards blossom, the drive is magnificent. Sand Bar Wildlife Sanctuary is located at the eastern approach to the islands, and three other state parks—Grand Isle, Knight Point and North Hero—are scattered along the route. There are beaches, hiking trails and outstanding views in all of them.

One of the first settlers here was Jedediah Hyde, Jr. He fought alongside his father at Bunker Hill and eventually found himself in the Corps of Engineers. The Hydes moved to Vermont in 1783 and were enlisted to survey these islands. The property had been parceled out to the Green Mountain Boys by the Allens, but the younger Hyde, liking what he surveyed, bought a few pieces for himself. He built a hand-hewn log cabin on one of them and, remarkably, it has survived, to be designated the oldest existing log cabin in the country. It has been moved, though, from its original location to the town of Grand Isle.

Vermont finally overcame its old misgivings about being linked too closely with New York when the bridge to Rouses Point was completed in 1937. Crossing the mouth of the lake, the road enters New York to begin its 500-mile hiatus until Michigan.

VISITING HOURS

MAINE

Bangor: Thomas A. Hill Museum, (207) 942-5766. South of U.S. 2 on Union St., at High St. Tuesday–Friday and Sunday, noon–4, mid-January–mid-December. Admission.

Isaac Farrar House, (207) 941-2808. South of U.S. 2 on Union St., at Second St. Monday–Friday, 9–4, all year. Admission.

Bethel: Moses Mason House, (207) 824-2908. On U.S. 2, at 15 Broad St. Tuesday–Sunday, 1–4, July–Labor Day. Admission.

Farmington: University of Maine-Farmington Art Galley, (207) 778-3501. On Main St., in Franklin Hall. Sunday–Thursday, noon–4, mid-September–mid-May. Free.

Lillian Nordica Homestead, (207) 778-2042. North on Maine 4, to Holly Road. Tuesday–Sunday, 10–noon and 1–5, June–Labor Day. Admission.

Old Town: Penobscot Indian Museum, (207) 827-6545. North of town, on Indian Island. Monday–Friday, 10–4, all year. Admission.

Old Town Canoe Company, (207) 827-5513. Off U.S. 2, at 58 Middle St. Monday–Friday, 1–4, July–August. Free.

VERMONT

Burlington: Fleming Museum, (802) 656-2090. North of U.S. 2 on Prospect St. to the University of Vermont campus, then east on Colchester Ave. Tuesday–Friday, 10–5; weekends, 1–5, all year. Free.

Ethan Allen Park and viewing tower, no phone. West from U.S. 2 on Main St., then north on North Ave. Wednesday–Sunday, noon–8, Memorial Day–Labor Day. Free.

Cabot: Cabot Farmers Co-op Creamery, (802) 563-2231. North of U.S. 2, just east of Marshfield, on Cabot Road. Monday–Friday, 8–4:30, all year. Free.

Grand Isle: Hyde Log Cabin, (802) 828-3226. On U.S. 2. Wednesday–Sunday, 9:30–5:30, July–Labor Day. Free.

Montpelier: State Capitol, (802) 828-2228. On U.S. 2 (State St.). Monday–Friday, 8–4, all year. Free.

Vermont Museum, (802) 828-2291. On U.S. 2, at 109 State St. Monday–Friday, 8–4:30; weekends, 10–4, all year. Free.

T. W. Wood Art Gallery, (802) 229-0522. East of U.S. 2, on East State at College Sts., at the Vermont College Art Center. Tuesday–Sunday, noon–4, all year. Free.

Richmond: Old Round Church, no phone. On U.S. 2. Daily, July 4–Labor Day, 10–4; weekends only, from Memorial Day. Free.

St. Johnsbury: Athenaeum, (802) 748-8291. On U.S. 2, at 30 Main St. Monday–Saturday, 9:30–5. Closes at 2, Saturday, July–August. Free.

Fairbanks Museum, (802) 748-2372. On U.S. 2, Main at Prospect Sts. Monday–Saturday, 10–4; Sunday, 1–5, all year. Admission.

Maple Museum, (802) 748-5141. East, on U.S. 2. Daily, 9–5, May–October. Charge for tour.

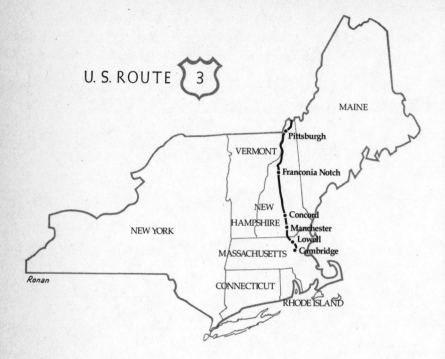

U. S. ROUTE 3

MAINE

VERMONT

Pittsburgh

Franconia Notch

NEW
HAMPSHIRE

Concord

NEW YORK

Manchester

Lowell

MASSACHUSETTS

Cambridge

Ronan

CONNECTICUT

RHODE ISLAND

Daniel Webster Country

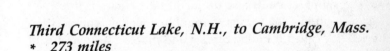

U.S. 3

Third Connecticut Lake, N.H., to Cambridge, Mass.
* 273 miles

This is the Daniel Webster Highway, and like the great statesman
and orator for whom it is named, it comes very near the heart of
New Hampshire. If you want to learn a lot about New Hampshire
in a hurry, you could do worse than drive U.S. 3. It runs the entire
length of the Granite State, from the near wilderness of the northern border to the magnificent mountain scenery of Franconia
Notch, to the central lakes, to the state capital, to the mill towns.
Virtually every aspect of the state can be found along the road.
The final miles in Massachusetts are something of an afterthought
by comparison, and many of them are freeway miles. But when
you break away to Lowell, Arlington and Cambridge, you get
some sense of the history and heritage of Massachusetts as well.

* **MILEPOSTS** *

The highway begins in forest, amid some of the wildest country in New England. U.S. 3 is the only road that penetrates the northern tip of New Hampshire, where the state narrows to a slender finger poking into Quebec. Here the Connecticut River springs from a series of three lakes surrounded by state forest. The road originates here too, at the border, in the shadow of 3,005-foot-high Deer Mountain. There is a lovely scenic turnout as the road passes Second Lake along a dam built in 1934.

This area is so remote that for a time it considered itself a sovereign nation. As in much of northern New England, the boundary between Canada and the United States was imprecise and in constant dispute after the War of 1812. In Maine, the disagreement led to the brief, bloodless Aroostook War. Here in New Hampshire, residents also decided to take matters into their own hands and in 1832 formed a republic independent of either country. They called it Indian Stream and placed the government in the village of Pittsburg, still the northernmost community in the state. This odd situation lasted about three years, until it turned dangerous, when an Indian Stream militia unit decided to move into lands claimed by Canada. This brought an immediate reaction from New Hampshire, which sent its own militia on a pacification mission. That calmed everyone down, and Indian Stream decided it would henceforth be part of New Hampshire. The Webster-Ashburton Treaty fixed the border in 1842, with Indian Stream safely tucked within the confines of the United States.

Near Stewartstown, the road bends south along the eastern bank of the Connecticut, with Vermont on the opposite side. The green summit of Mount Monadnock dominates the western horizon as the road nears Colebrook. The name of the mountain may sound familiar. Forget it. Wrong Mount Monadnock. You're probably thinking of the one lauded by several New England writers and poets, which is a couple of hundred miles south. This one is perfectly nice but a good deal farther from the main traveled roads. Colebrook once manufactured about 5 percent of the starch made in this country, but it is not nearly as stiff now, and tourism is the big industry. There is a covered bridge in nearby Columbia, noted for its unusually high, 75-foot roof.

The road continues through lightly populated country, occasionally running within sight of the river. **Lancaster** is the first town of any size along this road and was the first settled in northern New Hampshire. (See U.S. 2 for more information.) Like many communities in the area, it was pioneered by veterans of Rogers' Rangers, the band of backwoods fighters immortalized in Kenneth Roberts's novel *Northwest Passage.* They campaigned here during the French and Indian Wars and came back with hoes instead of muskets when hostilities ended.

Lancaster was the home of John W. Weeks, a member of both the Harding and Coolidge presidential cabinets. He came from an old New Hampshire family, one of whom is credited with naming the peaks of the Presidential Range of the White Mountains. Weeks was alarmed at the reckless way his state was wasting this treasure. Private lumbering concessions in the mountains were granted from 1867 on, and by the early years of this century the area was visibly lacerated. While in Congress, Weeks sponsored legislation to buy back vast portions of the area as national forest. The mountains had already been established as a resort, and many powerful public figures spent their summers there. They gave their support to Weeks's campaign, and many of them turned over some of their holdings as gifts to the government. The national forest now encompasses 753,000 acres of some of the finest mountain scenery in the country, protected for all time. Weeks's hilltop home on Mount Prospect is a state park, just south of Lancaster along the road.

Now the great peaks of the Presidential Range become visible to the east as the road rambles through the resort towns of Whitefield and Twin Mountain. Then it bends sharply southwest to enter **Franconia Notch**, the most celebrated patch of mountain greenery in New England. This gap between the rock walls of the Franconia and Kingman ranges was discovered in 1805 and by the Civil War years had become a leading tourist destination. The massive Victorian hotels that were built here—Flume House and

Profile House—have long since vanished. But the beauty of the land remains as it was, with one famed sight after another packed into an 8-mile stretch of road. Its admirers even managed to stop a freeway in the 1970s. Plans for Interstate 93, connecting Boston and northern Vermont, called for it to carve right through the notch. The public outcry was so great that the planners were sent back to the drawing boards. Now the freeway ends on either side of the notch, and old U.S. 3 is the only road to make the passage.

First stop is Echo Lake, the derivation of the name apparent from the acoustical excellence of the surrounding mountain walls. Cannon Mountain Aerial Tramway, with its 2,022-foot lift, ascends to the best views of the notch area. The Profile, also known as the Old Man of the Mountain and the Great Stone Face (after the short story written about it by Nathaniel Hawthorne), is the best-known feature of the area and the symbol of the state. This rocky outcropping, 1,200 feet above the lake that reflects its image, seems like the visage of the ancient mountains themselves. It's a powerful, deeply moving sight, no matter how many times you've seen it reproduced. The Basin is a deep, glacial pothole near a waterfall, reached by a short, pleasant trail. Finally, at the southern end of the notch is the Flume, a narrow gorge filled with tumbling cascades. A boardwalk is cut into the side of Mount Liberty along the wall of the natural chasm, enabling hikers to follow the canyon walk.

U.S. 3 now runs south from the notch alongside the bubbling Pemigewassett River. The narrow corridor cut by the stream is hemmed in on either side by national forest. Some of the commercial development is a bit obtrusive, but the concentration around North Woodstock does serve as a way of easing back into the ordinary world after the wonders we just traversed.

Plymouth is a pleasant college town on the border of the mountain country. Hawthorne died here in 1864 on a final journey to his beloved mountains. His longtime friend, the former president Franklin Pierce, accompanied him on the trip, hoping that it would buoy the great writer's failing health and spirit. But they only made it this far, with the great peaks rising hazily in the distance.

At Ashland, U.S. 3 abruptly parts company with Interstate 93 for a short detour east to the lake country. At the edge of Squam Lake, near **Holderness**, is the Science Center of New Hampshire, with miles of nature trails winding past exhibits of native animals in their natural habitat. The views across the lake, second largest in the state, open out on Mount Chocorua, named for a legendary chief who placed the white settlers under an eternal curse after they killed his son.

The road crosses a ridge and then drops down to Meredith on Lake Winnipesaukee, a body of water with such a complicated name that the spelling had to be fixed by an act of the state legislature in 1931. Its meaning may be "smile of the Great Spirit." Then again it may mean "good water with large pour-out place." I like the ring of the first one better, but the "pour-out place" version has historical authenticity going for it. It was there that Indians placed their nets to trap fish and gave the location its name, the Weirs. The first European explorers marked the spot in 1652 with a boulder that was supposed to fix the northern border of Massachusetts. The Endicott Boulder, to which members of the expedition affixed their initials, was found in a stream bed in 1833 and replaced in its original spot. The border had moved substantially south, however, when New Hampshire separated from Massachusetts in 1740. Cruises of the scenic lake leave from the docks of the Weirs, not far from the Endicott Boulder.

The boundaries of Laconia, next town along the road, spread over three lakes at the foot of Mount Belknap, but Laconia is as much a manufacturing town as a resort. It turns out a variety of products, from hosiery to printed circuitry. The highway runs along Winnisquam Lake after passing through town and turns west.

This may be called the Daniel Webster Highway, but not until it reaches **Franklin** does the road reach the man's native soil. Webster was born just south of here in 1782 in a cabin built by his father, Capt. Ebenezer Webster. The family moved just one year later, but that was long enough to fix the statesman's reputation to this place. In fact, Franklin was the second choice for the town name when it became incorporated. It wanted to name itself

Webster, but another village a few miles to the south had beat it to the punch, and Webster's hometown wound up honoring Benjamin Franklin instead.

Webster was regarded as the greatest orator of his age, at a time when this was the most popular form of public entertainment. Trained as a lawyer, his arguments before the U.S. Supreme Court in the Dartmouth College case (which established the inviolability of a contract even when a state wants to overturn it) won him a huge public following. He served in both branches of Congress and as secretary of state but was revered especially for his stirring defense of the Union. His debate with R. Y. Hayne on this issue in 1830 became a model for the study of rhetoric in American schools for years afterward, with students required to memorize huge portions of his declamation. He sacrificed his own popularity in the last years of his life by backing the Compromise of 1850 in a final, vain attempt to avoid war. But his legendary status in New England was celebrated in Steven Vincent Benet's short story "The Devil and Daniel Webster." A bust of the statesman sculpted by one of his descendants, Daniel Chester French, sits in front of Franklin's Congregational Church on Main Street. Webster's birthplace, 4 miles south of town, is reached by way of N.H. 127.

Webster began practicing law in Boscawen, the next town along U.S. 3. Boscawen was named after the American admiral in command of the British fleet that attacked the French fortress at Louisbourg in 1745.

Webster was opening his office at about the same time that neighboring **Concord** became the state's permanent capital. The seat of government was shifted here from Portsmouth in 1808. Eleven years later the statehouse was completed and is still going strong, the oldest capitol building in continuous use in the country. The original legislative chambers remain intact. Directly behind the capitol, on Park Street, is the New Hampshire Historical Society, with a variety of displays on the state's development. Among them is a Concord coach, the most widely used model of American stagecoach, which was manufactured here for 102 years. Designed by J. Stephen Abbot, its high-wheeled structure and suspension system made it an ideal conveyance for the old misshapen roads of the West. The most popular model carried nine passengers in excruciating discomfort, especially the ones who sat in the middle row with no back supports. The company was liquidated in 1928, but Concord still holds a Coach and Carriage Festival each June.

The town's name marks the resolution of a conflict that hindered development of New Hampshire for a good part of the eighteenth century. The Bow Controversy, involving duplicate colonial land grants, was litigated for decades before being resolved in 1765 and enabling clear titles to be set. Before that, the town had been called Rumford, and thereby hangs a tale.

Benjamin Thompson, a Massachusetts-born scientist, lived here for a while and married a local woman. Loyalist in sympathy, however, he returned to England, where he made pioneering studies in the fields of heat and friction. He was also a talented politician and held several government offices in the service of Bavaria, for which he was made a knight of the Holy Roman Empire. Thompson chose to be called Count Rumford, to honor his wife's home. The town had already changed its name by then, but somehow he felt Count Concord just didn't make it.

Its location on the Merrimack River made Concord accessible from most parts of the state, and the Middlesex Canal, which was built in 1815, also brought it a degree of industrial prosperity. Concord's most attractive output today, though, can be found in the gallery of the League of New Hampshire Craftsmen, housed in the Eagle Hotel. This was a popular gathering place for state politicians in the early nineteenth century and has been restored.

A few blocks away is the home of Franklin Pierce, the only New Hampshireman to become president. He lived in Concord from 1842 to 1848 and four years later was implausibly chosen as a compromise candidate at the deadlocked Democratic Convention. His life quickly became a disaster. A few weeks before his departure for Washington, his only son was killed in a rail accident. His wife never recovered emotionally from the shock, and Pierce, his personal life in a shambles, could not control the accelerating sectional conflict that was propelling the nation toward civil war.

He has come down through history as a mediocrity, the wrong man to hold the top office in dangerous times. It's hard to imagine how anyone could have contained those forces, but Pierce had the bad luck to be in charge at the time.

FOCUS
* * *

By the middle of the twentieth century, New England had become economically defunct, used up, obsolete. Its job base was disappearing, its cities in decline, its population moving elsewhere. The entire region seemed to be getting by on history and charm, a snippet of Robert Frost poetry and a fading print by Currier and Ives.

But within a generation everything turned around. By the 1980s, it had the lowest unemployment rate in the country. Its decrepit mill towns were riding the crest of the high-tech tide. People had rediscovered the attractiveness of its way of life, and several of its states experienced the fastest rate of population growth in their history.

This process did not reach everywhere in New England at the same time, and its results were spread unevenly throughout the area. But it happened first in **Manchester**. This has been New Hampshire's largest city since the mid-nineteenth century. As a small settlement on the Merrimack, it was best known as the home of John Stark, the Revolutionary War general who smashed a British force at Bennington, Vermont, and prepared the way for the critical victory at Saratoga. That era ended in 1810 when Judge Samuel Blodgett, inspired by the first cotton mill here, led a move to rename the place after the giant British industrial city.

For more than a century, that seemed prescient. The little cotton company was reincorporated in 1831 by Boston financiers and evolved into the huge Amoskeag Manufacturing Company, an industrial leviathan that became the largest textiles firm in the world. It eclipsed even the output of the city's British namesake, and totally dominated the life of Manchester.

Amoskeag occupied a mile-long row of mill buildings along the

Merrimack in the heart of the city. They were built over an eighty-year period in a unified, red brick mode, varying only in height. The restless hum of the mill machinery measured the pace of Manchester's life: 5 million yards of cloth a week, 8 million square feet of floor space, more than 700,000 spindles and 23,000 looms. The mills drew their power from the Merrimack rapids—and from the people of the city, who frequently entered them as children and left only upon retirement. On the next block up, Canal Street, the company built workers' housing in the same uniform style as the factory buildings. In one more block was Elm Street, the main commercial thoroughfare, its business district precisely paralleling the line of the mills. On these three streets, entire lives were played out.

But cracks began to appear in the monolith as the twentieth century began. The rate of capital investment slowed and the machinery became obsolete. Labor unrest led to strikes at many New England plants, so the owners accelerated their move to the South, where they found a more docile work force and an anti-union tradition. The competition from synthetics and imports increased. The industry was in decline by the 1920s, and when the Depression hit, it was finished. Amoskeag shockingly declared bankruptcy in 1935, and it seemed that Manchester would shrivel and die as well.

A civic committee bought the mill properties the next year at a knockdown price of $5 million. Slowly, painfully, as the effects of the Depression lifted, the group began to lure smaller businesses to town, filling the grim old buildings with a more diversified job base. That story has since been repeated all around New England. Nearby Lowell is another prime example. But Manchester was the model.

As you drive along Commercial Street today, you see the old mills restored to life. They are filled with clothing manufacturers, high-tech industries, plastics, an astonishing diversity of enterprises. Somehow the drive is most impressive on a weekend morning, when the only other traffic around is a biker or jogger, and all that mighty heart is lying still. The simple power of this concentrated mass of buildings is enormous. The knowledge that they were once empty for keeps makes the sight even more impressive.

There is a view of the Merrimack rapids from Loeb Square at the southern end of this complex. The space is named for Nathan Loeb, the feisty late publisher of the Manchester *Union-Leader.* His highly personal style of vitriolic journalism amazed and appalled the national media when it was exposed to him during the state's first-in-the-nation presidential primary. Near Philip Cote Street, watch for the sculpture of a young girl. She is on a flight of stairs, opposite the mills. She walks toward the dark buildings, but her face is turned away in a sweet, wistful look of longing. What does she see? Lost childhood? A home far away? It is a lovely, touching piece of art.

The Currier Gallery of Art is up the hill east of Elm. This is regarded as one of the finest small collections in New England. Housed in a jewel-like, late Renaissance–style chateau, it is named for Moody Currier, the local banker who founded the museum. He also wrote poetry and was governor of New Hampshire.

The Manchester Historic Association, two blocks east of Elm, contains displays illustrating the sweep of events over this city, including the drama of the Amoskeag shutdown and comeback.

* * *

The highway now enters Hillsborough County, one of the fastest-growing areas in the East. This part of southern New Hampshire is within commuting distance of Boston. It started to develop in the 1960s, as freeways made the population shift possible and the Massachusetts tax rate made it practical. New Hampshire has no state income tax, and the contrast with its neighbor, which came to be nicknamed Taxachusetts in this period, touched off the land rush. Some villages doubled in size within five years, and developers could barely keep pace with housing demand. A handful of these places have retained their charms, but many have been swallowed whole by the voracious megalopolis.

Thornton's Ferry is named for Matthew Thornton. He furnished transportation across the Merrimack here and went on to sign the Declaration of Independence. The highway completely bypasses Nashua, a lively manufacturing city that has become the commercial center of this regional boom.

From the state line to the Boston suburbs, U.S. 3 is a freeway. But that's no fun. Before the freeway was built, the old road followed the route now traced by Mass. 34. So cut over to that road at Tyngsborough and ride it into **Lowell**.

Maybe even more than Manchester, Lowell is the quintessential New England mill town. It was a planned community, set up by the Merrimack Manufacturing Company as a prototype of the modern factory town. Boston financier Francis Cabot Lowell had underwritten the development of a power loom, one that would dramatically expand the output of American textile plants. Existing locations were inadequate, so his associates selected this site on the Merrimack and built a new town. It was a wonder of its time. Delegations from Europe came over to study its features for adaptation.

However, it followed the pattern of other mill towns, planned and unplanned: exploitation of labor, strikes, heightened competition, obsolescence and collapse. Lowell lay prostrate for nearly half a century, but in the 1970s the community started to realize the tremendous potential of its historic buildings. The center of Lowell, with its canals and mills, was revitalized as Lowell National Historic Park in 1978. It contains a visitor's center, walking tours through the area, barge rides on the canals, old trolleys and historic displays. An adjacent state park complements these exhibits with demonstrations of vintage machinery in action. It is the most complete urban industrial museum in the country.

Mementoes of one who escaped the confines of the mill town are a few blocks away. James Abbott McNeil Whistler, the great portraitist, was born in the house at 243 Worthen Street in 1834. It is now a museum. Famed for his wit as much as for his brush, he left for Paris as a young man and spent the rest of his life in Europe. He is, of course, best remembered for the portrait of his mother that hangs in the Louvre and is formally titled *Arrangement in Black and Grey.* Coming from this town, those are the colors you'd expect him to use.

I would be remiss if I didn't point out that Lowell was also the hometown of a man who probably inspired more old road travelers than any other writer. Jack Kerouac, author of *On the Road* and the voice of the Beat Generation of the 1950s, was born here and is honored with a plaque in Eastern Canal Plaza.

The route runs through the suburbs of Billerica and Winchester. Then at Route 128, the electronics parkway that encircles Boston, Mass. 34 becomes U.S. 3 once more and enters **Arlington**. It runs past Mystic Pond before entering the business district and turning sharply east as Massachusetts Avenue. This is the route of the British retreat from Lexington and Concord in 1775. The Redcoats were harrassed all the way by Minute Men firing from concealment. But when they reached this town, then known as Menotomy, things got a lot worse. They were ambushed by the Old Men of Menotomy, a group of twelve elderly gents who had been left behind by the militia because they were deemed too old for battle. Stung by this slight, the senior citizens attacked the British supply train here and touched off the bloodiest fight of the long day. The Minute Men converged to reinforce them and grappled with the British at close quarters around the Jason Russell House. The British lost forty men in combat that was often hand-to-hand, and the colonials lost twenty-five. The house, a few blocks west of the U.S. 3 intersection and just south of Massachusetts Ave., is now a museum.

Nearby is the old Schwamb Mill, which has specialized in making oval picture frames for more than a century and is now an industrial museum of nineteenth-century woodworking.

The highway swings south as it enters **Cambridge** to become Fresh Pond Parkway. At the Charles River, the name changes to Memorial Parkway, and once past the Anderson Bridge you are just a few blocks south of Harvard. For a few years after its founding in 1630, this town across the Charles from Boston was the capital of the Massachusetts Bay Colony because its position was regarded as more easily defended. When it lost the government, it was awarded the colony's college and renamed Cambridge. (New England was fond of shaping its cities with British models in mind.) You have already seen how Manchester's industrial destiny was decreed by its name; similarly, Cambridge was to be a university center.

Actually, the school wound up here because of the popularity of the Rev. Thomas Shepard, a local minister who led the attempt to confound the heresies of Anne Hutchinson. His intellectual gifts were so highly regarded that it was felt a college to train the colony's ministers should be placed in his proximity. Another young minister, John Harvard, left his estate to found the library of the new school, and in 1636 Harvard opened as the first college in the New World.

It is still conceded to be preeminent. If you see nothing else of it, drive a few blocks north on John F. Kennedy Street and take a walk around Harvard Yard. Encircling this campus core are Massachusetts Hall, the university's oldest building, dating from 1720; University Hall, a Charles Bullfinch structure dating from about a century later; the imposing Widener Library, built in 1915 and perhaps the most readily identifiable building in the Yard; and the Fogg Art Museum. Harvard is regarded, with some justification, as the font of the intellectual tradition in American life. There is still no university credential that carries quite the same weight.

The school down the road comes close, though. U.S. 3 swoops around the great bend of the Charles and ends at the campus of the Massachusetts Institute of Technology. This center of research and applied science was established in 1916 by William Barton Rogers. As you near Harvard Bridge, you will see the distinct shapes of the MIT Chapel and Kresge Auditorium, both designed by Eero Saarinen. The cylinder and arches of the chapel and the three-cornered roof and floating dome of the auditorium are strong visual statements. They make appealingly civilized punctuation marks to end this drive down from the northern wilds.

VISITING HOURS

NEW HAMPSHIRE

Concord: Statehouse, (603) 271-2154. On U.S. 3 (Main St.). Monday–Friday, 8–4:30, all year. Free.

New Hampshire Historical Society, (603) 225-3381. West of U.S. 3, at 30 Park St. Monday–Friday, 9–4:30, mid-June–mid-September; open Saturday, at other times. Free.

New Hampshire League of Craftsmen, (603) 224-1471. On U.S. 3, at 205 N. Main St. Monday–Friday, 9–5, all year. Free.

Franklin Pierce House, (603) 224-9620. North, off U.S. 3, at 14 Penacook St. Monday–Friday, 11–3, June–Labor Day. Admission.

Franconia Notch: Cannon Mountain Aerial Tramway, (603) 823-5563. North end of notch, on U.S. 3. Daily, 9–4:30, Memorial Day–mid-October. Admission.

The Flume, (603) 745-8391. South end of notch, on U.S. 3. Daily 9–4:30, Memorial Day–mid-October. Admission.

Franklin: Daniel Webster Birthplace, no phone. South of town, then west from U.S. 3 on New Hampshire 127. Wednesday–Sunday, 9–5, late June–Labor Day. Admission.

Holderness: New Hampshire Science Center, (603) 968-7194. On U.S. 3, at New Hampshire 113. Daily, 9:30–4:30, July–August; Monday–Friday, 9:30–4:30; weekends, 1–4, May, June, September, October. Admission.

Lancaster: Weeks Estate State Park, (603) 788-4467. South, off U.S. 3. Wednesday–Sunday, 10–5, late June–Labor Day. Weekends only, rest of September. Admission.

Manchester: Currier Gallery of Art, (603) 669-6144. East of U.S. 3, at 192 Orange St. Tuesday–Saturday, 10–4; Sunday, 2–5, all year. Free.

Manchester Historic Association, (603) 622-7531. East of

U.S. 3, at 129 Amherst St. Tuesday–Saturday, 10–4, all year. Free.

The Weirs: Lake Winnipesaukee Cruises, (603) 366-5531. On U.S. 3. Memorial Day–mid-October. Call for schedule and rates.

MASSACHUSETTS

Arlington: Jason Russell House, (617) 648-4300. West of U.S. 3, on Massachusetts Ave., at 7 Jason St. Tuesday–Saturday, 2–5, April–October. Admission.

Schwamb Mill, (617) 643-0554. West of U.S. 3, on Massachusetts Ave. at Lowell St. Monday–Friday, 10–4, all year. Free.

Cambridge: Harvard University, (617) 495-1573. North of U.S. 3, on John F. Kennedy St. from Anderson Bridge. Call for tour information and hours. Most Harvard museums have an admission charge.

Massachusetts Institute of Technology, (617) 253-1000. On U.S. 3, Memorial Drive. Kresge Auditorium and MIT Chapel are open daily, daylight hours, all year. Free.

Lowell: Lowell National Historic Park, (617) 459-1000. North of Massachusetts 3A on Central St. to Merrimack St. Follow signs to Visitor Center. Daily, 8:30–5, all year. Free.

Lowell State Park, (617) 453-1950. Adjoins the National Historic Park. Daily, 8:30–5, all year. Free.

Whistler House, (617) 452-7641. North of Massachusetts 3A on Fletcher St. to Worthen St. Tuesday–Saturday, 1–4, July–August; closed Saturday, other times of year. Free.

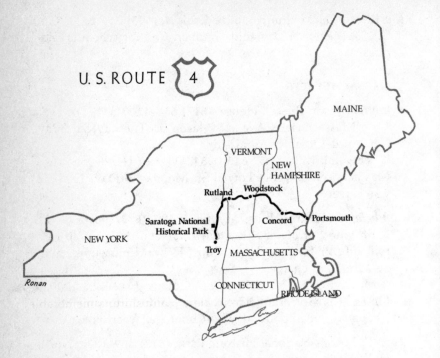

U. S. ROUTE 4

MAINE

VERMONT

NEW HAMPSHIRE

Rutland Woodstock

Concord Portsmouth

Saratoga National Historical Park

NEW YORK

Troy

MASSACHUSETTS

Ronan

CONNECTICUT

RHODE ISLAND

The Green Mountains

U.S. 4

Durham, N.H., to East Greenbush, N.Y.
* 256 miles

U.S. 4 is a chameleon. It changes its character with each state line it crosses. It is a pleasant ride in New Hampshire, a memorable mountain passage in Vermont and a journey into history in New York. The road begins by making its way through the old towns that lie just beyond the reach of metro Boston's explosion into New Hampshire. In Vermont it becomes the road across the Green Mountains and passes through classic New England scenery. Then in New York it shifts direction, dropping south to enter the upper reaches of the Hudson Valley. U.S. 4 is actually a connecting link in the old road system. It serves no major cities, connects no important points. It just fills in the gaps between the major highways, which is probably as strong a recommendation as an old road can have. Freeway intrusions are minimal and traffic usually not a problem.

* MILEPOSTS *

The road begins at the Spaulding Turnpike, northwest of Portsmouth, New Hampshire, on the banks of Little Bay, an estuary of the Piscataqua River. It was over these waters that a group of local patriots led by John Sullivan carried munitions stolen from Fort William and Mary in December 1774. The outbreak of war was still months away, but anti-British sentiment was growing and local revolutionaries were doing all they could to keep the pot simmering. In a rehearsal for his more celebrated ride, Paul Revere galloped into New Hampshire to warn Sullivan that the British were coming to get supplies of gunpowder stored at the seaside fort. The Sons of Liberty managed to get there first, seized the powder and carried it off by ship to the town of Durham. When the British discovered the theft, they tried to pursue but found their larger ships could not sail that far up the Piscataqua. The powder was later removed from its cache and used against its original owners at Bunker Hill. A tablet marks the site of the old meetinghouse in Durham where it was hidden. The town has been the home of the University of New Hampshire since 1893, when it split off from Dartmouth.

U.S. 4 runs along the route of the Portsmouth-Concord Pike, the first road to the state's interior, built in 1796. It passes through a succession of small towns, with occasional glimpses of the White Mountain peaks far to the north. After skirting the edge of Northwood Lake, it becomes a freeway east of Concord and bypasses the state capital. (Concord's attractions are discussed in the chapter on U.S. 3.)

Immediately after departing from the freeway, the road crosses the Merrimack River. Park on the bridge for a moment and follow a footpath to the island in midstream. This is where the indomitable Hannah Dustin, carried off in an Indian raid on her home in Haverhill, Massachusetts, turned on her captors and scalped ten of them as they slept. Then, with her nurse (she had given birth just a few weeks before) and a youth who had also been captured, she retraced their route along the river and enterprisingly peddled the scalps when she got home. This all happened in 1697, when life was a lot tougher in New Hampshire. The comparison to the story of Jael in the Book of Judges was not lost on religious commentators of the time, who turned the story into a parable repeated throughout the colony. Hannah is still well thought of in the area. You'll see her name on various roads and businesses in the southern part of the state. A statue on the island marks the spot where she took up her tomahawk. There are also nice views of the town of Penacook, on the far bank.

Past Boscawen, U.S. 4 enters an especially pleasant part of its journey, winding through one valley after another, around wooded slopes and through a succession of small towns. President James Monroe traveled this route in 1817. Upon reaching Salisbury, he was asked to leave his coach because the ladies of the town wished to see him. "By God," he replied, "I'd like to see your ladies." The president alighted, they all looked at each other, and satisfied, they proceeded on their ways.

Andover, another little town along the road, is the home of a prep school, Proctor Academy, and worth a short stroll.

The oldest mica, feldspar and beryl mine in the country is still operating near **Grafton**. There are, by someone's count, 150 varieties of minerals at the Ruggles Mine, and collecting is permitted.

Canaan has a pleasant historic district, with a venerable meetinghouse and church.

Mascoma Lake near the town of Enfield was once the site of a Shaker community. It lasted 141 years, not bad when you consider that the rule of celibacy radically shortened the sect's life expectancy. The Enfield group came up in 1782 from a larger settlement near Mount Lebanon, New York (see U.S. 20). Within ten years, they were established on the western edge of the lake, in the community now known as Lower Shaker Village. They reached a peak population of 330 before dwindling away to a handful of aged residents. The last of them moved out in 1923 and the town was taken over as part of the LaSalette Catholic Shrine.

The road runs through the busy manufacturing town of Lebanon and then across the Connecticut River into Vermont. White River Junction has been an important transportation center since 1863, when five New England rail lines placed terminals here.

There is still an Amtrak depot in town, and two Interstates converge on the place, creating some very complicated intersections. But U.S. 4 quickly climbs the hills to the west and enters the heart of Vermont.

Quechee Gorge is referred to in the tourist brochures as Vermont's Little Grand Canyon. Well, don't go expecting that. But there is a fine view from the 165-foot-high bridge on U.S. 4 of this mile-long chasm carved by the Ottaquechee River. Just across a nearby covered bridge is the town of Quechee, with some interesting shops in a converted mill and demonstrations of glass-blowing in the Simon Pearce Glassworks. There is another covered bridge across the Ottaquechee in the next town of Taftsville.

While the old covered bridges lend a nice air to the Vermont countryside, it is instructive to see what determined preservationist policy can accomplish in an entire town. That is the attraction of **Woodstock**, one of the most visually harmonious communities in the state. Grouped around its oval Green, laid out in 1830, are an assortment of historic homes, churches and public buildings, painstakingly maintained as closely as possible in their nineteenth-century setting.

Woodstock was one of the first places in Vermont, possibly in the nation, to understand the wealth it possessed in its past and the difficulty of keeping it in the face of strong pressures to develop. Easily accessible from the large cities of the East and with a premium value placed on its property, Woodstock made an early commitment to resist significant change and keep the look of the place as it was. Many similarly situated communities around the country didn't comprehend that until the charms that had attracted people were crushed beneath the onrush of the new. It wasn't until the 1970s that a preservationist ethos became rooted in America, and for many places the fight was already lost. But Woodstock's uncompromising plan for the town core made it secure for the future to enjoy.

There is a covered bridge here, too, but it dates only from 1968. Designed to harmonize with the town's style, it replaced an iron structure that was washed away. The Dana House is headquarters of the Woodstock Historical Society, and its rooms reflect the various sorts of decor popular in the nineteenth century. The town's main delight, however, is simply walking through it and feeling the present wash away like that old iron bridge.

Woodstock is surrounded by mountains, and if you drive a bit north on Vt. 12, you will soon be in the midst of them. This area was the birthplace, in 1934, of Vermont's downhill skiing industry. Until that time, the skiing familiar to Americans was the cross-country, Scandinavian variety. The sport didn't really take off in this country until the more exciting downhill style was introduced from Switzerland and Austria. A historical marker at Alpine Resort marks the spot of the first ski tow built in America. Also on this road is the Billings Farm, a museum that recreates every element of a working dairy farm in the 1890s. The farm was founded in 1871 by Frederick Billings, president of one of those railroads that once criss-crossed in White River Junction.

The road continues alongside the Ottaquechee, but you should cut south on Vt. 100A at Bridgewater Corners. This is the turnoff to **Plymouth** and the birthplace of Calvin Coolidge, thirtieth president of the United States. He was born here on the Fourth of July, 1872, and was on a visit home as vice president in 1923 when he received word that President Warren Harding had died. He was sworn into office in the family living room by his father, a notary public, in the flickering light of a kerosene lamp. That rustic beginning and Coolidge's Yankee taciturnity seemed to catch the country's fancy. It was all such a contrast to the raucous national mood. Silent Cal was the perfect foil for the boisterous excess of the Jazz Age. He was easily elected on his own in 1924, and when he stated in characteristic fashion, "I do not choose to run," prior to the 1928 election, the country was both charmed and disappointed. Ah, but Cal knew best. By retiring, he spared himself the anguish of becoming the Depression president and lived on, popularity undiminished, as a reminder of better times.

Coolidge's reputation goes up and down. For a time, he was vilified by historians as a do-nothing leader who chose to close his eyes to the business practices that were driving the country to disaster. Later it was argued that maybe laissez-faire hadn't been such a bad thing. He at least cleaned up the corruption left by Harding and restored public trust in the office. Plymouth is now a museum village, and Coolidge, who died in 1933, is buried nearby.

Rejoin U.S. 4 by way of Vt. 100 at West Bridgewater. You have now entered the heart of the Green Mountains, and the summit of Mount Killington rises to the west. At 4,241 feet it is second only to Mount Mansfield among the state's peaks. The resort area around **Killington** has expanded so fast that it eclipses the identity of the adjacent town of Sherborne Center, now called Killington Post Office. A gondola and chairlift elevate travelers to the summit all year long for a view of five states and a whole lot of sky. The base is just west of Killington on U.S. 4.

It was in this area that the Rev. Samuel Peters named the state, although there was a bit of a misunderstanding about that. Looking at the mountain greenery around him, he declared that it should be given the French name for green mountain, or Vermont. Later generations altered it to Vertmont for ease of pronunciation and spelling. Peters indignantly declared they had botched it up. The word *ver* in French means "maggot," he said, and it was certainly not his intent to name the place maggot mountain. He may have had a point, but he sounds like an unpleasant old fussbudget just the same.

From Mendon, the road descends to the Marble Valley and the city of **Rutland**. When rich deposits of marble were discovered north and west of here, Rutland became a boom town. By 1880 it was the largest city in the state, a distinction since relinquished to Burlington. Rutland became the finishing and shipping center for the stone quarried nearby and its business district a showcase for the local product. (For a discussion of the downtown attractions in Rutland, see U.S. 7.)

The Norman Rockwell Museum east of town contains more than 2,000 items relating to the work of the great artist and illustrator, who was a Vermont resident for many years.

Col. Redfield Proctor developed the quarries in Rutland but managed to have his holdings placed outside the town line. Like many other men of vision, Proctor understood that smaller communities are more susceptible than larger ones to gentle reason and arm-twisting when it comes to tax assessments, so the main quarries are located in West Rutland, along U.S. 4.

South of the road is Birdseye Mountain, named for a Colonel Bird who was a pioneer settler. He worked diligently to establish a sawmill on the mountain's well-treed slopes. Maybe too diligently. The first job handled by his mill was to prepare the wood for Colonel Bird's coffin.

The college town of Castleton is a feast for fanciers of early nineteenth-century domestic architecture. A home-grown genius, Thomas Royal Drake, began building homes here in 1807 and put his personal stamp on the place with a profusion of Federal and Greek Revival showplaces. They make the town a delightful place for a walk. This is also where Ethan Allen and the Green Mountain Boys planned their raid on nearby Fort Ticonderoga in 1775, the first success of colonial arms following the opening shots at Lexington and Concord.

Fair Haven grew rich on its slate and marble quarries and became an early industrial center. Its historic district around the Green includes several exemplary marble buildings. The town was also known as the home of combative Congressman Matthew Lyon, who settled here after marrying Ethan Allen's niece. An active anti-Federalist, he ran afoul of President John Adams and in 1798 was sentenced to four months in prison under the infamous Sedition Act. Lyon had his revenge, though. He was reelected while imprisoned, and it was his vote on the thirty-sixth ballot in the deadlocked presidential election of 1800 that elected Adams's successor, Thomas Jefferson. Lyon went on to become the only man ever elected to Congress from three states. He represented Kentucky from 1803 to 1811, then moved to Arkansas but died before he could assume the seat he had won.

The road enters New York at **Whitehall** and joins the route of the Hudson-Champlain Canal, one of the early-nineteenth-century projects that channeled commerce into New York and brought it national economic dominance. This was also the route followed by British Gen. John Burgoyne on his ill-starred invasion of the Hudson Valley in 1777. The campaign was crushed at

Saratoga, further along this road, and Burgoyne surrendered his army and was taken prisoner. Whitehall is an old canal town near the southern outlet of Lake Champlain. It was originally called Skenesborough after an early settler. When Philip Skene backed the Tories, the name was changed . . . but not until Burgoyne had safely surrendered. The Skenesborough Museum displays artifacts from the town's nautical past, including part of the shipyard where the first vessels used by a U.S. naval force were built in 1775. That gives Whitehall the claim of being birthplace of the navy. The museum also contains the hull of the U.S.S. *Ticonderoga,* raised from Lake Champlain in 1958.

Old locks from the canal lie just off the road as it enters Fort Ann. U.S. 4 reaches the Hudson at Hudson Falls, a papermaking center named for the highest cascade on the river, a drop of 70 feet.

The strategic position of **Fort Edward**, guarding the approach to the Hudson Valley from Lake Champlain, was critical to the British cause in the French and Indian Wars. The place was fortified then and became one of Burgoyne's major objectives. The Old Fort House, dating from 1772, was his headquarters during the British occupation and later served the same function for a succession of American generals, including Benedict Arnold and George Washington. After Burgoyne's advance south, the fort was seized by Gen. John Stark and his New England militia, blocking the British retreat north to Canada and forcing their surrender after Saratoga.

The road crosses to the west bank of the Hudson in a hilly area that squeezes the road into a narrow track along the river. It was here that Burgoyne marched his army into the trap that would change history.

FOCUS

* * *

So many of the decisive battles that shaped the world were fought in scenic places. It often seems, in fact, that if these places were not famous as historic battlefields they would have been preserved for their natural beauty. So it is with the Battle of Saratoga.

Of course this is no coincidence. The same elements of geography that lead us to admire a place's scenic charms make it important from a military point of view. Near the town of Schuylerville (originally named Saratoga), the hills close in on the Hudson. In many places the heights rise sheer from the water's edge. Further south on the river, between Albany and New York, where the Hudson inspired a school of painters, such scenes are familiar. But on the upper Hudson, the river passes through such a defile only in this stretch. It was enough to stop General Burgoyne and his army.

Through the summer of 1777, Burgoyne moved south from Lake Champlain on the road we have been following. He passed through Skenesborough and Fort Ann and Fort Edward. But while he advanced steadily, the other parts of his offensive plan were falling apart. A detachment sent into Vermont to obtain supplies and secure his eastern flank was smashed by John Stark's New England militia at Bennington. A support column heading overland from the west was held up at Oriskany in the Mohawk Valley and eventually turned back. Even more critically, the major force that Burgoyne thought was coming up from Manhattan to meet him did not exist. The commander in New York City, Lord Howe, decided that Philadelphia was the more important objective. He took the bulk of his troops to that area and left only a remnant to move up the Hudson and link up with Burgoyne.

The war was now two and a half years old. The colonial armies had achieved few successes. It seemed only a matter of time before the superior organization and experience of the professional British soldiers and their mercenaries would prevail. England's European rivals, particularly France, hung back. The French had been humiliated in North America twenty years before, losing their empire in Canada. They badly wanted to strike back at Britain and renew the war that had raged across the continent for the last century, but they waited for a sign of possible success from the Americans before committing troops.

Burgoyne crossed to the Hudson's west bank on September 13 and passed through the town of Saratoga. As he approached

Bemis Heights to the south, he realized he had entered a trap. The colonials, under the direction of the brilliant Polish engineer Col. Thaddeus Kosciusko, had beaten him there and fortified the heights. He could not pass without being torn apart by the American guns.

Burgoyne chose to attack. He advanced across a farm owned by John Freeman, a Loyalist who had gone north to join his army and now fought on his own fields. But Burgoyne could not dislodge the entrenched Americans, and for a time, a counterattack led by Benedict Arnold threatened to break his lines. Only the arrival of Hessian reinforcements saved him and forced the colonials to retreat. Burgoyne decided to dig in and await the arrival of the army that he thought was coming to assist him from the south.

When no help had arrived after eighteen days, his situation grew desperate. Unable to hold on much longer, he decided to risk everything on another assault. But colonial scouts detected the movement of troops immediately and a party of sharpshooters mortally wounded Gen. Simon Fraser, the commander of the main offensive. The loss of Fraser threw the British into confusion, and again Arnold led a counterattack. This time the colonials managed to break through the line, with Arnold himself leading the final charge over the fortifications. Darkness saved the main body of the British force, and the next morning Burgoyne began to retreat north. But he was quickly surrounded by the steadily swelling force of American troops, and on October 17, outnumbered and cut off, he surrendered. France entered the war soon afterward, tipping the balance in America's favor.

Saratoga National Historic Park sprawls over 2,700 acres in present-day **Schuylerville** and Bemis Heights. On a hill just west of Schuylerville is a 155-foot monument marking the spot where Burgoyne surrendered to Gen. Horatio Gates. On the southern edge of town is the home of Gen. Philip Schuyler, one of the American commanders. (The original building was burned down during the British retreat. This one was built a few months after the battle.) The town was renamed in Schuyler's honor in 1831.

The entrance to the battlefield itself is 8 miles further south of Schuyler house. A side road climbs the heights and leads to the park entrance. A visitor's center, with orientation displays and self-guiding maps for a loop drive, is located here. The drive leads to ten stopping places, each illustrating a different aspect of the battle and the terrain. If you're in a hurry, stop at least at the Freeman Farm—the center of the British line—and adjacent Neilson Farm, where the Americans were entrenched. These rocky slopes offer a graphic illustration of how the Revolution literally turned neighbor against neighbor. While Freeman fought with Burgoyne, John Neilson bore arms with Gates against him. Neilson's house has been rebuilt to its appearance of those days. Nearby is a monument to Kosciusko, a gift from Poland in 1936.

Stop also at the Breymann Redoubt, scene of the final American breakthrough. Arnold was shot in the foot, through his boot, as he stormed this position, after galloping through crossfire to take part in the climactic assault. The official park brochure says that if Arnold's wound had been fatal, "posterity would have known few names brighter." Instead of a dead hero, Arnold was to be a live traitor, however. A memorial near the redoubt consists of a single sculpted military boot. On the back is a dedication to "The most brilliant soldier of the Continental Army." No name appears on it anywhere.

* * *

The river is still rather narrow as it passes Stillwater, with its old homes backing up to the water. The landmarks in this area are associated mostly with the Revolutionary War, but Mechanicville has a Civil War item of note. The first Union officer killed was Col. E. E. Ellsworth, of this town, who died in a skirmish in Alexandria, Virginia. There is a monument to him in the local cemetery.

Past the big General Electric silicone plant, the road enters Waterford, another of those places that for a time was a gateway to the West. This is where the Mohawk flows into the Hudson, the starting point of the Erie Canal's journey to the Great Lakes. The opening of the canal in 1825 made the towns in this area jumping-off points for all those headed out to open the new lands in Michigan and Wisconsin. It created new cities all along its route and made New York City the unchallenged commercial center of the country. In Waterford, Cohoes and Troy, it touched off an economic boom that lasted almost a century.

Troy has not been a major city for many years, but it was once major league. It has the distinction of being the smallest city ever to have had a baseball team in the National League. The Haymakers represented the town from 1879 to 1882. Despite the presence of two future Hall of Fame pitchers, Tim Keefe and Mike Welch, they never finished higher than fourth place and were absorbed by the New York Giants. Part of Troy's prosperity was based on an item that also vanished with the old century—detachable shirt collars for men. It was known for a time as the Collar City.

The road crosses back to the east bank of the river to enter the Lansingborough area of Troy. This was the first settlement in the area, dating back to 1771, but it didn't become part of Troy until 1901. It is a narrow district, wedged in between the river and hills and filled with space-saving row houses. Defining its eastern edge is Oakwood Cemetery, best known as the final resting place of Uncle Sam. It is fairly well documented that the life model of our national symbol was a man named Sam Wilson who supplied meat to federal troops during the War of 1812. The stamp *U.S.* on his product was jokingly taken to stand for Uncle Sam, and the name caught on. Caricatures of Wilson drawn at the time reflect the familiar face of the white-bearded gent who has adorned patriotic posters for more than a century. The 87th Congress made it official, adopting a resolution that gave Wilson national avuncular honors.

U.S. 4 runs through the center of downtown Troy, an area undergoing extensive renovation. Its ornate Victorian facades came through the decades remarkably intact, and they now make up one of the most visually complete nineteenth-century business districts in the country. Strolling these streets is like returning to the city where the Haymakers played and collars rolled out of the factories.

In the Hart-Cluett mansion, you have a strong reminder of what wealth those shirts and collars produced. The Federal-style house was built in 1827 and presented as a wedding gift to Betsey

Howard Hart. It was bought by George Cluett in 1892 after he made a fortune in the shirt business and is now a museum of local history, concentrating on interior furnishings.

A few blocks south along Second is the Washington Park area, a lovely urban square surrounded by warm old brownstones and, toward Fourth Street, pastel-shaded row houses. The highway continues south through Troy on Fourth, then swings east to the heights as it reaches Hudson Valley Community College. As it runs along this crest above the river, there is a fine view of the Albany skyline across the water. In a few more miles, U.S. 4 intersects with the combined highways of U.S. 9 and 20 and comes to an end.

VISITING HOURS

NEW HAMPSHIRE

Grafton: Ruggles Mine, (603) 523-4275. North, on U.S. 4. Daily, 9–5, mid-June–mid-October. Weekends only, May and early June. Admission.

VERMONT

Killington: Gondola and Chair Lift, (802) 422-3333. Gondola is west, on U.S. 4. Daily, 10–4, September–mid-October. Weekends only, 10–4, July–August. Admission. Chairlift is south from U.S. 4, on Killington Road. Daily, 10–4, July–mid-October. Admission.

Plymouth: Calvin Coolidge Home, (802) 828-3226. South of U.S. 4, on Vermont 100A. Daily, 9:30–5:30, Memorial Day–mid-October. Admission.

Rutland: Norman Rockwell Museum, (802) 773-6095. East, on U.S. 4. Daily, 9–5, all year. Admission.

Woodstock: Dana House, (802) 457-1800. On U.S. 4, at 26 Elm St. Monday–Saturday, 10–5; Sunday, 2–5, May–October. Admission.

Billings Farm, (802) 457-2355. North, on Vermont 12. Daily, 10–5, May–October. Admission.

NEW YORK

Fort Edward: Old Fort House, (518) 747-9600. On U.S. 4, at 29 Lower Broadway. Daily, 1–5, July–August; Sunday only, June and September. Donation.

Schuylerville: Saratoga Monument and General Schuyler House, (518) 695-3664. Entrance to the monument is west of U.S. 4, on New York 29. The Schuyler House is south on U.S. 4. Daily, 9–5, Memorial Day–Labor Day. Free.

Troy: Uncle Sam's Grave, in Oakwood Cemetery. No phone. East of U.S. 4, in northern end of town, on Oakwood Ave. Daily, 9–4:30, all year. Free.

Hart-Cluett House, (518) 272-7232. West of U.S. 4, at 59 Second St. Tuesday–Friday, 10–4, all year. Donation.

Whitehall: Skenesborough Museum, (518) 499-0754. North of U.S. 4, on New York 22. Daily, 10–5, July–Labor Day. Admission.

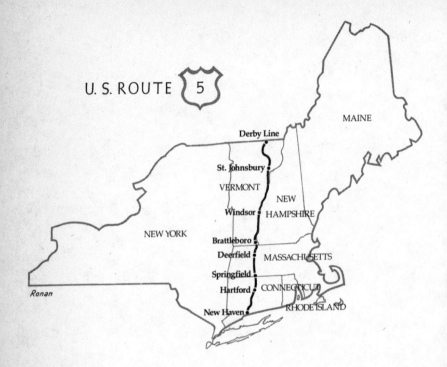

U. S. ROUTE 5

Derby Line

St. Johnsbury

VERMONT

NEW
HAMPSHIRE

Windsor

NEW YORK

Brattleboro

Deerfield

MASSACHUSETTS

Springfield

Hartford

CONNECTICUT

New Haven

RHODE ISLAND

MAINE

Ronan

The Connecticut Valley

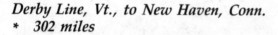

U.S.5

Derby Line, Vt., to New Haven, Conn.
★ 302 miles

For most of its passage through central New England, U.S. 5 is
smothered by the Interstates. It is rarely out of sight—or sound—
of I-91, the freeway that haunts its route. The benefit is that the
freeway draws off the heavy traffic that once choked this old road.
The drawback is that it's always there. Nonetheless, this is the
road that runs down the Connecticut River Valley and it is one
of the most attractive and historic drives in the Northeast. If you
can ignore the distant rumble and the franchise signs poking
above the treetops, you will find elements of wonder all along this
road.

★   **MILEPOSTS**   ★

It begins at the border between the United States and Canada,
surely one of the friendliest in the world, but even this amiable
frontier has few places like **Derby Line**. The international line

meanders right through town, in some cases right through the middle of a house. The Haskell Free Library and Opera House is the epitome of this easy attitude, with the audience sitting in Vermont and the cast performing in Quebec. It may be the only place in the world where an actor can justly claim to be an international favorite after one performance.

Newport is another town with a library of note. The Goodrich Memorial Library was built here in 1899 during the peak of the lumbering boom. It is now a museum and historic landmark. The city is built along a bay of Lake Memphremagog, perhaps the most misspelled body of water in the state. It means "beautiful waters" and it certainly lives up to the billing here, with the 3,360-foot summit of Owl's Head looking down on it from the west. Best views of the area are from the Church of Ave Maria Stella, on Prospect Hill. It is located off U.S. 5, near the center of town.

Between Newport and East Barnet, the road follows the path of Rogers' Rangers on their retreat from the St. Francis raid of the French and Indian Wars. Robert Rogers and his corps of backwoods fighters set out from the British fort at Crown Point on Lake Champlain, September 13, 1759. Moving undetected through the wilderness, they reached St. Francis, a major Indian settlement in Canada, in three weeks. Because allies of the French had raided the Connecticut Valley from this base for a century, Rogers' goal was to remove it by annihilating the population. Surprise was complete, and about two hundred Indians were slaughtered. But the survivors were able to regroup and with reinforcements set out in pursuit of Rogers and his band. Rogers reached Newport ten days after the raid and from here began a desperate race with the Indians to the Connecticut River and the safety of British settlements. He reached safety unscathed.

It should be noted here that Rogers was not quite the heroic figure depicted by Spencer Tracy in the old movie *Northwest Passage.* His honesty and sobriety were frequently called into question. When he later commanded the Mackinac outpost, he was removed and charged with conspiring against the Crown. Nonetheless, in this brilliant campaign he managed to hold his command together with daring and cunning, returning to rescue many of his fighters after reaching safety himself.

You can take a short side trip out of Orleans, further along the road. Follow the signs to **Brownington**, a village in the hills, to visit the Old Stone House. This four-story structure was built in 1836 as a dormitory for a local grammar school, and like the surrounding town, it hasn't changed much since. The building was scheduled for demolition but was saved to become a historical exhibit center for a number of little towns in the county.

Past Barton, the road runs along the shore of Crystal Lake, with a state park beach. The Passumpsic River runs through the center of Lyndonville, and there are five covered bridges within the town. Lyndon State College is situated on a scenic hilltop campus, with fine views east to New Hampshire's White Mountains. The attractions of St. Johnsbury, which you'll drive through next, are discussed in the chapter on U.S. 2. The road reaches the Connecticut River at Barnet and never strays far from its side, all the way to Hartford.

Ethan Allen and his family dominate the history of western Vermont, and Jacob Bayley would be an equivalent figure for this side of the state. He settled in Newbury, in the middle of the oxbow country where the Connecticut twists back upon itself, making lazy loops in its course through the wild hills. Bayley and his family moved into the area just before the Revolution. He later helped build the Hazen-Bayley military road, which connected the river to Lake Champlain and Canada. A frequent target of attempted Tory ambushes, Bayley narrowly escaped capture once when a friend passed a note to him as he walked to his fields. Knowing they were being watched and trying to keep things cryptic, the friend had written "The Philistines be upon thee, Samson." The Loyalist raiders, waiting for him in concealment in his fields, went away empty-handed as Bayley heeded the warning from the Book of Judges. The Newbury area is studded with reminders of Bayley. The home built by his son, Isaac, is part of the Bayley Historic District just north of South Newbury, and the Oxbow Historic District, south of that, has more buildings dating from his time, as well as wonderful views of the river.

Samuel Morey is a figure from the dawn of the industrial era who never quite made it to high noon. Around the town of Fairlee, it is firmly believed that he operated a steamboat along the Connecticut as early as 1793, a full fourteen years before Robert Fulton launched his first model on the Hudson. Moreover, it is documented that Fulton conferred with Morey before his own boat, the *Clermont,* took to the water. But the Vermonter got little credit and no cash whatsoever for his hard work and in a fit of despondency sank his boat in a nearby lake. Since renamed Lake Morey, this lake to the west of the road is now a resort area. Every so often, someone reports a vision of a ghostly steamboat gliding across its moonlit waters.

Norwich once had a college of its own but lost it twice. Norwich College was founded here in 1819 but decamped to Middletown, Connecticut, six years later. It came back home in 1829, only to leave again right after the Civil War. This time it moved permanently to Northfield, Vermont, where it remains and is still called Norwich College. Its namesake contents itself with being a residential suburb to the college town across the river—Hanover, New Hampshire, home of Dartmouth College.

The road runs through the transport center of White River Junction and passes south into Windsor.

FOCUS

* * *

The summer of 1777 was a desperate time in Vermont. The British had recaptured Fort Ticonderoga in New York, seized two years before by Ethan Allen, without resistance and were pursuing its fleeing defenders into Vermont. Its petition for statehood had been rejected by the Continental Congress. The territory was internally convulsed by unending disputes over conflicting land claims granted by New Hampshire and New York.

Amid this confusion, the holders of the New Hampshire grants decided to convene in **Windsor** to try to unify in the common struggle against both England and the New Yorkers. These disputed claims dated back to the previous century when colonial boundaries were, at best, loosely defined in the face of vast geographic ignorance. George III weighed in on the side of New York, upholding its claims to the land, which fired the zeal of Allen and other settlers who had moved up from Connecticut as holders of the New Hampshire grants. They even called the area New Connecticut.

The delegates met in a tavern owned by Elijah West, which was then in the center of Windsor. As they hurried to meet the threatened British invasion, they ratified a constitution that declared Vermont an independent republic. It was the first document in America that outlawed slavery and granted universal manhood suffrage without property requirements. Both of these notions reflected the tough, independent frame of mind that would later be regarded as characteristic of the Vermont nature.

The British threat was repelled at the battles of Hubbardton and Bennington, and for the next fourteen years Vermont carried on as a nation apart from the other former British colonies. New York refused to relinquish its land claims and used its clout in Congress to block Vermont's statehood. Finally, Alexander Hamilton managed to use his influence to frame an agreement, and in 1791 Vermont entered the Union as the first new state after the original thirteen. The West Tavern, now known as Constitution House, has been moved to the northern outskirts of town, along U.S. 5. It is a museum of the historic gathering held here.

In the first years of statehood, Windsor shared the designation as state capital with Montpelier and was the state's largest city. It lost the seat of government, but prosperity continued. Asahel Hubbard began making hydraulic pumps here in 1829, thereby establishing a solid industrial base. By mid-century, Windsor was famous for its skilled machinists and precisely made products. Under the guidance of Richard S. Lawrence, one of the developers of the repeating rifle, it became a major firearms producer. Spurred by the boom in his business caused by the Mexican War, Lawrence opened a three-story armory on the southern edge of town. It was the most modern facility of its kind in existence, equipped with newly developed machine tools that allowed vastly expanded production and complete interchangeability of parts. The company demonstrated its products at London's Crystal Palace Exhibition in 1851 and signed a large arms contract to supply weapons to Britain. The speed and quality with which the contract was met astonished the British, who sent a Parliamentary commission to Windsor to study how it was done. From then on, the method was known as the American System of production and established a reputation for industrial quality that was the highest in the world.

The old armory is now the American Precision Museum, an unusual celebration of the machine tools that made the process possible. It exhibits a wide variety of nineteenth-century tools, as well as the products they made. The museum is a forest of lathes and mills and presses. More than that, it is an exhibit of changing attitudes toward the workplace and its tools. The first machine tools were regarded as works of art, proudly decorated and embellished. Their makers hadn't quite realized that the process they were creating would soon render the individual craftsman anonymous.

The core of Windsor is made up of a delightful assortment of older buildings. The Vermont Crafts Center occupies the old Windsor House, built in 1840 and regarded at the time as the finest public accommodation between Boston and Montreal. This crafts center is one of only two in the state. Just south of the business district, on Bridge Street, is the longest covered bridge in the country, crossing the Connecticut River to Cornish, New Hampshire. It was built as a toll bridge in 1866. The good news is that there is no more toll. The bad news is that it is closed to all but foot traffic.

*　*　*

Just south of Windsor, Mountain Road leads to the 3,144-foot-high summit of Mount Ascutney and its view over this southeastern corner of the state. Past the town of Ascutney, Wilgus State Park has a pleasant riverside location and nature trails.

Now you enter a sparsely settled part of the river valley, with hills coming right down to the water's edge. Even **Bellows Falls**, the next community of any size, is tightly wedged between heights and river. A flight of stairs climbs to the residential part of town from the business district in the flats. The falls plunge 50 feet here and have been used to power a papermaking industry for better than a century. They were also a formidable obstacle to navigation and resulted in the first canal project in America, started here in 1792. The canal took ten years and nine locks to complete but cleared the river for passage all the way to Barnet. The falls were also a favorite fishing spot for early Indian settlers, and their petroglyphs are still visible in the rock walls, just below the bridge.

The most famous resident of Bellows Falls early in this century was Hetty Green, the Witch of Wall Street. New England's treatment of witches has not always been cordial, but Hetty was accorded an almost mystical respect. She was known as the richest woman in America, and when she managed to increase her holdings during the Panic of 1907 she became a legendary figure. She lived under a number of assumed names to confound the tax assessors and sat for hours in her bank vault sorting through her fortune in stocks and bonds. Born Hetty Robinson, she moved to Vermont after marrying a local man. Both had inherited fortunes, but her husband made the mistake of losing his. She dumped him at once and moved back to New York to pursue her accumulation of wealth and her eccentricities. Her old home in Bellows Falls, at School and Westminster, is now a bank.

Before the Vermonters signed their constitution in Windsor, they held a preliminary meeting at Westminster. This town was a focus of tension between New York and New Hampshire land grantees. When a New York–appointed sheriff fired into a mob that had seized the courthouse, killing one of the rioters, it was called the Westminster Massacre. It led to an initial declaration of independence here and then to the Windsor constitution a few months later.

Putney is a lively cultural center during the summer months, with theater, dance and musical performances held at the River Valley Playhouse and Yellow Barn. But it isn't half as lively as when John Humphrey Noyes lived there. He established his colony of Perfectionists at Putney in 1838. The group practiced communism, free love and other activities that local residents regarded as anything but perfect. Noyes and his followers were thrown out in 1847 and moved to Oneida, New York.

Forty-five years later, Rudyard Kipling moved into the neighborhood, although he wasn't terribly thrilled about it. The famed British writer married Cardine Balestier, of Brattleboro, and they moved into a home near Dummerston in 1892. Kipling called the house Naulahka after one of his early stories. It was a productive time for him professionally. He wrote some of *The Jungle Book* and his New England novel, *Captains Courageous,* while living there. But this chronicler of Empire never felt comfortable in Vermont and in 1896 he and his wife returned to England permanently. Later on, he wrote some rather harsh things about his American experience, mostly because he was angry with his brother-in-law, who had sued him. Families can ruin just about any locale. Dummerston celebrates an apple pie festival each summer.

Sir William Dummer, for whom that community was named, was the first settler in **Brattleboro**. The city bills itself as Where Vermont Begins, since the Dummer settlement of 1724 was the first English-speaking community in the state. The slogan also holds up geographically, since Brattleboro is the first town of any size for travelers entering Vermont from the south on U.S. 5. A busy manufacturing center, the town was once best known as the home of the Estey Organ Company, the best-selling brand in the country. The Estey display is the centerpiece of the Brattleboro Museum, housed in the old railroad station, at Main and Vernon.

The town was the birthplace of Larkin Mead, the sculptor whose statues of Ceres and Ethan Allen are displayed in the state capitol. His brother, William, was a top architect, a partner in the firm of McKim, Mead, and White, whose ornamented, neoclassical style set the standard at the turn of the century. Brattleboro was also home to another artistic brother act. William M. Hunt introduced the French landscape artists of the Barbizon school to an American audience and was himself widely admired as a painter. His brother, Richard, was an architect whose best-known work was the Tribune Building in New York. Like Bellows Falls, Brattleboro also had its Wall Street wizard. James Fisk, whose shenanigans helped bring on the Black Friday crash of 1869, when thousands of investors were ruined, is a native son.

Guilford was another community where the passions of the Vermont land disputes erupted. At one time it had two sets of town officers, one from New York and one from New Hampshire. Ethan Allen, in his engaging way, threatened to level the place unless the New Yorkers capitulated. When Vermont became a state, this was its largest city, but so many disgruntled New Yorkers left when their claims were set aside that it shrank to the village it remains today. The place saw some humor in its situation, though. One condition of the New Hampshire grants was that the governor of New Hampshire be given 500 acres in each town. Guilford obliged and gave him the top of a nearby hill, still named Governor's Mountain.

The highway crosses into Massachusetts along the eastern slope of the Berkshires. Just north of Greenfield, it crosses Mass. 2, called the Mohawk Trail, the first road in the country designated as a scenic highway. On High Street, near the intersection, is a lookout tower called Poet's Seat. It was named for Frederick Goddard Tuckerman, who celebrated in verse the kind of scenery visible from the perch.

This river valley was the chief line of north-south communication in colonial times. It was also the path of Indian raiders from the north, who swooped down upon the exposed outposts of the British frontier. We have seen how Rogers' Rangers settled accounts with one source of these attacks in their massacre at St. Francis in 1759. That raid effectively ended the last threat to the valley. But the cycle of massacre and reprisal had begun long before that, and some of the bloodiest chapters were played out in **Deerfield**.

This village is regarded as a treasure now, a perfectly preserved piece of the eighteenth-century New England frontier. It was actually settled before then, however. In 1669 it was established as the northwestern limit of Massachusetts. Six years later, the raiders struck, and the first of the conflicts that would come to be known collectively as the French and Indian Wars burst upon it. Deerfield was right in the path of Indian raiders from Canada. The initial attack was beaten off, and the residents, believing they still had time, began to salvage what food they could from their fields before moving to a safer place. While they worked, the Indians surrounded them. As the loaded wagons forded a brook south of town, the Indians struck, killing sixty-four of the ninety men in the party. The survivors were so demoralized that the town was abandoned for seven years.

A generation later, the rebuilt town was struck by the calamity that has come down through history as the Great Deerfield Raid of 1704. On a clear winter night, the sleeping town, never dreaming danger was near, was attacked again. This time forty-nine inhabitants were killed immediately, and more than a hundred more, mostly women and children, were marched through the snowy woods in captivity. Many died along the way, most of the town was burned, and ever afterward Deerfield seemed suspended in time.

Old Deerfield Street, referred to simply as the Street, is lined with twelve museum homes administered by Historic Deerfield. This stretch of elm-shaded village street has remained almost unchanged for two centuries. It looked like this when Deerfield Academy, a leading prep school, was established here in 1797. John Quincy Adams pronounced it "the finest view I have ever seen, not excepting the Bay of Naples." There is an orientation program in the Hall Tavern, and it is a good idea to stop there first. It will give you some idea of the range of homes that are open and allow you to choose which ones best appeal to your interests. The Memorial Hall Museum, in the first Deerfield Academy building, has many exhibits, including the tomahawk-scarred door of a house that survived the Great Raid.

The site of the first massacre, known as Bloody Brook, is marked by a sign along the road in South Deerfield.

As if the Indians weren't trouble enough, this part of Massachusetts also had Jonathan Edwards to contend with. **Northhampton** was the home pulpit of this Calvinist minister who scared the living daylights out of New England in the mid-eighteenth century. His classic sermon, "Sinners in the Hands of an Angry God," stirred congregations to the depths of their souls. Speaking in a low voice, his burning eyes fixed on a point somewhere toward the back of the church, Edwards spoke movingly of predestination and the horrible torments that awaited the damned. His recitation of them in a matter-of-fact style made them all the more horrifying. "Infants, if they are out of Christ, are in God's sight young vipers, and infinitely more hateful than vipers," he said. It is claimed that children swooned in the streets at his approach. No wonder.

Edwards was a leader of the Great Awakening, a religious fever that swept across the colonies after 1740. Old church hierarchies broke down under the strain, and new sects with new ideas became rooted in America. Some historians feel that the Great Awakening was a prelude to the main theme of Revolution, making a generation of Americans accustomed to the idea of defying a long-established central authority.

This frenzy spent, Northhampton settled down to a more peaceful life. It was noted for the serenity of its setting. When the great coloratura soprano Jenny Lind honeymooned here in 1852, she called it "the Paradise of America." The Reverend Edwards would certainly not have approved.

A few years after Lind's visit, Sophia Smith, who lived in the nearby town of Hatfield, left half a million dollars to found a college for women in Northhampton. (Hatfield, although a tiny place, also produced the founder of Williams College and the first president of Princeton.) The vista that so impressed Jenny is part of the Smith campus, Paradise Pond. Smith is now the largest privately endowed women's college in the country. Its fine museum of art is located on Elm Street.

In this century, Northhampton is best recalled as the place where Calvin Coolidge got his political start. The thirtieth president is most closely identified with his native Vermont, but he began his career as mayor of this city and retired here in 1929. The Forbes Library, on West Street, has a room full of Coolidge memorabilia, including the Indian headdress he wore in the classic deadpan campaign photograph of 1924.

Now the 1,214-foot-high bulk of Mount Tom, which dominates this portion of the valley, becomes visible on the southwest. As U.S. 5 squeezes between mountain and river, a road branches off to a reservation on the slope, with lookouts, hiking trails and a natural history museum.

The road skirts the western edge of the industrial city of Holyoke. (For a description of its attractions, see U.S. 202.) As it approaches Springfield, U.S. 5 becomes a divided road and then a freeway. Just before it swings over to the river's eastern bank, though, cut off at Memorial Avenue in **West Springfield** on Mass. 147. This leads to Storrowton Village, a collection of buildings from around New England reassembled here in a village setting on the grounds of the Eastern States Exposition. There are homes, a church, a blacksmith shop—sort of an instant tour of the region. The Exposition itself, the largest fair held in the East, goes on during twelve days each September.

Cut back to U.S. 5, which runs through Springfield as a freeway. Once out of the city, it again becomes a two-lane road, passes through the town of Longmeadow and arrives in Connecticut. Here it is a tobacco road, running through the remainder of the Northeast's largest production area of that crop. Tobacco was established here late in the eighteenth century, and by 1810 cigar factories had opened in Windsor. The industry enjoyed its greatest prosperity from around 1870 to 1890, when the broad-leaf variety grown here was especially esteemed for cigars and large quantities were exported to Germany. But tastes shifted towards cigarettes in the new century and shifted again in recent years toward abstinence. The suburbs of Hartford have also pushed back the old tobacco fields, and the largest source of smokes in the area today is backyard barbecues. Tobacco continues to be grown, though, and the patchwork pattern of the fields makes a pleasant seasonal vista.

The first great barrier to navigation on the Connecticut River was the rapids south of Enfield. All cargoes had to be unloaded at the rapids' southern end, which came to be known as **Warehouse Point**, then transported overland for reloading at Thompsonville. A canal project here, along with the one at Bellows Falls, made the river navigable from its outlet in Long Island Sound to northern Vermont. But when rail transport replaced the barges, the canals were diverted to industrial use. There are now plans to rebuild the Enfield locks and open the river again to pleasure boats as far as Springfield. Enfield won earlier fame as the place where

Jonathan Edwards first delivered his "Angry God" sermon to an astonished congregation.

Warehouse Point was where William Pynchon established his portage service around the Enfield rapids in 1636. Now two museums concerned with transportation share a tract in the town. The Connecticut Trolley Museum and Connecticut Fire Museum contain collections of vintage vehicles from each field. They are located on Conn. 140.

The highway widens as it sweeps into the industrial suburb of East Hartford, famed for its association with pioneer aircraft plants. U.S. 5 becomes a freeway, recrosses the river on the Charter Oak Bridge south of downtown Hartford and finally turns sharply away from the Connecticut for the final leg of its journey.

Now it is called the Berlin Turnpike as it speeds four lanes wide through the belt of Hartford suburbs. Berlin was the home of the first Yankee peddlers, those shrewd and hearty forerunners of the traveling salesman, who carried their line in backpacks along the old roads of frontier America. Yankee is an odd word, probably of Hudson Valley Dutch derivation, that came to be applied specifically to anyone from Connecticut. Eventually its usage widened to include any New Englander, then anyone from the North and, finally, in its overseas evolution, anyone from America. The prototypes of the crafty Yankee peddlers were the Pattison brothers, Edward and William, who began making their tinware here around 1740, and first came up with the notion of selling it door to door in the nearby towns.

The road squeezes between Lamentation Mountain on the east and Silver Lake on the west, then enters Meriden. The first silver in North America was found in this part of Connecticut, and these towns along U.S. 5 became leaders in working that metal. Pewter was being made here by 1794, and the Rogers brothers invented the electroplating process in Meriden, giving them dominance in the manufacture of kitchen silverware. The International Silver Company, which combines several of these old firms, is still active here.

Wallingford, another old silver town, is also known as the home of Choate-Rosemary Hall prep school.

The road enters the Quinippiac River Valley, passing a series of state parks and the bulk of Sleeping Giant Mountain to the west. Wharton Brook makes a delightful spot to rest along the road and go for a quick wade to cool off.

After a jog through North Haven, U.S. 5 enters New Haven as State Street. (For more on New Haven, see U.S. 1.) There is one more stop to be made before coming to journey's end in this old college town. Follow the signs to East Rock Park, the largest public park in the city. The land was originally owned by Seth Turner, a local hermit who was found frozen to death in his hilltop hut in 1823. Now the park contains the Pardee Rose Gardens. From Indian Head Peak, there is a wonderful view across the entire city, down to the harbor and the sparkling waters of Long Island Sound.

VISITING HOURS

VERMONT

Brattleboro: Brattleboro Museum, (802) 257-0124. On U.S. 5 (Main St.) at Vernon St., in the Union Railroad Station. Tuesday–Friday, noon–4; weekends, 1–4, May–early November. Donation.

Brownington: Old Stone House, (802) 754-2022. North of U.S. 5, from Orleans. Daily, 11–5, July–August; Friday–Tuesday, mid-May–June and September–mid-October. Admission.

Derby Line: Haskell Free Library and Opera House, (819) 876-2471. At the Canadian border, off U.S. 5. Tuesday–Saturday, 1–5, all year. Free.

Newport: Goodrich Memorial Library, (802) 334-7902. On U.S. 5, at 70 Main St. Monday–Saturday, 10–5, all year. Free.

Windsor: Constitution House, no phone. On U.S. 5, at 16 N. Main St. Daily, 10–5, mid-May–mid October. Free.
American Precision Museum, (802) 674-5781. South edge

of town, on U.S. 5. Daily, 10–5, Memorial Day–October. Admission.

Vermont Crafts Center, (802) 674-6729. On U.S. 5 (Main St.). Monday–Saturday, 10–5, all year. Free.

MASSACHUSETTS

Deerfield: Old Deerfield Historic Homes, (413) 774-5581. On "The Street," off U.S. 5. Monday–Saturday, 9:30–6; Sunday, 11–6, July–October. Closes at 4:30, other times of year. Admission.

Memorial Hall, (413) 774-7476. On Memorial St., off U.S. 5. Monday–Friday, 10–4:30; weekends, 12:30–4:30, May–October. Admission.

Northhampton: Smith College, (413) 584-2700. West from U.S. 5, on Massachusetts 9. The Art Museum is open Tuesday–Saturday, noon–5; Sunday, 2–5, all year. Free.

Coolidge Room of the Forbes Library, (413) 584-8550. Off U.S. 5, on Massachusetts 66, at 20 West St. Monday–Friday, 9–9; Saturday, 1–5, all year. Free.

West Springfield: Storrowton Village, (413) 787-0136. Exit U.S. 5 at westbound Massachusetts 147 (Memorial Ave.). Monday–Saturday, 11–4, mid-June–Labor Day. Admission.

CONNECTICUT

Warehouse Point: Connecticut Trolley Museum, (203) 623-7417. East of U.S. 5 on Connecticut 140 (North Road). Monday–Saturday, 10–4; Sunday, noon–6, Memorial Day–Labor Day. Weekends, noon–5, at other times. Admission.

Connecticut Fire Museum, (203) 623-4732. Adjoins the Trolley Museum. Monday–Saturday, 10–4, Sunday, noon–6, June–August. Weekends only, noon–5, April, May, September, October. Admission.

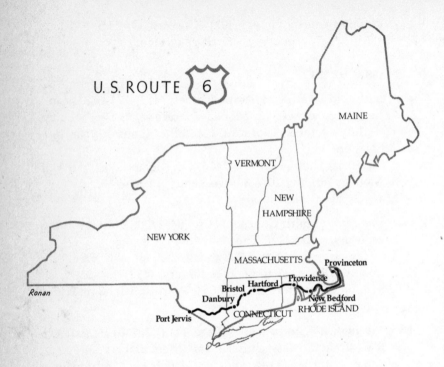

U. S. ROUTE 6

MAINE

VERMONT

NEW HAMPSHIRE

NEW YORK

MASSACHUSETTS

Provinceton

Providence

Bristol Hartford

Danbury

New Bedford

Port Jervis

CONNECTICUT RHODE ISLAND

Ronan

From the Cape to the Catskills

U.S.6

Provincetown, Mass., to Port Jervis, N.Y.
* 345 miles

U.S. 6 was once the longest of the old roads, running from the Massachusetts beaches to Long Beach, California. But in the late 1960s, route designations were changed in California. Instead of continuing all the way into the Los Angeles area, U.S. 6 was cut short at the town of Bishop, just across the state line in the Sierra Nevadas. That was enough margin to allow U.S. 20 to edge past in total mileage and drop this road back to second place.

The eastern segment of U.S. 6 starts at the farthest end of Cape Cod and follows its hooked arm around the northern shore. It runs through the seafaring town of New Bedford and the industrial city of Fall River, then quickly traverses Rhode Island through the middle of Providence. The road wanders lazily through Connecticut, running through hill country, historic towns and manufacturing centers whose roots reach back to the foundation of American industry. The road crosses the Taconic range in New York and skirts the southern edge of the Catskills before it reaches the Delaware River, passing into Pennsylvania and out of this book.

* MILESTONES *

The Old Cape Cod that Patti Page warbled about in her 1950s hit record is hard to find. Travelers who show up on the Cape in midsummer and hope to locate "quaint little villages here and there" and "winding roads that seem to beckon you" often go away feeling as if they'd seen nothing but a crush of humanity and jammed highways. The charms celebrated in the song sometimes seem to have disappeared, victims of the greater accessibility the Interstates have created. The charms are still there, but the slender arm of the Cape is a fragile place, and not entirely at its best in July and August. This is definitely an area to explore off-season, or if that isn't possible, along the north shore, where development has not been quite as intensive as in the south.

U.S. 6 runs the entire legnth of the Cape's arm, but at Orleans, it becomes a freeway, heading away from the shore through the center of the Cape. So we'll follow the old route of U.S. 6 (now designated Mass. 6A), which makes its way through the cluster of towns that cling to the northern coastline, before we rejoin the main road at the Cape Cod Canal.

Provincetown is the start, and since Highway 6 bypasses the town on its way from Herring Cove Beach, you'll want to begin the trip on 6A, which runs through Provincetown as Commercial Street. As you probably know, Provincetown was almost the start historically as well as geographically. The Pilgrims anchored here in November 1620 and stayed for five weeks before choosing another harbor at the far end of Cape Cod Bay. While they rested, they signed the Mayflower Compact and recorded the birth of the first European child born in Massachusetts, Peregrine White. The Pilgrims had planned to land in Virginia, but storms had blown them far off course; now they were preparing to enter a remote wilderness about which they knew nothing. The Compact reflects this sense of entirely new beginnings. It is regarded as a seminal democratic document, one that logically led to a continuing expansion of representative government. This first group of settlers was drawn from Britain's laboring class. They had no aristocratic pretensions. It was probably natural that given the chance to establish a new order in a new world, their impulse would be toward a free society—or as free as their church would permit.

The ship anchored three-quarters of a mile offshore, and many Pilgrims waded to land through the frigid waters. Dorothy Bradford, the wife of the first governor, drowned on one of these excursions. Eventually it was decided that the position here was too precarious. A party exploring the farther shore in a small boat came upon Plymouth harbor, and it was considered a more suitable permanent site. The Pilgrims' Monument remains in Provincetown, though, a 252-foot-high granite shaft, with a historical museum at the base containing exhibits on the landing here and the town's development.

Provincetown remained an isolated outpost for years after the Pilgrims left. In the nineteenth century, it attracted a population of Portugese fishermen who were the basis of the local economy. Right after the turn of the century, though, it was discovered by a group of artists and became a summer colony. By 1915, when the Provincetown Players were founded and Eugene O'Neill was working here, it was established as a seasonal center for Bohemian lives. The alternative culture in all its varieties and hues dominated the summer life of Provincetown by the 1960s and still does. After Labor Day each year, though, the craziness ebbs and Provincetown once more reverts to being a little town way out at sea. The place is a delight then. In recent years, whale-watching expeditions leaving from MacMillan Pier have extended activities well into the autumn. The pier is named, by the way, for Donald B. MacMillan, the Arctic explorer who lived here while not on the road to Ultima Thule. Exhibits relating to his trips and pioneering ethnological studies among the Eskimo tribes of Greenland are displayed in the museum near the Pilgrim Monument. Also in town is the Seth Nickerson House, noted for its age (built in 1746) and for its furnishings (constructed of material scavenged from shipwrecks).

Leaving Provincetown along Highway 6A, you'll come to Pilgrim Spring, part of Cape Cod National Seashore. This is where the Mayflower passengers supposedly first filled their casks with fresh water after the long ocean voyage. There are self-guiding nature trails and other displays nearby. The turnoff east to Highland Light, built in 1797, comes in North Truro, on Highland Road. This is a lonely portion of the Cape's Atlantic shoreline, with rolling sand hills stretching down the coast and few signs of human habitation. It is an ideal setting for this powerful light, which is visible 20 miles at sea. A small museum is also on the property.

Just north of Truro, watch for a hill with two nineteenth-century church buildings, one of them now the town hall, at its crest. This is one of the more dramatic vistas on this windswept spit of land. Truro itself was once a good-sized port, but the restless sand silted over its harbor in about 1850, and that finished off the fishing business.

The Cape narrows once more at **Wellfleet** harbor. This was the first alternative explored by the Pilgrim party sent out from Provincetown, but it was regarded as no more advantageous for settlement. It became a major oystering center from 1830 to 1870, but one local seafarer gathered another food that had all New England going bananas. Lorenzo Dow Baker, born in Wellfleet, engaged in a modest trade with the West Indies. On a return voyage from Jamaica in 1840, he loaded up with green bananas, hoping to sell some in Boston as a curiosity. But when Boston got a taste of the ripened fruit, it demanded more. Baker dropped everything else and began shipping nothing but bananas back home. From that beginning grew the gigantic U.S. Fruit Company, an empire that would control most of the trade and some of the governments of the Caribbean Islands and Central America.

Another visitor to the area who had long distances in mind was Guglielmo Marconi. He came here in 1901 after doing some early work on long-wave radio signals. He wanted to send a wireless transmission across the Atlantic and selected Wellfleet as the point where he'd encounter the least interference. The station he built for this first transoceanic test still stands east of town on the National Seashore. Additional Marconi memorabilia are in the

Historical Society Museum on Main Street. The Audubon Society also operates a refuge with nature trails, just off the road south of town.

The Old Windmill in **Eastham** has been grinding corn since 1793 and is one of the most familiar sights on the Cape. The Pilgrim exploration party also came ashore here and sighted their first Indian. There is a National Seashore visitor's center at Salt Pond, and on the Atlantic side of this narrow segment of Cape Cod is Nauset Beach, one of the best public facilities on the entire Cape.

The road becomes a freeway past Eastham, but continue straight ahead on 6A, the Cranberry Highway, into **Orleans**. Marconi's idea of setting up a transatlantic communications post in this area was not original. Orleans was the American end of the undersea cable to France for seventy years. Opened in 1890, the station remained in operation until 1959 and is now a museum of that era in communications, which began to fade when Marconi's first message began crackling across the ocean air.

A French connection came naturally to Orleans. It was named for the Duke of Orleans who visited the area in 1797, a refugee from the revolution that had taken away his title and guillotined his father. Foreign visitors also showed up in 1918: Orleans was the only American city to be shelled by a German U-boat in World War I. It sank some coal barges and gave the place a good scare, but there were no other casualties.

Now you begin to run along the Cape's northern shore and into the town of **Brewster**, with its fine sea captains' homes, a good museum of the Cape's natural history and a Fire and History Museum. This last facility contains the fire-fighting apparatus collected by the late Boston Pops conductor Arthur Fiedler, a great fire buff.

Part of the supporting cast of any decent Thanksgiving feast is the cranberry sauce. The fruit is a symbol of Massachusetts, and it was in the bogs around **Dennis** that it was first cultivated. The berries had grown wild for two centuries and were familiar all along the Cape. But in 1816 a local farmer, Henry Hall, got the idea of covering the vines with loose sand. This improved productivity and made them profitable as a cash crop. The town was named for a minister, the Rev. Josiah Dennis, and his home, built in 1736, has been restored. Just south of town is Scargo Hill, with a fine view back down the Cape's forearm. Dennis is also a theatrical and artistic center, and for years its summer playhouse has been a well-known training ground for aspiring actors.

Yarmouth Port has lots of old elms and a few old homes. The one built by Capt. Bangs Hallet, who amassed his fortune at sea before the town's decline as a port, is now a museum. The area is also a focus for old legends about Norse landings on the Cape about six hundred years before the Mayflower got here. Some area historians are convinced Leif Erickson came ashore here and that his brother, Thorvald, was killed by Indians at Yarmouth. This first Vikings-Redskins match took place, supposedly, in 1007.

Barnstable is one of the larger towns on the Cape and the commercial center for its north-central district. The best-known landmark is Sturgis Library. Organized in 1645, it is the oldest in the country, with priceless genealogical material on Cape families. In neighboring **West Barnstable** is West Parish Congregational Church, the oldest building of that denomination in the United States. The parish was organized in London in 1616 and this building erected in 1717.

Now you enter an area of salt marsh, with white sand dunes rising behind the marshes to front the bay. This is, once again, sparsely settled country. It first attracted settlers because livestock thrived on the salty marsh hay.

Provincetown was the first anchorage, but settlement of the Cape actually progressed west to east, from the inside out. **Sandwich**, near the western edge, was the first town planned, with the surveying work credited to Miles Standish in 1637. The Hoxie House was built that same year and is the oldest habitation on the Cape. Sandwich was best known for its pressed glass, made here from 1825 to 1888. Work was halted during a strike and never resumed and now the glass is highly esteemed as a collectible. A museum in town has a wide-ranging display. Sandwich also was the home of children's author Thornton W. Burgess, who wrote

Peter Rabbit. His residence, a restored eighteenth-century house, is filled with memorabilia of his career. Burgess was a devoted naturalist, and the Green Brier Nature Center near town is dedicated to him. The Old Brier Patch Trail, named after one of his stories, is a self-guiding nature walk.

Building a canal across the shoulder of Cape Cod was discussed as far back as 1697. It would have been an obvious benefit, sparing Boston-bound travelers the long swing around Cape Cod. But it took another 217 years to get it built. The area at the Cape's shoulder had been a lively crossroads ever since 1627 when the Aptuxcet Trading Post was established near what is now **Bourne**. Here Pilgrims met with Dutch traders from Manhattan, and both bartered with local Indians. This was among the first business ventures entered into by the Plymouth Colony as a way of repaying debts to its London sponsors. It operated for about thirty-five years. The post was restored in 1930 and contains artifacts from the area.

Tourism on the Cape received a big boost in the 1960s when President John F. Kennedy set up the summer White House in his family's compound of homes near Hyannisport. But seventy years before that, another president also summered on the Cape. Of course, there was nothing as formal as a summer White House when Grover Cleveland occupied his home, Grey Gables, in the 1890s. It was just a place he enjoyed spending the summer. He chose the Bourne area, the story goes, because of a slight to a good friend. The famed actor Joseph Jefferson was turned down by a property-holder's association in Sandwich, whose members wanted no one as disreputable as an actor living nearby. So Jefferson bought land near Bourne instead and the president did likewise. Who knows? Sandwich might have found him unsuitable, as well. (Jefferson took his final bow in Sandwich, though. He is buried there, and the lease is eternal.) The rail terminal Cleveland used for his trips to Bourne is now part of the Aptuxcet restoration.

Once across the canal, U.S. 6 turns west along the northern shore of Buzzard's Bay, not the ideal name from a chamber of commerce point of view, but a pleasant body of water nonetheless. You'll pass **Wareham**, where the Tremont Company has been making nails since 1819 and runs a visitor's center and company store at its plant site.

The road continues to the town of Mattapoisett, on the bay, through Fairhaven, and across the Acushnet River into **New Bedford**. Although a good-sized fishing fleet still sails from this port, New Bedford is best known for a sea hunt that ended long ago. For forty years, from 1820 to the Civil War, New Bedford was home port to the greatest whaling fleet this country ever saw. The era was captured in Herman Melville's classic *Moby Dick.* (The author acquired his whaling experience, by the way, aboard a ship named the *Acushnet,* for New Bedford's river.) New Bedford was home to Captain Ahab and the good ship *Pequod.* To those who waded through all the heavy symbolism in some long-ago American Lit. class, the town offers a few familiar echoes. The Seamen's Bethel, with its pulpit shaped like a ship's prow, can be found on Johnny Cake Hill, just south of U.S. 6 as it enters the city. Father Mapple delivered his sermon to the crew of the outward-bound *Pequod* here. The Bethel, a New England term for a seaman's chapel, was built in 1832, or nineteen years before the novel was published. Down the block is the Whaling Museum, with its full-scale reproduction of a whaling ship, skeleton of a humpback whale and dozens of other exhibits relating to that era.

Other reminders of New Bedford's glory days can be seen along County Street, just west of downtown. Melville wrote that "all the brave houses and flowery gardens of New Bedford" were brought up from the bottom of the sea by the whaling boats. The Rotch-Jones-Duff House was built in 1834 in the midst of that age of plenty. Named for the three families who owned it in turn, it is now a museum, surrounded by formal gardens, and the starting point for walking tours of the other fine homes in this historic district.

The nautical history of New Bedford predates whaling. From its boatyards in 1767 came the *Dartmouth,* a ship that would soon become famous when a cargo of tea was dumped from its decks in Boston Harbor. The town was a base for privateers during the Revolution, and it was burned in retaliation in 1778. Whaling began to decline in the 1850s as the great mammals were slaughtered into scarcity and the first Pennsylvania petroleum fields began to provide a cheaper source of oil. The last of the wooden whalers, the *Charles Morgan,* was built here in 1882 and was rescued from decay in the 1940s by Mystic Seaport. It is now one of the top attractions at that Connecticut museum (see U.S. 1).

Fall River's fame rested on spindles rather than harpoons. As New Bedford declined in importance after the Civil War, its neighboring town to the west rose to replace it. By 1875, its 120 mills accounted for the greatest textile production in the country. During the Depression, the city entered the same cycle of decline experienced by New England's other textile centers. Now the old mills have been turned to other uses. The city boasts that as it once led the country in textile production, it now leads the way in factory outlet store sales. Every weekend, bargain hunters throng to the once dreary factory district and fill the grim old streets with more sparkle than they ever had when the looms were humming.

The town's textiles legacy is examined in Fall River Heritage State Park, with a variety of exhibits. Adjoining the park on Mount Hope Bay at the western end of town is Battleship Cove, with sailing craft from the area's nautical past and a collection of vessels that served in World War II. Most prominent among them is the U.S.S. *Massachusetts,* commissioned in 1942 and a veteran of both the Atlantic and Pacific theaters. It is the state's official war memorial.

Fall River occupies a lovely site on hills between an inland pond and the bay. It was called Troy for a while but reverted to the English translation of its old Indian name, Quequechan, in 1834. The name comes from a stream that rushed down a chasm in the heights. The views from the old mansions in the hilltop district may remind a few travelers of San Francisco. In one of these old mill-owners' homes, on Rock Street, a few blocks up from the bay, is the Historical Museum. There is a wide assortment of exhibits, but the one that draws most people relates to Fall River's best-known native daughter, Lizzie Borden. The reputed double parricide of 1892 has an enduring fascination, and the bit of

doggerel enumerating the number of ax whacks given to mother
and father Borden remains as familiar as a Mother Goose rhyme.
The Borden house is private, but still stands at 234 Second Street.
Ms. Borden, by the way, was acquitted of the crime and died here
in 1927. Unsurprisingly, she never married.

The highway has run close to Interstate 195 since Wareham, but
west of Fall River it practically crawls into the concrete with it.
Just over the Rhode Island line, the two roads join and run coter-
minously into Providence. U.S. 6 passes through the state capital
as a freeway. The pre-Interstate route would have led you across
the Providence River on the Point Street Bridge. Just across this
span is Davol Market Square, a onetime rubber factory that has
been converted into an entertainment area and shopping mall. But
this is the only significant point of interest along the way, and it
gets a bit complicated retracing the old route on Westminster
Street to its link with the current U.S. 6. A better idea may be to
stop at Davol Square, then return over the bridge to the freeway
and run through the rest of town that way. (For a more complete
discussion of driving through Providence, see U.S. 44.)

Once out of the city, the road becomes Grand Army of the
Republic Highway. About 2 miles past Interstate 295, in **North
Scituate**, is Brown Avenue, the turnoff to Dame Farm and Snake
Den State Park. This is a historic farm run by the state, which
shows a family operation from the period 1870 to 1915 with
equipment used at the time.

The road passes Moswaniscut Pond and an arm of the vast
Scituate Reservoir as it continues west. It even gets into some hilly
country, a rarity in this state. Rhode Island's highest elevation is
only 812 feet, at Jerimoth Hill just to the north.

After entering Connecticut, U.S. 6 heads west through a string
of towns leading to the Thread City (see below). Some of these
places had a fling with industry but didn't succeed. South Kill-
ingly, for example, was the home of Mary Kies, who held the first
patent ever granted to a woman in this country for her straw-and-
silk weaving machine of 1809. Two years before that, a family in
nearby Danielson opened a mill and entered the cotton business.

But the Tiffanys would find greater treasure by dealing in jewelry in New York.

Israel Putnam always seemed to be leaving hastily for one reason or another during the Revolutionary War. The Connecticut-born general had to escape down a gully when British troops surprised him at Greenwich in 1779. Four years before that, while working his farm in Brooklyn, he received news of the battle at Concord. Leaving his plow in the furrow, he galloped off on horseback to join the cause. Putnam died in 1790 and is buried in Brooklyn, his memory saluted with a statue on the Green. It is, of course, an equestrian statue.

This is the most sparely settled corner of Connecticut. The road dips and darts through rolling countryside and tiny villages snuggled up to rushing streams. It brushes the edge of the James L. Goodwin State Forest and finally reaches **Willimantic**. This was known as the Thread City because of the dominance of the American Thread Company, formed here in 1854. It was the largest mill of its kind in the country. The Wincham Textile and History Museum, at Union and Fair, preserves the memories of those days. U.S. 6 bypasses the town by freeway, but dip down on Conn. 66 to make a visit.

The road swings back north, along the Hop River, and passes through the scenic area of Bolton Notch. This marks the entry into the Greater Hartford area. Right at the foot of the notch is **Manchester**, the first city of any size along this road in Connecticut and another place with memories of early industry. Once it was known as the silk capital of the country. The Cheney brothers established their mills here in 1838, and within fifty years they dominated national production. The six Cheneys grew up in the home built by their clockmaker father, Timothy. This is now a museum, just south of the highway as it passes through town. The mills closed after World War II, but by then Manchester, like so many of these Connecticut towns, had diversified its economic base to maintain a high level of prosperity. No longer the capitals of anything in particular, these cities instead just go about amassing capital.

West of here, U.S. 6 quickly becomes a part of Interstate 84 and crosses the Connecticut River into **Hartford**. It doesn't emerge from the freeway until it has passed through the city, which is not a good way to see Hartford. So I suggest leaving the Interstate at the Farmington Avenue exit, the former route of the highway, which is now designated Conn. 4.

In a few blocks you'll see the domed headquarters of the Aetna Insurance Company, built in 1929, the largest Federal-style structure in the country. The city's name is practically synonymous with insurance. As you came into town, the tallest building on the skyline was the Traveler's Tower, and dozens of smaller firms are scattered about the landscape. The industry had its modest beginnings here with marine insurance, and Hartford Fire, organized in 1794, became the first major firm. Forty years later it paid off all its claims on a major fire in New York City. This well-publicized performance established its reputation and brought business rushing its way. Hartford became a byword for reliability, and the companies based here are among the most powerful economic forces in late-twentieth-century America.

Right across Farmington Avenue from Aetna is St. Joseph's Cathedral, a contemporary house of worship noted for the twenty-six stained glass windows along its nave.

The Hartford *Courant* is the oldest continuously published newspaper in the country. It hasn't missed an issue since 1764. Charles Dudley Warner was its editor in the 1870s, and his reputation as a man of letters attracted a large number of writers to the city. They formed a small colony in the Farmington-Forest area, down the block from Warner's home.

Harriet Beecher Stowe was the first to settle in, then Samuel Clemens (Mark Twain) moved right next door. The area was called Nook Farm, and Mrs. Stowe's home—more of a cottage, actually—reflects the sense of tidy comfort in that name. She built the house in 1873 and lived here for the last twenty-three years of her life, not turning out any significant works of literature but working tirelessly for her favorite causes, temperance and woman's suffrage.

Her neighbor Samuel Clemens had just enjoyed his first national success with *Innocents Abroad* when he chose to build here.

His home was a good deal more elaborate than Mrs. Stowe's and somewhat unorthodox in appearance. He chose, for example, to place the kitchen beside the front entrance rather than in its customary place in the rear, "so the servants can see the circus going by without running into the front yard," he explained. He said it would also save the carpeting. Hartford was a bit baffled by the man. But while living here he managed to write *The Gilded Age* with Warner and also batted out *The Adventures of Tom Sawyer.* After that, it really didn't make any difference what Hartford thought. He moved out in 1879, and the nineteen-room house, along with the Stowe cottage, is now a museum with mementoes of both writers in profusion.

The area was regarded as Hartford's most fashionable in those years. The actor William Gillette, famed for his portrayal of Sherlock Holmes, lived nearby, and actress Katharine Hepburn was born a few blocks away, in the home of her physician father.

Reliability and predictability are the basis not only of insurance but of communications as well. This observation takes us into the suburb of **West Hartford** and the home of the man who first standardized the written word in America, Noah Webster. His name has become the generic term for any dictionary, but that wasn't the work that occupied his time while living here. His *Grammatical Institute of the English Language,* best known for its first part, the blue-backed *Elementary Spelling Book,* became the basis for a nationwide system of standard spelling. With its messages of moral uplift taken from the lessons of history, the book became the very model of a nineteenth-century elementary school text. The blue-backed speller appeared in 1783, and for the next twenty years of his life Webster labored at the dictionary. It didn't appear until 1806, long after he had moved to Amherst, Massachusetts. But his residence here, just south of U.S. 6, has become a shrine to the lexicographer who gave Americans their own language. A statue of Webster by Korczak Ziolkowski, who also worked on Mount Rushmore and the Crazy Horse Memorial, is on the town hall lawn.

The destination of the avenue we have been traveling since Hartford, as you may have guessed, is **Farmington**. Once a linen and hatmaking center, its industrial dreams ended when land-slides closed the canal connecting it to the Connecticut River. It is now an expensive residential suburb with the aristocratic aura of old New England evident on its blocks of fine old homes. Part of that cachet is also supplied by Miss Porter's School, established in 1844 for young ladies of high quality and big bucks, by Sarah Porter. Her father, the Rev. Noah Porter, was pastor of the Congregational Church for sixty years, and that white-spired building, erected in 1771, still stands on Main Street. The colonial showplace in town is the Stanley-Whitman House on High Street, with its 18-inch overhang and other unique ornamentations of the early eighteenth century. An exceptionally fine small museum is Hill-Stead, at Farmington and Mountain. It was built by architect Stanford White for local industrialist A. A. Pope, an avid collector of French Impressionists. The appearance of a private residence is preserved, with the artwork shown off as it would be in a home.

FOCUS
* * *

Connecticut's old nickname and a sort of unofficial state slogan was Land of Steady Habits. Sounds exciting, huh? But it was more than just a slogan here, it was a way of life, almost a guiding principle of Connecticut conduct. It was really no accident that this state became the center of America's insurance industry or that Noah Webster, who labored to give order to the language, was born here. A distinct culture developed here, which became known for its high degree of craftsmanship and the reliability of its products. A Made in Connecticut stamp was a guarantee of dependability. Writer William Manchester once speculated that if the auto industry had been based in Connecticut instead of the Midwest it would have developed with the emphasis on precision rather than size and style. He was probably right. Slow and steady wins the race.

If any part of the state best symbolizes this attitude it is proba-bly this stretch of U.S. 6, through the towns of Bristol, Terryville and Thomaston. This was the cradle of American clockmaking, and if any item stands for steady dependability, it is one of the sonorously ticking clocks that came from these workshops.

As in so many early Connecticut industries, the proximity of Eli Whitney's work on mass production led to its implementation here. In the 1790s, when clock production in the **Bristol** area was begun by Gideon Roberts, it was still a slow, laborious process. Britain led the world in the quality of its handcrafted timepieces, and America could not hope to compete. But where it could find an edge was in cost. Eli Terry was the first Connecticut man to grasp the principle that quality clocks could be made with existing machine tools. The tolerances were wide enough to permit mass production with similar if not precisely interchangeable parts. He set up his shop in 1803 with the goal of turning out, not a few clocks a year, but the unbelievable total of 1,000. He was scoffed at, but within five years he had managed to increase that to 4,000 and was making a large profit. Then the scoffing stopped and the innovations began.

Terry developed the shelf clock, dropping the sales price from $25 to $5 and widening his market immeasurably. It became a staple item of the Yankee peddlers, small enough to fit into their knapsacks and useful enough to be a reliable seller. It was through these roving salesmen that Connecticut clocks spread throughout the country. The state and the product became inextricably linked.

One of Terry's students, Chauncey Jerome, was the first to switch to brass from wood for the interior workings. That raised initial costs but resulted in a smaller and more accurate clock, one that would not be affected by changes in weather. Soon he was turning out 40,000 a year, priced so cheaply that he was able to export to Britain. British contempt turned quickly to alarm when clockmakers learned that this mass-produced competitor was underselling their own products, even with import duties tacked on, and exploiting a mass market they hadn't even tried to reach.

By the end of the century, mass production techniques were being applied to watches. The Bristol-based Ingraham Company charted sales of $80 million between 1911 and 1960. But as in so many maturing industries that began in New England, rising costs and shifts in taste eventually caused production to drop off and then leave the area entirely. The last of the Bristol clockmakers stopped ticking in the 1960s. But the Clock and Watch Museum here is an extensive and delightful review of what they made. It is located on Maple Street, two blocks south of U.S. 6.

There are more than 2,000 timepieces on display. The rhythm of their ticking, like a chorus of mechanical crickets, is a bit overpowering when you enter, and if you happen to be walking through on the hour, when hundreds of them are set to chime at once, better keep some earmuffs handy. But soon it all blends in and the fascinating displays, emphasizing Connecticut products, absorb your attention. There are timepieces of every size and shape from around the world; everything from stately grandfather clocks to miniscule wristwatches to novelty items that no one in their right mind would use to tell time. There are also recreations of early clock stores.

Eli Terry set up his first production facility in Plymouth, just to the west, and the area where he established his factory became known as **Terryville**. His son, James, found that the principles his father had applied to clocks could also be used effectively in making locks. His Eagle Lock Company started here, and the Lock Museum of America, on Terryville's Main Street, traces the evolution of the industry from its beginnings.

Thomaston, further along the road, was home base of the Seth Thomas factory, named after a student and partner of Terry's. But this, too, has become a place from which tempus has fugit.

*   *   *

Black Rock State Park, south of Thomaston on U.S. 6, was named for old graphite mines in the vicinity. There are good hiking trails in the gently rolling terrain.

At the end of the American Revolution, the issue of religious identity was very much in question. The Anglican Church, after all, was one with the Crown: state and church were unified. With political ties to Britain severed, what would become of the former colonial churches?

One of the answers came in the town of **Woodbury** at Glebe House, the former Episcopal rectory. Most of the clergy in the colonies were Loyalist in sympathy. Glebe House, in fact, had a secret passageway leading underground to a nearby hill so that its occupant, the Rev. John Rutgers Marshall, could flee from local rebels if the need arose. It was here that Samuel Seabury was elected America's first Episcopal bishop in 1783. He refused consecration in England, however, because he would not take the required loyalty oath to the king. His stand symbolized the break in religious as well as civil ties with the former homeland and was a step on the way to religious freedom in America. Some state governments would continue to grant privileges to specific churches, but there would be no national established church. Glebe House, built in 1740, is now a museum of the era and of Seabury's historic election.

The road winds through hill country as it approaches the Housatonic Valley. At **Southbury** is the Bullet Hill School, among the oldest in the country. It closed in 1942, but records have traced its beginning as far back as 1789, and it may predate the Revolution.

U.S..6 crosses the Housatonic as a freeway, then opens out on lovely hillside views across Taunton Pond, west of Newtown.

In 1777 a British raid burned **Danbury** to the ground, so families from this area were given tracts on Connecticut-owned land in the future state of Ohio as compensation, and that area is still known as the Firelands. The city was wiped out a second time when American men started going bareheaded. Danbury had become the center of hat production in the country; from 1790, when Zadoc Benedict set up a beaver hat factory here, to the 1930s, when Danbury's plants turned out seven-hundred-dozen hats daily, this was headware headquarters. When styles changed after World War II, the hatmakers resisted. In fact, hatless salesmen were refused admittance to some factories in the 1950s. Such stern measures did no good. Now the only remnant of the Danbury hatters is the Scott-Fanton Museum, on Main Street. Among other local historical exhibits is the Dodd Shop, showing how hats were made here for 150 years.

The road briefly runs as a freeway after entering New York State, then narrows as it comes to the town of **Brewster**. This area is dotted with reservoirs from which New York City draws its water supply. It was originally dotted with farms from which the city drew its food, but most of the old farm towns have turned into outposts of suburbia, with land prices exceeding anything in the wildest dreams of agriculture. It was in this area in the 1850s that Gail Borden began to produce evaporated milk. He got the idea while sailing home from England (and an unsuccessful attempt at marketing a meat biscuit) and seeing the impossibility of keeping sea travelers supplied with fresh milk. After several experiments, he hit upon the idea of condensing milk in a vacuum pan. He received patents on the process in 1856 and found a ready acceptance of his new product in New York City, recently shaken by a scare involving contaminated milk. He won the contract to supply condensed milk to the Union Army, and before you knew it, there was Elsie, the smooth-talking cow, and Borden's had become an American standby. One of the first condensaries is exhibited at the old Southeast Town Hall on Main Street in Brewster. If you don't want to stop for that one, there is another old Borden's setup in the neighboring town of **Mahopac**'s Agricultural Museum.

The road makes its way past several of the reservoirs before dropping out of the hills and into the Hudson Valley at Peekskill. There it heads north on a ridge above the river, with great views of the water and of Bear Mountain on the far bank. U.S. 6 crosses the Hudson at Bear Mountain Bridge, built in 1924, and continues west as Palisades Interstate Parkway. Turn off at Seven Lakes Parkway, which leads into Perkins Memorial Drive, a road that climbs to the crest of Bear Mountain and offers a magnificent view over this part of the Hudson Valley. Then return to U.S. 6 along the same route.

The highway turns into a freeway west of here, but you should follow the original route, now designated N.Y. 17M. Past **Monroe** is the Museum Village of Orange County, a recreation of a nineteenth-century crossroads settlement, with working crafts people, stores, workshops and a lineup of family activities.

Horse racing may be the sport of kings, but harness racing gives it a peculiarly democratic spin. It is the quintessential county fair event, with horses harnessed as if for work taken out to race for amusement instead. The Historic Track in **Goshen** was the birthplace of American-style harness racing—as distinguished from the Ben-Hur style. Races have been held here since 1838 and an annual meet still goes on from mid-May to mid-July. Nearby is the Museum of the Trotter, housed in historic stables, with prints and displays of the greatest names in the sport.

The road now angles southwest, past the Shawangunk Mountains, and reaches the Delaware River at the old canal town of Port Jervis. It was named for John B. Jervis, head engineer of the Delaware and Hudson Canal project, which opened the anthracite coal fields of northern Pennsylvania to the markets reached by the Hudson River. From here, the road continues into Pennsylvania for the next stage of its transcontinental voyage.

VISITING HOURS

MASSACHUSETTS

Barnstable: Sturgis Library, (508) 362-6636. On Massachusetts 6A (Main St.). Monday–Saturday, 9–5, all year. Free.

Bourne: Aptuxcet Trading Post, (508) 759-5379. On Shore Road, west of U.S. 6 from the Bourne Bridge, Cape Cod Canal. Monday–Saturday, 10–5; Sunday, 1–5, mid-April–mid-October. Closed Wednesday, except July and August. Admission.

Brewster: Fire and History Museum, (508) 896-5711. West, on Massachusetts 6A. Daily, 10–5, mid-June–Labor Day; weekends only, 10–3, to mid-October. Admission.
   Museum of Natural History, (508) 896-3867.

Dennis: Josiah Dennis Manse, (508) 385-2232. Off Massachusetts 6A, at 77 Nobscusset Road. Tuesday and Thursday, noon–5, July–August. Donation.

Eastham: Old Windmill, no phone. On U.S. 6. Monday–Saturday, 10–5; Sunday, 1–5, late June–mid-September. Free.
   Salt Pond Visitor Center of the Cape Cod National

Seashore, (508) 255-3421. On U.S. 6. Daily, 9–5,
March–December. Free.

Fall River: Heritage State Park, (508) 675-5758. South of U.S.
6, along the east bank of the Taunton River, at Davol St.
Tuesday–Sunday, 9–8, Memorial Day–Labor Day; 9–4:30, at
other times. Free.

Battleship Cove, (508) 678-1100. Adjacent to Heritage
State Park. Daily, 9–7, July–Labor Day, 9–4:30, at other
times. Admission.

Historical Museum, (508) 679-1071. South of U.S. 6, at
451 Rock St. Tuesday–Friday, 9–4:30; weekends, 2–4,
April–November. Closed Sunday, March and December.
Free.

New Bedford: Whaling Museum, (508) 997-0046. South of
U.S. 6, from the western end of the harbor bridge, at 18
Johnny Cake Hill. Monday–Saturday, 9–5; Sunday, 1–5, all
year. Admission.

Seamen's Bethel, (508) 992-3295. Adjoins Whaling
Museum. Monday–Saturday, 10–5; Sunday, 1–5, June–Labor
Day. Closes at 4, May and September–mid-October.
Donation.

Rotch-Jones-Duff House, (508) 997-1401. Off U.S. 6, at
396 County St. Tuesday–Friday, 11–4; Sunday, 1–4,
June–August. Sunday only, April, May, September, October.
Admission.

Orleans: French Cable Station, no phone. South of U.S. 6, on
Massachusetts 28, at Cove Road. Tuesday–Saturday, 10–5,
July–Labor Day. Admission.

Provincetown: Pilgrim Monument, (508) 487-1310. One block
north of Massachusetts 6A, on Town Hill. Daily, 9–4,
March–November. Admission.

Nickerson House, (508) 487-1228. On Massachusetts 6A,
at 72 Commercial St. Daily, 10–5, June–mid-October.
Admission.

Whale Watch Cruises, (508) 487-1582. Leave from

MacMillan Pier, on the harbor. Daily,
mid-April–mid-October. Call for times and rates.

Sandwich: Glass Museum, (508) 888-0251. South of
Massachusetts 6A, at 129 Main St. Daily, 9:30–4:30,
April–November. Admission.

Burgess Museum, (508) 888-4668. South of Massachusetts
6A, on Massachusetts 130, at 4 Water St.
Monday–Saturday, 10–4, Sunday, 1–4, April–November.
Donation.

Hoxie House, (508) 888-1173. South of Massachusetts 6A,
on Water St. Monday–Saturday, 10–5; Sunday, 1–5,
mid-June–mid-October. Admission.

Wareham: Tremont Nail Co., (508) 295-0038. Off U.S. 6, at 8
Elm St. Monday–Saturday, 10–5; Sunday, noon–5,
June–December. Closed Monday, at other times. Free.

Wellfleet: Marconi Wireless Station, (508) 349-3785. South on
U.S. 6, then east to Cape Cod National Seashore. Site may
be visited all year. Free.

Historical Museum, (508) 349-3346. West, off U.S. 6, on
Main St. Tuesday–Saturday, 2–5, late June–mid-September.
Admission.

West Barnstable: West Parish Meetinghouse, (508) 362-3511.
South of Massachusetts 6A, on Massachusetts 149. Daily,
10–4, Memorial Day–mid-October. Free.

Yarmouth Port: Bangs Hallett House, (508) 362-3021. South of
Massachusetts 6A, at 8 Strawberry Lane. Monday–Friday,
1–4, July–August. Admission.

RHODE ISLAND

North Scituate: Dame Farm, (401) 949-3550. East on U.S. 6,
then north on Brown Ave. Sunday, 1–4,
mid-May–mid-October. Donation.

CONNECTICUT

Bristol: Clock and Watch Museum, (203) 583-6070. South of U.S. 6, at 100 Maple St. Daily, 11–5, April–October. Admission.

Danbury: Scott-Fanton Museum, (203) 743-5200. South of U.S. 6, on Connecticut 53, at 43 Main St. Wednesday–Sunday, 2–5, all year. Donation.

Farmington: Stanley-Whitman House, (203) 677-9222. South from Connecticut 4, at 37 High St. Tuesday–Sunday, 1–4, May–October. Sunday only, March, April, November, December. Admission.
   Hill-Stead, (203) 677-4787. South from Connecticut 4 on High St., then east on Mountain Road. Wednesday–Sunday, 2–5, mid-February–mid-January. Admission.

Hartford: Nook Farm, (203) 525-9317. West, on Connecticut 4 (Farmington Road) at Forest St. Daily, 10–4:30, June–August. Tuesday–Saturday, 9:30–4; Sunday, 1–4, at other times. Admission.

Manchester: Cheney House, (203) 643-5588. South from U.S. 6, on Connecticut 83 (Main St.), then west on Hartford Road. Thursday and Sunday, 1–5, all year. Admission.

Southbury: Bullet Hill School, (203) 264-2993. South, on U.S. 6. Open by appointment.

Terryville: Lock Museum of America, (203) 589-6359. On U.S. 6, at 130 Main St. Tuesday–Sunday, 1:30–4:30, May–October. Admission.

West Hartford: Noah Webster House, (203) 521-5362. South of Connecticut 4, at 227 S. Main St. Monday, Tuesday, Thursday and Friday, 10–4; weekends, 1–4, mid-June–September. Thursday–Sunday, 1–4, at other times. Admission.

Willimantic: Windham Textile and History Museum, (203) 456-2178. South from U.S. 6, on Connecticut 66, at Union and Main Sts. Tuesday–Sunday, 10–4, all year. Admission.

Woodbury: Glebe House, (203) 263-2855. Off U.S. 6, on Hollow Road. Saturday–Wednesday, 1–4, April–November. Donation.

NEW YORK

Brewster: Southeast Town Hall Museum, (914) 279-7500. On U.S. 6 (Main St.). Tuesday–Thursday, noon–4; weekends, 2–4, March–December. Free.

Goshen: Historic Track, (914) 294-5333. Exit U.S. 6 at northbound New York 207, to Park Place. Daily, 10–4, all year. Admission. Meeting is held mid-May–July. Call for times.

Museum of the Trotter, (914) 294-6330. North of U.S. 6, at 240 Main St. Monday–Saturday, 10–5; Sunday, 1:30–5, all year. Donation.

Mahopac: Agricultural Museum, (914) 628-9298. West on U.S. 6, at Baldwin Place Road. Daily, 10–5, March–December. Admission.

Monroe: Museum Village, (914) 782-8247. West of town, on New York 17M. Wednesday–Sunday, 10–5, mid-April–October. Admission.

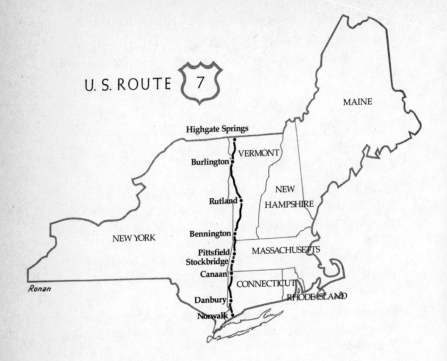

U. S. ROUTE 7

Highgate Springs

Burlington

Rutland

Bennington

Pittsfield
Stockbridge

Canaan

Danbury

Norwalk

MAINE

VERMONT

NEW
HAMPSHIRE

NEW YORK

MASSACHUSETTS

CONNECTICUT

RHODE ISLAND

Ronan

The Berkshires

U.S. 7

Highgate Springs, Vt., to Norwalk, Conn.
* 318 miles

For old road drivers, this is as close to perfection as it gets. U.S. 7 defines the best of the old roads. It has unforgettable scenery, associations with some of the most memorable figures in our history, art and literature and, except for a few miles at its northern end, no Interstates. It skirts Lake Champlain, runs along the western edge of the Green Mountains, through the heart of the Massachusetts Berkshires and finally follows the course of the Housatonic River through Connecticut's Litchfield Hills. There are no large cities on the way, no seasonal traffic backups. This is truly a road to enjoy as the panorama of America unfolds outside the car window.

* MILEPOSTS *

Swanton has always had a rather cozy connection with the nearby Canadian border. This site, at the falls of the Missisquoi River, was one of the bases of the St. Francis tribe of Canada. Their main villages were across the line in Quebec, but from these forward positions they raided freely through the Connecticut River Valley under French patronage. Many captives of the Great Deerfield Raid of 1704 (see U.S. 5.) were brought here to Swanton, and a bell stolen from Deerfield was placed in a chapel built here by the Jesuits. After Rogers' Rangers devastated the main St. Francis village with a surprise raid in 1759, the chapel was moved to Ste. Hyacinthe in Canada. Vermont farmers, with whom the War of 1812 was not especially popular, carried on a brisk smuggling trade in livestock with the enemy across this border. Then in the 1920s, Swanton was an especially lively port of entry for illegal Canadian liquor.

Just west of town is a covered railroad bridge across the Missisquoi. At 369 feet, it is the longest in the country. Built in 1898 by the St. Johnsbury and Lake Champlain Railroad, the bridge was part of a larger rail complex. Its ruins are visible on the far side of the span.

The relations of **St. Albans** with Canada were not nearly as cordial. When a populist revolt in Quebec was crushed in 1837, many of the insurgents fled to this town. They harbored resentment toward the Canadian authorities for years and in the 1860s supplied a base and refuge for the Fenians, an Irish revolutionary group, which planned to strike a blow for the homeland by invading Canada. It was an odd concept, but the border agitation grew so serious that President Andrew Johnson was compelled to send troops to restore calm.

None of this ill will was helped at all by the raid of 1864, one of the strangest episodes of the Civil War. A band of Confederate soldiers stormed into St. Albans from Canada on October 19, held up the town's banks and killed a man as they fled north. Eventually, twenty-two of the raiders were captured in Canada. Vermont was infuriated when they were tried and acquitted, their actions judged legitimate acts of war. It was, by quite a distance, the most northern action of the war. The Franklin County Museum, in the town historic district near Taylor Park, has mementoes of the raid and other aspects of the town's past. The most violent thing that goes on around St. Albans today is probably the woodchopping contests held during the annual Maple Sugar Festival in April.

Georgia Center was the home of Gen. George Stannard, whose 16th Vermont Brigade broke Pickett's Charge at Gettysburg in 1863. Past this village, as the road runs by Arrowhead Mountain Lake, the outline of Mount Mansfield, the highest peak in Vermont at 4,393 feet, becomes visible to the east.

Once his warring days were done, Ira Allen, the brother of Ethan, decided to go into business. He picked the town of Winooski and built a mill at the falls of the river in 1786. Many others followed, and for a time they thrived. But in the familiar pattern of decline, the last one closed in 1954. Blighted for years, the old mills have been converted to malls. What a difference a vowel makes. Winooski's downtown redevelopment program has won several national awards, and blight has become delight.

The road runs through the middle of Burlington, Vermont's largest city (see U.S. 2), then passes several attractive residential areas before following the shore of Lake Champlain along Shelburne Bay.

Every so often, in parts of the country where roots run deep, you come upon a family that influenced a community so profoundly that the place is forever changed. That's what happened with the town of **Shelburne** and the Webbs. Dr. Seward Webb made a fortune in railroads and consolidated those holdings with his marriage to Lila Vanderbilt, whose family also dabbled in rails. In the last years of the nineteenth century, they assembled a 4,000-acre estate on a ridge overlooking Lake Champlain just west of Shelburne. The grounds were laid out by the foremost park planner of the time, Frederick Law Olmstead, and the forestry work was supervised by Gifford Pinchot, soon to head the U.S. Forestry Service. The estate was topped off by a 110-room mansion, Shelburne House; a horsehoe-shaped, five-story livestock barn; and another barn entirely for carriages. Shelburne Farms was regarded as the finest country estate in Vermont.

Their daughter-in-law, Electra Havemeyer Webb, used the area as a base for collecting folk art. Passionate in this pursuit, she gradually amassed one of the largest collections in the country.

She concentrated on New England—paintings, scrimshaw, quilts, cigar store Indians. In order to adequately display her eclectic, enormous ingathering, she formed the Shelburne Museum Foundation in 1947. Both the farm and the museum are now open to the public, although separately operated and about a mile and a half apart. The museum has grown to include thirty-five buildings, transported here from all over northern New England, and the old sidewheeler S. S. *Ticonderoga,* brought over from the nearby lake. Together, the farm and the museum make up a remarkable family legacy to the area.

One of the museum exhibits is the Hezekiah Barnes Tavern, brought here from the neighboring town of **Charlotte**. The tavern was once a primary stop on the stagecoach run from Burlington, Vermont, to Troy, New York, along this road. For a time, Charlotte was larger than Burlington because of the activity it generated. Although the tavern is gone, enough remains of Charlotte to form a historic district, just east of the highway. Nearby is the Vermont Wildflower Farm, a vast blanket of ever-changing seasonal colors spread over the rolling acreage of fields and gardens. There are also special exhibits on herbal remedies and Indian legends of flowers.

Lake Champlain is out of sight now, but not if you take to the heights. Just south of Charlotte, you'll find the entrance to Mount Philo State Park. The view from the summit takes in the southern portion of the lake, all the way to the crests of the Adirondacks in New York.

The writer who most enduringly stamped the image of the Vermont character on the national mind was Rowland E. Robinson. His nineteenth-century portraits of rural life in what was then an isolated part of America won him a wide following and formed the popular picture of the idiosyncratic, laconic Vermonter. Originally a magazine illustrator, Robinson lost his sight, but that only seemed to sharpen his perceptions of the people around him. His home, Rokeby, is now operated as a historic site and museum in **Ferrisburg**.

The falls of Otter Creek attracted the first settlers to **Vergennes**, named for the French foreign minister during the American Revolution. During the War of 1812, the fleet that defeated the British at the pivotal battle of Plattsburgh, on Lake Champlain, was assembled here under the direction of Commodore Thomas Mac-Donough. The historic district of Vergennes includes an unusually wide assortment of nineteenth-century structures, including the Bixby Memorial Library, with exhibits of local history.

Middlebury was settled in 1761 and given its name because it lay at the midpoint of the road between two other new communities, New Haven and Salisbury. It is now a community that falls midway between the Vermont that was and the Vermont that is being made. The "was" part is easy to find. Middlebury has the state's largest historic district, with nearly three hundred buildings. Its Congregational Church, with a 136-foot spire, is the best proportioned in Vermont. The Sheldon Museum, in a home dating from 1829, contains an outstanding collection of decorative arts from the state's past. Middlebury College occupies the area just west of the business district, and on its campus is Painter Hall, built in 1816, the oldest college building in the state.

Middlebury College has also been one of the leading engines of change. The school was founded in 1800, but the woman who would most directly shape its history arrived seven years later. Emma Hart Willard came here to direct the Female Academy, a local women's school, and did so much to raise the standard of women's education that the college eventually absorbed the school. A cousin of her husband's boarded with them while attending classes at Middlebury. When Willard dipped into his textbooks, she was astonished and then outraged to learn what women were being deprived of in higher education. She dedicated her work in Middlebury to proving to a dubious world that women were capable of competing with men academically at the highest levels. She left in 1818 to establish her own college in New York, but the reputation she built at Middlebury has endured. It is now regarded as the archetype of the small, excellent liberal arts school. It also has a renowned writing program.

The Frog Hollow Crafts Center grew out of the school's curriculum. In a restored mill on Otter Creek, more than two hundred crafts workers have studios and exhibit space. Established in

1971, it was the first center of its kind in the state and typifies the sort of outlook brought to Vermont by the thousands of newcomers who have given Vermont the greatest growth rate in its history. If any part of America has truly "greened," it is the Green Mountain State. The chatty yuppie is as familiar a local character now as the laconic farmer.

One part of the legendary Vermont countryside that endures, though, can be found on the University of Vermont's Morgan Horse Farm. It is 3 miles northwest of Middlebury on Vt. 23 and is dedicated to sustaining and improving the Justin Morgan breed. The horse that is Vermont's pride was developed in the late eighteenth century, and Col. Joseph Battell began breeding Morgans here about a hundred years later. He traced pedigrees, established the Morgan Register and, in 1906, left his farm to the federal government for the purpose of preserving the breed that makes horse-fanciers rhapsodic. Vermont took the farm over in 1951 and has carried on the work. The farm gives the traveler an excellent chance to view Vermont's Official State Animal in its Official State Habitat.

South of Middlebury, take the turnoff to Lake Dunmore for an exceptional view across the water to the peaks of the Green Mountains. Return to the main highway by way of Salisbury.

If election results are any gauge, Stephen Douglas won the most famous series of political debates in the country's history. But he takes second billing to Abraham Lincoln, the man he defeated for the U.S. Senate seat from Illinois in 1858. The debates gave Lincoln a national reputation, and two years later the men opposed each other again as presidential candidates. With the Democrats split over the slavery issue, Lincoln won the election, and as far as reputation is concerned, the one in 1858 too. Douglas grew up in the town of **Brandon** and attended the local academy here before moving to Illinois at the age of twenty. His birthplace is now a museum. Douglas, who was four years younger than Lincoln and a good 12 inches shorter, died in 1861 and took his place forever as the second banana in one of the country's most memorable campaigns.

Pittsford has an especially pleasant triangular Green and a most complete collection of antique maple-sugaring instruments in its New England Maple Museum. But in this part of the state, it was marble, not maples, that was tapped for riches.

Just south of Pittsford, turn off on Vt. 3, the Marble Valley Highway, to **Proctor**. The town was named for Redfield Proctor, who organized the Vermont marble industry in the 1880s. The towns in which marble was quarried and processed, Proctor and Rutland, became showcases for the product, with buildings, sidewalks, bridges and curbstones all made of the local stone. The Vermont Marble Company operates the Marble Exhibit next to its Proctor factory. From the visitors' galleries, you can watch the huge uncut slabs arriving from the quarries and going through the stages of the finishing process. A sculptor-in-residence works in a nearby room, and an adjacent gallery gives an idea of the enormous range of uses to which the finished product is put. A movie explains the origin and subterranean portion of the marble's trip to Proctor and shows some of the celebrated structures worldwide that are fashioned of Vermont stone.

South of town, along West Proctor Road on the way to Rutland, is Wilson Castle, a high-Victorian hodgepodge of every style and architectural eccentricity under the sun. Part Gothic castle and part Arabian fantasy, it contains thirty-two rooms, eighty-four stained-glass windows and innumerable peacocks wandering the grounds. The castle was built in 1867 and has undergone recent restoration.

Turn east on U.S. 4 for a few miles into the heart of **Rutland**. You will hit U.S. 7 again at its junction with Main Street. This was the rail and financial center of the marble industry, and the heart of town is literally made of marble. Drive along Main Street, north and south, to get the feel of how it was used in both public buildings and private residences. Stop at the Chaffee Art Gallery, opposite Main Street Park. You can take a pleasant break here, either to visit the museum or to wander about the park and its adjacent historic district.

Wallingford has been known for its garden tools for more than a century. This is the home of the True Temper Company, and the

Old Stone Shop on the town's broad, tree-lined main street is where the firm got its start.

Not all the writers who lived along this road drew their inspiration from New England themes. The village of Danby became the home of Pearl Buck, who started her career as an American missionary in China and ended it, in effect, as a Chinese missionary to America. Her moving novels of that faraway land were enormous successes in this country, roused tremendous sympathy for the Chinese and won her the Nobel Prize for Literature in 1938. In her last years, she moved to this village, and the foundation she funded restored many of its buildings, making a perfectly preserved nineteenth-century vista. Prior to Miss Buck's arrival, Danby's literary laurels went to Thomas Rowley, poet laureate of the Green Mountain Boys, who were very active in this area. The town is noted now as an antiques center.

East Dorset is another of the area's marble villages. The quarries on nearby Mount Aeolus provided the stone for the New York Public Library.

U.S. 7 branches to the east here and becomes a freeway. Ignore that and remain instead on highway 7A, which is infinitely more interesting.

In **Manchester**, you come to the bedrock of Vermont's tourist industry. The gentle hills of this state have always appealed to those who passed through. Even some of the soldiers who were called on to fight here had nice things to say about the scenery. But only in the late nineteenth century, in the years after the Civil War, did people begin making trips to Vermont specifically to look at it. Manchester, in its verdant valley between the Taconic range and the Green Mountains, became an early resort destination. Its Equinox Inn was founded in 1769 as an overnight stop for weary overland travelers. In the succeeding century, though, it became known as a place to linger and restore the spirit. The inn still dominates the center of Manchester. Vacant for many years, a recent restoration has turned it again into prime resort property.

Bromley ski resort has brought a rush of sports-minded travelers into the area in more recent decades, but it has long been

famous for its fishing, and the Orvis Company, a leading manufacturer of tackle, has established the American Museum of Fly
Fishing in Manchester. It contains old prints, hand-crafted equipment and celebrity fishing gear, from Ernest Hemingway's to
Herbert Hoover's, which is quite a range.

Mount Equinox shelters the town on the west and gave its
name to the old inn. At 3,816 feet, it is the highest of the Taconic
peaks. A paved road, Equinox Mountain Drive, leads to the summit and a viewpoint, from a turnoff just south of Manchester.

Near the turnoff is Hildene, the home of Robert Todd Lincoln.
How odd that the son of the sixteenth president would move to
this particular area, along the same road and just a few miles from
the birthplace of his father's great political opponent, Stephen
Douglas. Lincoln moved here in 1904, and family members continued to occupy the classic Georgian mansion until 1975. The
interior has been preserved virtually intact, with many Lincoln
family possessions. The exterior features formal gardens and
wonderful views of the surrounding mountains.

I mentioned a few miles back that even soldiers came away
impressed with Vermont's scenery. The most significant example
of such tourism in arms occurred in **Arlington**. A British officer,
it is said, was so taken by the western landscape here that he
carved the scene on his horn drinking cup. The engraving then
became the basis for the mountain scene depicted on Vermont's
State Seal. Whether that's true or not, there was a more pacific
local resident who unquestionably reproduced Vermont's charms
for a wider audience. Norman Rockwell lived here from 1939 to
1953, and many of his best-known magazine covers, as well as
The Four Freedoms series of paintings, were done in Arlington, using
local residents as models. There is an exhibition of his works in
a former church on Main Street. (Rockwell's career is discussed
more fully under Stockbridge, Massachusetts, farther down the
road.)

Still another Arlington resident was Dorothy Canfield Fisher,
whose books and articles defined the state for a twentieth-century
readership, much as Rowland Robinson's had done in the previous century. Robinson emphasized the quirky, ruggedly indepen-

dent nature of the Vermonters. But by Fisher's day, these manner-
isms had come to be regarded with affection, as part of the state's
unique charm, a slice of bygone America. Her portraits of the state
and its people were a key factor in introducing its attractions to
a growing stream of new residents in the years after World War
II.

The writer who became the most profound interpreter of northern New England to the rest of the world was Robert Frost, however. For a time the poet lived in South Shaftsbury, in a stone
house near the highway, but he soon retreated deeper into the
region's heartland. His final resting place is a bit farther along this
old road, in **Bennington**.

The road we have traveled from the north of Vermont is called
the Ethan Allen Highway. In Bennington (named for New Hampshire's governor Benning Wentworth), it crosses the Molly Stark
Trail from the east. This junction is a fulcrum of the state's history, as well. Here Allen's Green Mountain Boys met Gen. John
Stark's militiamen to repel the British invasion of the state in the
summer of 1777 and open the way for the colonial triumph at
Saratoga. The road is named for Stark's wife. He had been a
capable leader in the war's early months, but when younger,
better-connected officers were promoted over him, he went home
to New Hampshire to sit it out. He changed his mind, though,
when he learned that a major British force was coming down the
Hudson Valley under the command of Gen. John Burgoyne.
Recognizing the mortal danger to New England that this represented, Stark hastened west, raising local militia along the way.
In trying to get to the main body of the colonial forces, he found
the British first. Burgoyne had sent a force under a Hessian officer,
Lt. Col. Friedrich Baum, to raid Vermont for horses and provi-
sions. By the time they reached Bennington, Stark was already
holding the town and waiting for them. Taking the initiative, he
moved northwest of town to meet them. "There are the Red
Coats," he exclaimed. "They will be ours or tonight Molly Stark
sleeps a widow."

There were many widows made in that engagement, but Mrs.
Stark was not one of them. Her husband's victory, instead, won

her a kind of immortality. In a two-hour battle, Baum was killed
and the British and Hessians routed. As Stark's exhausted troops
returned to town with their prisoners, though, they were attacked
by a reserve column of enemy soldiers. As they gave ground, Seth
Warner's Green Mountain Boys entered the battle and again
forced the British into flight. The victory ended any hope Burgoyne had of provisioning his army from the land. Moreover, it
created a battle-tested force on his flank, one that would eventually bottle him up and force his surrender.

The battle monument in Bennington dates from 1891, and at
the time its 306-foot limestone shaft was the tallest of its kind in
the world. There is an elevator to an observation platform for a
superb view over the countryside. The battleground was actually
a few miles from this spot; the monument marks the location of
a storehouse that was the British objective. The famed Catamount
Tavern, where Stark met with his officers to plan the attack, was
situated nearby. According to legend, British officers had sent
word to the Catamount to prepare a victory dinner for them
following the battle. When they were led past the tavern that
evening as prisoners, the proprietor called out, "Gentlemen, dinner is waiting." It's a good story but it sounds like one of those
things you wish you had said but didn't think of at the time.

The Old First Church, near the monument, is one of the most
photographed and most graceful in the state. It was designed by
the great Federal-era architect Asher Benjamin. Although the
church was not built until twenty-eight years after the battle,
those who fell in the engagement are buried in the churchyard.
So is Robert Frost, whose epitaph reads "I had a lover's quarrel
with the world." Down the hill, on West Main Street, is the
Bennington Museum, containing large collections of regional
glass and furniture, memorabilia from the battle and a gallery of
paintings by Grandma Moses, who lived just over the state line
in Eagle Bridge, New York.

The road joins the Hoosic River at the town of Pownal and,
running with the stream, sweeps across the state line into Massachusetts.

Ephraim Williams had a premonition that he would not be

coming home, as he prepared to go fight the French in 1755. So he left a bequest to found a college, on condition that the designated locality change its name from West Hoosac to **Williamstown**. Sure enough, Williams fell leading his troops at the battle of Lake George in New York. But it took another thirty-eight years for Williams College to actually be established. The man had a good eye for a college town, though. This mountain-rimmed setting in the Berkshires is close to ideal.

Williams used to be known as the "college of gentlemen," which isn't such a bad thing but is hardly the sort of reputation a contemporary school wants bandied about. While strolling its tidy campus, watch for the Thompson Chapel, with its 120-foot tower, and Chapin Hall and Library, with its collection of rare books, including the country's four founding documents, and the Paul Whiteman collection, containing memorabilia of the bandleader who applied symphonic treatment to jazz in the 1920s and conducted the debut of *Rhapsody in Blue*. Just south of the campus is the Sterling and Pauline Clark Art Institute, with a large collection of French Impressionists. The Clarks were especially fond of Renoirs, and more of them are assembled here than anywhere else in the country.

Mount Greylock, the highest peak in Massachusetts at 3,491 feet, rises on the east in the midst of a state reservation as you head south on U.S. 7. The village of Lanesborough was the birthplace of Henry Wheeler Shaw. That might not mean anything to you unless I add that he wrote under the name of Josh Billings. That might not mean anything to you either unless you happen to like thumbing through books of famous quotations. Billings is always good for a few citations. He was the leading rustic humorist of his time (right after the Civil War), a field of whimsy that went into decline before being revived in recent years by Garrison Keillor. "It's better to know nothing than to know what ain't so" is one of Billings's lines. So is "There is no man so poor but what he can afford to keep one dog. And I have seen them so poor that they could afford to keep three." Well, it was regarded as great stuff a century ago.

At Pontoosuc Lake, there are wonderful views west to the Taconic range in New York.

Pittsfield is a good-sized manufacturing city, the commercial center of the Berkshires, but it also has rather impressive literary credentials. Oliver Wendell Holmes inherited property along the Housatonic River here in the 1830s and later averred, "The best of tonics is the Housatonic." Holmes had already written his poem "The Last Leaf," and his model for this sketch of a generation's final living member was a Pittsfield man, Maj. Thomas Melville. Melville had moved to Boston years before, participated in the Tea Party and was reputed to be the last man in America to wear a cocked hat. Melville's brother still lived in the area then and one of his nephews was an aspiring writer. Herman Melville wasn't making enough to live on, but the family advanced him the money to buy a farmhouse in the area, about half a mile from Holmes' place.

He took up residence in Pittsfield in 1850 and began work on a new book about whaling for which he had some hopes. He also did a lot of writing on the wall near his chimney, much of it still visible. These jottings were later collected and published under the title *I and My Chimney.* Melville lived there for thirteen years and called his house Arrowhead, from the number of old Indian relics he gathered on the property, a pastime also pursued by his neighbor Holmes. Arrowhead is now a museum, off U.S. 7 on Holmes Road, and more Melville memorabilia are contained in the Berkshire Athenaeum in the middle of town.

Pittsfield's early prosperity was based on the more mundane pursuit of wool carding. The trade embargo that resulted from the War of 1812 created a huge demand for American-made textiles. The development of a mechanized carder, which separates the fibers before the spinning process, speeded up a tedious procedure and made Pittsfield something of a boom town. Its chief product now is electric transformers, and the guidance equipment for the Polaris guided missile system was put together here.

A few years before the carder came to town, in 1810, Pittsfield started an American tradition by holding the first county fair. Elkanan Watson is credited with dreaming up this agricultural get-together, which was held under the elms on the town's Green. The biggest of the elms was 214 years old then, and when it had to be cut down in 1861 there was lamentation in Pittsfield. A historic plaque marks the site of this great tree, as well as the first fair held beneath its branches.

South Mountain, at the southern edge of town, has been the site of chamber music concerts since 1918 when they were started by Elizabeth Sprague Coolidge, wife of the future president. They have become a part of the rich Berkshires' musical tradition.

More of that is evident in **Lenox**, summer home of the Boston Symphony since 1939 and site of the annual Tanglewood festival. A full menu of musical delights is presented on the festival grounds during July and August. In one corner of the 210-acre estate is a cottage now used as a music studio. This is where Nathaniel Hawthorne lived in the 1850s and wrote *Tanglewood Tales.* He and Melville developed a rather distant friendship when they both lived in the Berkshires. The same summer that one was writing *Moby Dick,* the other was busily scribbling away here on *House of the Seven Gables.* Hawthorne was a reclusive man, ill at ease in literary gatherings. It is said that Holmes rode over to Tanglewood one day for a visit, went off to locate Hawthorne and returned to find the writer holding his horse. "Is there a greater honor in America than to have the author of *The Scarlet Letter* hold your horse," he observed. Hawthorne didn't think it was very funny.

Edith Wharton did much of her work in the Lenox area and set her tragic novel *Ethan Frome* in the town. She co-authored a book on planning houses in 1897 and four years later began work on the ideal home visualized in the text. The Mount was completed in 1902, its gardens and design laid out by Wharton. They remain an ongoing tribute to a woman who brought to life not only the characters but the buildings of her imagination.

FOCUS

* * *

There is an old story about a Broadway musical with a score so derivative that people entered the theater humming the tunes.

Something like that happens in **Stockbridge**. People enter the Norman Rockwell Museum knowing in advance what they will see; and they can hardly wait to see it. The images are as familiar as the flag and as comforting as old memories. The visitors have seen them countless times on old magazine covers and in book-sized collections. Maybe they even have reproductions of one or two of them hanging in their homes.

Here is the young couple filling out the marriage license form, all nervous eagerness, while the elderly clerk, bored and amused at the same time, prepares to close for the weekend. Here is the little runaway boy with his knapsack, sitting on the diner stool next to the overstuffed cop who will soon take him safely home. Here is the young girl, primping at her mirror in complete dissatisfaction, as she glances at the photo of a Hollywood queen in the open fan magazine beside her. The images are so familiar they bring an involuntary smile when we see the original paintings here. Familiar, yet larger than life, too. It's as if you came upon the face of an old friend beaming down at you from the wall of a museum.

Rockwell moved to this town in the Berkshires in 1953, at the height of his fame, and remained here for the last twenty-five years of his life. If you've been traveling this road from its start, you know that he lived in Arlington, Vermont, for fourteen years and did much of his best work there. A museum in Arlington displays many of the most famous covers. Stockbridge, however, shows off the originals, even those that were done in Arlington. Rockwell's best-known Stockbridge piece is probably the picture of the town at Christmas time, which first appeared in McCall's in 1962. The view of Main Street today is not much changed.

The Rockwell Museum is housed at the corner of Main and Elm. The building is historic in its own right. It has been occupied by descendants of Cyrus Field, a Stockbridge man who laid down the first transatlantic cable, including novelist Rachel Field, whose best-seller, *All This and Heaven, Too,* was set in this town and largely based on her family. But because of space limitations, works can only be displayed here on a rotating basis. In 1991, the new Norman Rockwell Museum is scheduled to open in expanded quarters in the Glendale district of town, a few miles west of its present location.

It will then be near Chesterwood, the home of another famed American artist, sculptor Daniel Chester French. His best-known works are the Minute Man at Concord Bridge and the seated Lincoln in the Memorial in Washington. Most of the work on Lincoln was done here from 1914 to 1917, and the studio is still filled with the casts used in its design. French bought an old farmhouse in the area in 1896 and spent the next nine years transforming it into this elegant estate. The view toward Monument Mountain on the west was also a favorite of British poet Matthew Arnold, who lived on the property in 1886. The Berkshire landscapes here have been compared to those of Britain's Lake Country. Maybe that's what appealed to Arnold. Judging from his subsequent writing, not much else about America did. Chesterwood has been open to the public since 1955.

The first European to settle in the area was the Rev. John Sergeant, who opened a mission there in 1739. His home, Mission House, was moved to Main Street in 1926 from its original setting on a nearby hill, and it's now open to the public. The painstaking restoration was the project of Mabel Choate. Her family's home, Naumkeag, is a chateaulike mansion built in 1886 for her father, the famed lawyer and ambassador to Great Britain, Joseph Choate. A true American aristocrat, Choate was known for his regal bearing and impressive mien in the courtroom. One opponent warned the jury not to be impressed with "Mr. Choate's Chesterfieldian, urban manner." Choate, knowing the man had recently moved to an exclusive New York suburb, replied that neither should it be impressed with his adversary's "Westchesterfieldian, suburban manner." At a later date, when asked who he would wish to be if he were not Joseph Choate, he responded, "Mrs. Choate's second husband." Don't you like a man who can think on his feet? He was ambassador to the Court of St. James from 1899 to 1905 and his home, designed by Stanford White, is now open to the public. Most of the gardens were designed by his daughter, Mabel. The house is located north of town, just off U.S. 7.

For refugees from the 1960s, Stockbridge also fondly recalls Alice's Restaurant, the dining spot of Arlo Guthrie's hit record, at which "you can get anything you want." A movie based on the song was shot here using local figures in supporting roles, but both Alice and her restaurant are gone with the hippies.

* * *

The highway runs on, through wonderful scenery, past the flank of Monument Mountain to **Great Barrington**. In a setting made for poets and philosophers, this town has had its share. William Cullen Bryant came here as a young attorney in 1816 and served as town clerk. He was just about to burst into international literary fame with the publication of his poem "Thanatopsis," at the age of twenty-three. The work caused a sensation, was hailed in England as the first great American poem, and the obscure lawyer in this secluded town was lionized as a prodigy. He never approached that level of poetry again, although his "To a Waterfowl" will have a familiar ring to aging American Lit. students. Instead Bryant went off to New York City and changed the course of American journalism as editor of the *Post*. Great Barrington is now the home of the Albert Schweitzer Center, a wildlife refuge and a museum dedicated to that remarkable man. Another writer and activist and the first black man ever to earn a Ph.D. from Harvard, Dr. W. E. B. DuBois, also was born here in 1868.

Another landmark in American black history is preserved in the town of **Ashley Falls**. Col. John Ashley, who gave his name to the place, built his home here in 1735. A black servant in his house filed the test case that abolished slavery in Massachusetts in 1781, making it the first state to do so. Nearby is Bartholomew's Cobble, a nature preserve and garden area along the Housatonic.

The road follows the river closely as it winds through northwestern Connecticut along the route of the old Housatonic Valley Railroad. When its promoters completed this line, from Stockbridge to Bridgeport, in 1844, they had great hopes for the industrial development of the valley. Fortunately, the hopes were thwarted. Instead, this has remained some of the wildest country on the entire drive, a delightful area known as the Litchfield Hills.

In **Canaan**, the old railroad depot, built in 1872, is still in service. It is the oldest terminal in continuous use in the country. Although it opens now only for sightseeing rides along the river, that is worth the fare.

As you continue south, it's easy to see why the settlers named this area Canaan. The promise of the land is immediately apparent. On a back road just northeast of the cluster of little towns named with variants of Canaan, there is a village called Sodom. I'll leave that for you to check out. The Canaan Mountains seal off this valley to the east, and to the west are the slopes of Mount Riga.

The next series of towns are the Cornwalls. The oldest covered bridge on the Housatonic, built in 1837, is in West Cornwall. This is a bit confusing, because a bit further up the road is a town named Cornwall Bridge. That old bridge was washed away, though, in the great flood of 1936. Between these two towns, the road runs through Housatonic Meadows State Park, an idyllic spot with hiking trails along the river. Another lovely state park, Kent Falls, lies on the far side of Cornwall Bridge. The river cascades over a series of rock ledges here in a beautifully secluded setting.

Kent Furnace is named for the ruins of an iron production plant built here in 1826. The ruins are now part of the Sloane-Stanley Museum, which also includes antique farm implements and the studio of the late artist Eric Sloan. Kent's delightful setting has attracted artists for many years, and there are several galleries in the town.

The road swings wide to the west, almost to the New York line, near another covered span at Bulls Bridge and through constantly impressive mountain scenery. A concentration of crafts galleries enlivens the town of **Brookfield**. The Crafts Center is housed in four colonial-era buildings and features demonstrations by several working artisans.

U.S. 7 shoots through Danbury as a freeway. (The city is described in the chapter on U.S. 6.) Just south of Danbury, cut to the west along Conn. 35 for a side trip into **Ridgefield**. There is a strong artistic presence in this town, too, with the Aldrich Museum of Contemporary Art on Main Street. This is prime New

York suburban territory, and if you want a shock to the system, take a look at the prices of the houses pictured in the real estate offices along Main Street. Benedict Arnold tried to barricade this street in 1777 as he pursued the British raiding party that burned Danbury to the ground. The British fought their way free, though, and killed Gen. Daniel Wooster in the skirmish. Wooster Mountain State Park, north of town, is named for him. So is the city of Wooster, Ohio, which was part of the Western Reserve lands given to victims of the war in this part of Connecticut. The Keeler Tavern in Ridgefield still shows off a British cannonball embedded in its wall, left as a parting shot by the retreating Redcoats. The building, once owned by architect Cass Gilbert, has been restored to its colonial appearance.

The highway rejoins U.S. 7 near Wilton and the road rushes to its end, in the midst of suburban bustle, in Norwalk.

VISITING HOURS

VERMONT

Arlington: Norman Rockwell Exhibition, (802) 375-6423. On Vermont 7A (Main St.). Daily, 8–7, June–October; 10–5, at other times. Admission.

Bennington: Battle Monument, (802) 447-0550. West on W. Main St. from U.S. 7, then north on Monument Ave. Daily, 9:30–5:30, April–October. Admission.
Bennington Museum, (802) 447-1571. Adjacent to Monument. Daily, 9–5, March–November. Admission.

Brandon: Stephen Douglas Home, (802) 247-6501. On U.S. 7, at 2 Grove St. Open by appointment.

Charlotte: Vermont Wildflower Farm, (802) 425-3500. North, on U.S. 7. Daily, 10–5, May–mid-October. Admission.

Ferrisburg: Rokeby, (802) 877-3406. On U.S. 7. Wednesday–Monday, 9–5, mid-May–mid-October. Admission.

Manchester: Museum of Fly Fishing, (802) 362-3300. On Vermont 7A, at Seminary Ave. Daily, 10–4, March–October; Monday–Friday, at other times. Donation.

Equinox Mountain Drive. South, off Vermont 7A. Daily, 8 a.m.–10 p.m., May–November. Toll.

Hildene, (802) 362-1788. South, on Vermont 7A. Daily, 9:30–5:30, mid-May–late October. Admission.

Middlebury: Sheldon Museum, (802) 388-2117. Off U.S. 7, at 1 Park St. Monday–Saturday, 10–5, June–October; Wednesday and Friday, 2–4, at other times. Admission.

Frog Hollow Crafts Center, (802) 338-3177. Off U.S. 7, in town. Monday–Saturday, 9:30–5, all year. Free.

Morgan Horse Farm, (802) 388-2011. West, on Vermont 23. Daily, 9–4, May–October. Admission.

Pittsford: New England Maple Museum, (802) 483-9414. North, on U.S. 7. Daily, 8:30–5:30, mid-May–October; 10–4, from mid-March, and November–Christmas. Admission.

Proctor: Marble Exhibit, (802) 459-3311. West of U.S. 7, on Vermont 3, at 61 Main St. Daily, 9–5:30, Memorial Day–late October. Admission.

Wilson Castle, (802) 773-3284. West of U.S. 7, on Vermont 3, then south on West Proctor Road. Daily, 8–6, mid-May–October. Admission.

Rutland: Chaffee Gallery, (802) 775-0356. On U.S. 7, at 16 S. Main St. Daily, 10–5, mid-June–October. Donation.

St. Albans: Franklin County Museum, (802) 527-7933. Off U.S. 7, on Church St. Tuesday–Saturday, 10–5, July–August. Admission.

Shelburne: Shelburne Farms, (802) 985-8686. West from U.S. 7, on Harbor Road. Daily, 9–5, June–mid-October. Admission.

Shelburne Museum, (802) 985-3344. On U.S. 7. Daily, 9–5, mid-May–mid-October. Admission.

Vergennes: Bixby Memorial Library, (802) 877-2211. West of U.S. 7, in town. Monday–Friday, 12:30–5, July–August. Free.

MASSACHUSETTS

Ashley Falls: John Ashley House, (413) 229-8600. West of
Massachusetts 7A, on Cooper Hill Road.
Wednesday–Sunday, 1–5, late June–Labor Day. Weekends
only, after Memorial Day and before mid-October.
Admission.

  Bartholomew's Cobble, no phone. North, off
Massachusetts 7A. Daily, 9–5, mid-April–mid-October.
Admission.

Great Barrington: Albert Schweitzer Center, (413) 528-3124.
South on U.S. 7, then west on Taconic Ave.
Tuesday–Saturday, 10–4; Sunday, noon–4, all year.
Donation.

Lenox: Tanglewood, (413) 637-1940. West from U.S. 7, on
Massachusetts 183 (West St.). Festival is held in July and
August. Call for schedule. Hawthorne Cottage is on the
Festival grounds and is open prior to concerts.

  The Mount, (413) 637-1899. South, on U.S. 7.
Tuesday–Friday, 11–4; weekends, 9:30–4, Memorial
Day–Labor Day. Friday–Sunday, 10–4, through October.
Admission.

Pittsfield: Arrowhead, (413) 442-1793. South on U.S. 7, then
east on Holmes Road. Monday–Saturday, 10–4:30; Sunday,
11–3:30, Memorial Day–Labor Day. Closed Tuesday and
Wednesday, after Labor Day through October. Admission.

  South Mountain Temple of Music, (413) 442-2106. South,
on U.S. 7. Concerts are held on weekends, August and early
September. Call for schedule.

Stockbridge: Norman Rockwell Museum, (413) 298-3822. On
U.S. 7 (Main St.). Wednesday–Monday, 10–4:30, except for
last two weeks in January. Admission.

  Chesterwood, (413) 298-3579. West on Massachusetts
102, then south on Massachusetts 183. Daily, 10–5,
May–October. Admission.

  Mission House, (413) 298-3239. On U.S. 7 (Main St.).

Tuesday–Saturday, 10–4:30; Sunday, 11–3:30, Memorial Day–mid-October. Admission.

Naumkeag, (413) 298-3239. North on Massachusetts 102 (Prospect St.). Tuesday–Sunday, 10–4, late June–Labor Day. Weekends only, after Memorial Day and before mid-October. Admission.

Williamstown: Sterling and Francine Clark Museum, (413) 458-9545. Off U.S. 7, at 225 South St. Tuesday–Sunday, 10–5, all year. Free.

CONNECTICUT

Brookfield: Craft Center, (203) 775-4526. East of U.S. 7, on Connecticut 25. Monday–Saturday, 10–4; Sunday, noon–5, all year. Free.

Canaan: Housatonic Railroad Co., (203) 824-0339. Depot is on U.S. 7 at Connecticut 44. Call for schedule and rates.

Kent Furnace: Sloane-Stanley Museum, (203) 927-3849. North, on U.S. 7. Wednesday–Sunday, 10–4:30, mid-May–October. Admission.

Ridgefield: Aldrich Museum, (203) 438-4519. On Connecticut 35, at 258 Main St. Wednesday–Friday, 2:30–4:30; weekends, 1–5, April–November. Closed Wednesday, at other times. Admission.

Keeler Tavern, (203) 438-5485. On Connecticut 35, at 134 Main St. Wednesday and weekends, 1–4, all year. Admission.

U. S. ROUTE 9

Rouses Point
Plattsburgh
VERMONT
NEW HAMPSHIRE
Saratoga Springs
Albany
MASSACHUSETTS
Hudson
NEW YORK
Kingston
Hyde Park
RHODE ISLAND
Newburgh
West Point
CONNECTICUT
U.S. ROUTE 9W
Tarrytown
U.S. ROUTE 9N
New York
MAINE
Ronan

Echoes of the Hudson Valley

U.S. 9

This is the road that links New York City to Montreal, the valley of the Hudson to the valley of the St. Lawrence. It was the strategic pivot of the entire Northeast, as British and French, Indians and Yankees struggled in three wars for control of the vast inland empire to which these rivers led. Whoever was master of the road that became U.S. 9 controlled the continent. It was hardly coincidental that the U.S. Military Academy was established along its length. But you will find more than the faded banners of old battles and the echoes of distant trumpets here. In its northern portion, along Lake Champlain and Lake George, it is the gateway to the Adirondacks, the largest public recreation grounds in the region. To the south, it passes the edge of the Catskill Reserve and river scenery that inspired an American school of landscape artists. Eventually the highway runs the length of New Jersey, skips across Delaware Bay by a ferry connection and ends near the town of Laurel, Delaware.

THE HUDSON VALLEY

Rouses Point to Tappan, N.Y.
* 336 miles

The first part of this route runs along the western shore of Lake Champlain, then becomes the only old road to penetrate the Adirondacks, through New York's finest mountain scenery. After passing the classic resort of Saratoga Springs and the capital city of Albany, it becomes U.S. 9W and heads down the western bank of the Hudson's most majestic stretch. You'll pass some of the old Dutch towns where the legends of the Catskills were born, then head into the magnificent vistas of Storm King Highway, West Point and Bear Mountain. The area is sometimes called America's Rhineland, and on this drive you'll see why.

* MILEPOSTS *

Since the construction of Interstate 87, the major crossing point to Canada has shifted to the town of Champlain. But in the days of the old roads, U.S. 9 began, instead, at the historic crossing of Rouses Point, where Lake Champlain narrows to form the Richilieu River. This segment is now designated N.Y. 9B. Nonetheless, it is where we'll begin. The border here was always hotly disputed. Even after the war to settle the matter was over, it wasn't over. Border fortifications were being erected after the War of 1812 when the federal government learned to its embarrassment that the land it was fortifying belonged to Canada. The outpost was abandoned and referred to thereafter as Fort Blunder. Its ruins are on a point of land just north of town, visible from the eastbound bridge to Vermont.

All Jean Framboise wanted to do was grow apples. But when the British came marching through **Chazy** in 1777 on their way to disaster at Saratoga, Framboise was forced to flee his land. He returned after the war, and when he finally got the chance to cultivate his orchards he made up for lost time. The MacIntosh plantations that developed on his holdings around Chazy are the largest in the world.

The Miner family also left the fruits of their labors in this area. William H. Miner made a fortune in railroads, and a portion of it funded an agricultural and environmental research center. The Miner Institute, just west of Chazy, has self-guided tours around the property. The Alice Miner Collection, located in the middle of town in a house built in 1824, displays the results of his wife's intense interest in colonial artwork.

Samuel de Champlain did not make a favorable first impression on the native tribes in this area. On his voyage of exploration around the lake that bears his name, in 1609, he shot two of their chiefs in a get-acquainted encounter. The dead leaders were allied with the powerful Iroquois Confederacy, and the hostilities that grew out of that incident changed the pattern of North American settlement. French trading routes were forced to the north, away from Iroquois territory, and that part of the continent was stamped with a strong Gallic legacy. The British capitalized on this enmity and allied themselves with the Iroquois, a partnership that would last through the Revolutionary War. The Iroquois were a powerful buffer between the two great colonial powers and insured the supremacy of an English-speaking culture in New York. A statue of Champlain, who started all the trouble, stands on the waterfront in **Plattsburgh**.

It's an ironic location, because the big lake was the focus of English policy in North America for years, a strategic factor in both the Revolution and the War of 1812. By capturing the lake and moving down the Hudson Valley, Britain felt it could detach New England from the rest of the country. Its first attempt to do that ended in the autumn of 1776, when a makeshift colonial fleet assembled at the town of Skenesborough (now known as White-hall) and held up the British just long enough for winter to arrive. The British returned the following summer, capturing the lake and its fortifications at Ticonderoga and Crown Point before being mauled at Saratoga, but the year's delay bought vital time for the colonial cause. The British pursued a similar strategy in September 1814 when they sent a combined naval and land force south out of Montreal. But U.S. Commodore Thomas Mac-Donough inflicted a crushing defeat on their fleet off Plattsburgh, by using lighter vessels with more maneuverable guns. The name of his flagship, significantly, was the *Saratoga*. MacDonough's monument is in front of Plattsburgh's city hall.

When the British were stripped of naval support in 1814, the land forces, although superior in numbers, had to retreat. Among the articles abandoned in the rush back to Canada was a silver chest. It is displayed in the Kent-Delord House, which the British had seized as a military headquarters. Built at the end of the eighteenth century, the home overlooking the lake remained in the Delord family until 1913 and is now a museum of decorative art and portraiture. A member of the Kent clan also figures in another local museum. Although artist Rockwell Kent came from Tarrytown, much further south along this road, he did a lot of his work in the nearby Adirondacks, and a gallery of his paintings is displayed at S.U.N.Y.-Plattsburgh.

The area south of town, near Cliff Haven, the scene of the Revolutionary naval battle, has been a federal military reservation since 1815. It is now a Strategic Air Command base. Cumberland Bay State Park, with swimming facilities on the lake, is also located in the Plattsburgh area, along U.S. 9.

AuSable Chasm was one of the first beauty spots in the Adirondacks to be commercially developed. At the northeastern edge of the vast Adirondack Park, it was opened to the public in 1870. Generations of tourists since then have walked past the rock formations and waterfalls, along the paths cut into the canyon walls. The trip is about a mile and a half long, part of it by boat and the rest by foot.

The road now enters Adirondack Park, set aside as a forest preserve in 1885 to protect this region of mountain and forest from exploitation. It covers more than 6 million acres, virtually the entire northeastern quadrant of the state, and one-third of that is under state control. U.S. 9 runs along a corridor in which some private development has been allowed, but it is limited. You can only imagine what this area, so close to the huge population centers of the East, would have become without the protection of the preserve. The more grotesque manifestations of shlock tourism are kept outside its boundaries. This is the only old road to penetrate the park, and it runs in tandem with Interstate 87.

Elizabethtown lies at the base of Hurricane Mountain, and a hurricane of sorts did storm out of this area in the 1850s. This was home country for the fiery Abolitionist John Brown (who always considered his primary occupation to be sheep farmer). His body lies moldering in the grave on his former farm in nearby Lake Placid. After his hanging in 1859, following the raid on the arsenal at Harper's Ferry, he was brought here to lie in state. Now the town is noted for the Adirondack Center Museum, concentrating on the region's history, with adjacent gardens modeled on designs of the colonial era.

The Bouquet River Drive, south of town, is the most scenic portion of mountain greenery traversed by U.S. 9. The crest of Mount Marcy, highest peak in the state at 5,344 feet, is just to the west. The road then follows the western shore of 10-mile-long Schroon Lake. Private development here has been fairly widespread, but there is a public beach at Eagle Point, beyond South Schroon.

Warrensburg was part of the early lumbering industry in the area. It was founded as a mill town in 1804 by Joseph Warren and is now an antiques center that carefully cultivates its rustic appearance. This was the hometown of aviation pioneer Floyd Bennett, who made the first flight over the North Pole with Admiral Richard Byrd in 1926. He died two years later after coming down with pneumonia on an Antarctic expedition. The risks of the trade.

The Last of the Mohicans contains one of the most horrifying passages in American literature, describing the massacre of settlers leaving Fort William Henry under a safe conduct pass during the French and Indian Wars. It is difficult to associate that grim scene of slaughter with the bright holiday pleasures that surround the old fort near **Lake George** today. This is an extremely popular resort area, and Beach Drive along the lakeshore is speckled with recreational facilities. But it used to command the direct portage trail between Lake Champlain and the Hudson and was a strategic prize. Sir William Johnson fortified the place for Britain at the outbreak of war in 1755. The garrison and additional militia then managed to beat back an initial French incursion in the Battle of

Lake George. Two years after that battle, the French returned, this time led by the brilliant general Louis Joseph de Montcalm. Striking overland from Lake Ontario, Montcalm took Fort William Henry in a campaign that marked the apogee of French success in the war though the massacre that followed was a dark stain on the French triumph. But an energetic new British prime minister, William Pitt, alert to the danger of losing North America, poured renewed effort and material into the war. Within two more years, Montcalm fell at the walls of Quebec and the French empire in America was finished.

The old fortification has been restored, and there are demonstrations of what life was like in an outpost of that period. An abridged film version of the Cooper story is also shown. The ruins of Fort George, built on the earlier battlefield when the British reclaimed the area in 1759, are nearby.

Lake George was first sighted by Champlain but was not explored until missionary Isaac Jogues circumnavigated it in 1646. He was martyred in that same year by the Mohawks and became the first American saint in 1925. Prospect Mountain Highway, just south of Lake George Village, leads to an overlook across the entire lake area.

The cascades at **Glens Falls** are about 10 feet lower than the cataract at nearby Hudson Falls, highest on the river at 70 feet. Still, they were a big enough nuisance that the Indians called the place Chepontuo, "a difficult place to get around." The falls made it an easy place for industrious settlers to live, though. The British burned out the first community here, but in 1788 the intrepid Col. John Glen led the resettlement of the area and gave his name to the falls. It soon became a major paper and pulpmaking center, a position it retains today. The Hyde Collection displays artwork spanning five centuries in the magnificent Italianate mansion of their collector, just east of downtown.

Ulysses S. Grant came to **Wilton** as a dying man in 1885. The military hero of the Civil War, his popularity undimmed by two scandal-ridden presidential administrations, was racing his mortal clock to finish the final volume of his memoirs. He moved into a small cottage in this village in the Adirondack foothills, a few miles from the fashionable resort of Saratoga Springs, where he had so often been feted. Grant made his deadline, and never was the word so apt, by a matter of days. The two-volume autobiography has fared far better among historians than his presidency did and is considered among the leading military histories ever written by a participant. Grant Cottage is a now a state museum, with many family possessions exhibited.

FOCUS

* * *

There was a marvelous party once in **Saratoga Springs** and all the best people came. Although it went on for more than half a century, it ended too soon. And while the Springs is no longer the haunt of Vanderbilts and Astors, the afterglow lingers to illuminate the town.

Saratoga Springs was the First Resort of the Gilded Age. An appearance during the August season was imperative for those who counted. The wealthiest families in America came to take the waters, race their horses and build their mansions out on North Broadway. Those with slightly fewer resources checked in at the luxurious hotels built to serve them.

It may be a little hard for Americans in the last quarter of the twentieth century to understand the appeal of the place. Our concept of the ideal vacation is altogether different from the Victorian one. We demand sports facilities and a guarantee of lots of sun to bake in. But in the nineteenth century, it was understood that one visited a resort for a rest. And for the waters.

Hydropathy was a respected branch of medicine then. It was regarded as a matter of scientific fact that ingestion of and immersion in the proper waters would cure any disease. This attitude survives today in Europe, and many labor unions there have regular vacation time at such spas built into their contracts. But while the concept of a spa survives in the United States, its most common application now is to a resort that features nutritional and exercise programs. The heyday of Saratoga Springs called for far more leisurely vacations.

The springs here were known to the Indians. Animals were attracted by them, which made the area around the springs a prime hunting ground. But it was believed that the Mohawks, too, thought the waters possessed restorative powers. Sir William Johnson, who commanded British forces around Lake George, came here in 1771 to take the waters, suffering from an old wound. Johnson recuperated and began spreading the word. Among those who heard was George Washington, who supposedly tried to purchase land around the springs.

It wasn't until 1802, however, that Saratoga began to develop. Gideon Putnam discovered a new spring, purchased the surrounding property and built a hotel nearby. The railroad reached the place in 1832, giving visitors from New York City ready access. In another ten years, the first horse track was added, and by the time of the Civil War, Saratoga had become the preeminent spa in the nation. Three months after the South's surrender, U. S. Grant attended the ball that opened the opera house. In 1870, former bare-knuckle heavyweight champion John Morrissey opened the first casino near Putnam's spring in what had come to be called Congress Park.

Finally, its very popularity caused the spa to fall from favor. The right crowd moved elsewhere as fashions changed. Commercial exploitation of the springs started in the early twentieth century, and the sinking of too many wells dried up some of them. The resort was in serious decline until the State of New York stepped in to begin a program of conservation and development in 1933. A new generation has now rediscovered the Victorian charm of the place, and a good part of the business district has been restored and infused with new enthusiasm. The annual race meeting in August remains a high spot on the national sports calendar, and then the town is jammed to capacity. But Saratoga has also developed a year-round convention business.

U.S. 9 runs through the center of town as Broadway. North of the business district, it passes the extraordinary row of mansions built by the wealthy in the Springs' greatest years. Also in the vicinity is the campus of Skidmore College, on a wooded 650-acre tract.

The central part of town lies just beyond the major intersection with Arterial Road (N.Y. 50). Several of the rambling old hotels still occupy the western side of the street, while a variety of new businesses have opened in the vintage storefronts along the way. At the southern edge of this area is Congress Park, with its historic spring and casino. The core of this building is Morrissey's original casino, but it was greatly enlarged after being purchased by Richard Canfield in 1894. Canfield was known as the Prince of Gamblers, but he bet wrong this time. He got into the game just as the major players were about to pull out. He sold the casino back to the city in 1911, and it is now a fascinating museum of the town's social history and the gamblers who played here. You can even see some of boxer Morrissey's gym equipment on the upper floor.

The building also houses a museum dedicated to the Walworth family. Reuben Hyde Walworth was New York's last chancellor, a powerful position at the head of the state's equity court. His home, Pine Grove, was the meeting place of New York's rich and famous from 1828 to 1848. It also nurtured a family whose history reads like a soap opera, with divided Civil War loyalties and a celebrated murder case as part of the brew.

A few blocks to the east of Congress Park, along Union Avenue, is Saratoga Race Course, a landmark of the sport and the oldest thoroughbred track in the nation that's still in use. It dates to 1864. Nearby is the National Museum of Racing, with mementoes of the sport's greatest horses, jockeys, trainers and owners, as well as the Hall of Fame. Also in the vicinity is Yaddo, with its splendid rose gardens. The estate itself is a retreat for artists and writers and is not open to the public.

Back on U.S. 9, heading south out of town, you'll pass the National Museum of Dance. As you would guess, the place showcases historic exhibits and special events relating to dance. The summer home of the New York City Ballet is just a few blocks away, at the Saratoga Performing Arts Center on Ballston Avenue, and the museum works closely with the company on special shows when it is in residence.

The entrance to Saratoga Spa State Park is a bit further to the south. You come in through a scenic Avenue of Pines, which leads to two enormous bathhouses, occupying the center of the 2,200-acre reserve. This is a spa based on the European model, but with most American amenities. The Roosevelt Bathhouse is open all year, the Lincoln Bathhouse only during the summer. Both feature private rooms for taking a dip in the carbonated water and massage. There is also an 18-hole golf course on the property, as well as two swimming pools and the state-run Gideon Putnam Hotel.

* * *

Once past Saratoga Springs, the road widens in a four-lane rush toward Albany. You cross the old Erie Canal near the town of Crescent, just down the road from Halfmoon. Cruises leave from the bridge area to explore the Mohawk River and the canal's double lock at Vischer Ferry. Now U.S. 9 enters the suburbs of the state capital and divides soon after passing the city limits. The course of U.S. 9 through downtown Albany and along the eastern bank of the Hudson is covered in the second segment of this chapter. On this ride stay with U.S. 9W, which weaves through outlying portions of the city, then leaves town as Southern Boulevard.

The Dutch settlers of **Coxsackie** were an impatient lot with no great love for the British Parliament. So in January 1775, more than two hundred of them gathered to draft a declaration of independence, opposing "recent oppressive acts." The action anticipated the formal severing of ties in Philadelphia by a year and a half. Among the first settlers in this area was Pieter Bronck, a member of the family that gave its name to the Bronx. The buildings on his farm, some of which date back to 1663, now give an overview of three centuries of Dutch settlement on the Hudson. The most famous structure in the complex is Bronck's 13-sided barn.

From here, cut over to the river road, N.Y. 385, which heads to Athens. Like many towns on this part of the Hudson, Athens once built its prosperity on shipping ice downriver to Manhattan. This is a delightful little place, tucked away on a cozy cove of the river, with several old homes and churches, a lighthouse and an old ferry dock.

You are now in the Catskill country of the old legends. The dark, wooded hills that so stirred the imaginations of the early settlers rise to the southwest. It was in these mountains, behind the town of **Catskill**, that a townsman named Van Winkle settled down for a twenty-year nap. The bridge across the Hudson here is named for Washington Irving's henpecked snoozer. This vicinity was far livelier in later years. In the 1920s it became an operations center for a number of bootleggers from New York, and the storied gangster Legs Diamond was tried in the Catskill courthouse.

The town was also the home of Thomas Cole, credited with being the founder of the Hudson River School of painting. The brooding scenery that characterizes these landscapes begins on this section of the river. Even though Cole insisted that the natural beauty of the American scene should be rendered faithfully, he could not resist adding a few ruined castles to his own works to give them a more European flavor. He believed that great paintings should teach moral lessons and explained that the ruins pointed up the transitory character of Man's works in the face of Nature. Cole's home, built in 1814, is now a museum.

Saugerties, the "town of sawyers" in Dutch, was a busy port in its time. It now carefully tends to its wealth of Victorian homes and shops and its historic riverfront along the mouth of Esopus Creek. To give you some idea of how art along the Hudson has changed since Cole's time, visit the Opus 40 and Quarryman's Museum. It encompasses 6 acres of environmental sculpture rising out of a bluestone quarry, centered around a 9-ton rock. There is also a display of quarrying tools. No moral lessons are offered.

As the British raided throughout New York in 1777, the state government tried to stay one jump ahead of them and moved from place to place as enemy advances dictated. The government arrived in **Kingston** in February and stayed eight months, long enough to adopt a constitution, inaugurate a governor and hold a legislative session. On October 7, with a British force moving up from Manhattan in an attempt to link up with Burgoyne's army at Saratoga, the government had to flee once more. Nine days later the town was burned. The Senate House escaped destruction, though, and this stone building, dating back to the Dutch settlement of 1676, is now a museum of Kingston's term as capital. It also contains paintings by the Hudson River School and exhibits of regional history. George Clinton was the governor who took the first oath of office here, and he rests nearby in the graveyard of the Old Dutch Church. Clinton also served as vice president of the United States from 1805 to 1813 in two different administrations, those of Thomas Jefferson and James Madison. Only one other man, John Calhoun, ever did that. The church itself dates from 1852, but the congregation was organized in 1659 and the graveyard dates from that period.

Kingston was a major coaling port in the early nineteenth century, the outlet of the Delaware and Hudson Canal, which carried anthracite up from the Pennsylvania mines. When that trade died off, it became a cement producer, but around 1900 the local product lost its market to the faster-drying Portland variety. For years the old cement plants near the mouth of Rondout Creek were a crumbling eyesore. Now the area has been restored as Rondout Landing, with a maritime museum, trolley rides and sightseeing cruises along the river.

John Burroughs was a naturalist who roamed the world from his farmhouse near West Park. But sometimes the world closed in on him, and for those occasions when he wanted to get away while at home, he built Slabsides. This was his rustic retreat, a cabin where he could escape the press of celebrity. Burroughs was an intimate of presidents and millionaires. Theodore Roosevelt came to call, and the two walked together from the Hudson ferry dock to Slabsides. In later years, Burroughs delighted in joining Henry Ford and Thomas Edison on rustic hikes through various parts of the country. But Burroughs became known as the Sage of Slabsides and felt most comfortable in its simple shelter. The cabin is preserved as a memorial to him, about a mile west of highway 9W. The grounds are open daily, all year.

To make the comparison with the Rhineland complete, the area between **Highland** and Marlboro is studded with vineyards. Half a dozen of them offer tastings, with Hudson Valley Winery in Highland and Cagnasso in Marlboro located right on the highway. In Milton, the Royal KEDEM winery occupies a site overlooking the Hudson, for those with a taste for kosher wine.

Most people would identify the Battle of Yorktown as the end of the American Revolution. But it really ended in **Newburgh**, almost two years later, when Washington gave the final order to disperse and go home to his army camped nearby. This town was the general's headquarters from April 1782 to October 1783, as the country awaited the outcome of peace talks in Paris. The British still occupied New York City. There had been no combat since the surrender at Yorktown, in October 1781, but the army was kept intact. While his troops camped at nearby Vails Gate, Washington moved into the Hasbrouck House in Newburgh. The house was built by the Mynders family in 1725 and purchased by Hasbrouck, whose family was prominent in this part of the Hudson Valley, thirty years later. Washington was joined there by his wife and used the guest bedroom as an office. This is where he turned down the offer to become king and rebuked the officers who made it. The house has been returned to its appearance of those years, with a museum of the Continental Army adjoining it. Also on the grounds is the Tower of Victory, erected on the centennial of the war's end.

If you want to round out the tour of the Revolution's last roundup, head west on N.Y. 32 to New Windsor Cantonment. This is where Washington came to deliver his "law and order" address. Certain officers had suggested redressing their grievances against the Continental Congress by taking up arms against it. In the middle of a stern reprimand to these men, Washington paused, put on his spectacles and remarked, "I have grown gray in the service of my country and now, as you can see, I am growing blind." The emotional effect of that gesture ended any talk of rebellion. (There are other versions of what Washington said on this occasion, and the above quote may be a later literary invention. But the gist was the same.) The Cantonment is now a National Historic Site.

The natural and cultural history of this part of the river are combined in the Hudson Highlands Museum, just west of **Corn-wall-on-Hudson**. There are exhibits of native animals in one wing, regional art in the other.

The turnoff here, marked as N.Y. 218, is the famed Storm King Highway, among the most scenic roads in the country. Climbing 1,400 feet above the river, on the brow of the mountain that was known in less romantic times as Butter Hill, it opens out on extraordinary views of the river below and the Taconic Mountains to the east.

The road leads to **West Point**, a name synonymous with the U.S. Army. Here, at the Hudson narrows, the Continental Army decided to secure the river by the simple device of stretching a great chain, 1,700 feet long, from one bank to the other. The engineering genius Thaddeus Kosciusko, who had supervised the fortifications at Saratoga, directed the construction of the chain and had it floated downriver in the spring of 1778. The links were 2 feet long and 2¼ inches square. With their fleet bottled up in the river's southern reaches, the British tried to take West Point by land but were dislodged from their foothold at Stony Point. (We'll get to that in a few more miles.) What they couldn't gain by arms, they almost accomplished by treachery. The Point was under Benedict Arnold's command and it was here that he turned against the colonial cause and plotted to betray it to the British in 1780. The denouement of that drama also awaits us a bit further along the road.

West Point has been the site of the U.S. Military Academy since 1802 and one of the most venerated spots in American patriotic lore. The stern Gothic buildings on a bluff high above the Hudson also make up one of the nation's most beautiful campus settings. The barracks, classrooms and administration buildings are closed to visitors. But the museum, with its unmatched exhibits of military history, is open daily. It was recently moved to expanded quarters in Olmsted Hall. Also open is the Old Cadet Chapel, with shields of Revolutionary War generals on the walls. Fort Clinton, the restored Revolutionary stronghold, is part of the Academy grounds. Parades are generally held in April, May, September and October, but there may be other special occasions on which you can see the cadet corps assembled. Check with the information center at Thayer Gate for maps and a schedule of the day's activities.

The road rejoins U.S. 9W at Highland Falls and then makes its way along the haunch of Bear Mountain. At **Stony Point**, which you'll reach next, was the British base that threatened West Point in the summer of 1779. While discussing strategy, Washington asked Gen. Anthony Wayne if he could take the place by assault. "I'd storm hell, sir, if you made the plans," Wayne replied. Washington dryly responded that he would try Stony Point first. Wayne was wounded in the successful attack and carried into the fort on the shoulders of his men. From then on he was known by his nickname of Mad Anthony. A museum is now on the battlefield site.

Near Haverstraw is the ridge of High Tor, celebrated in Maxwell Anderson's fanciful 1937 play of the same name about the ghosts of Dutch settlers and the destructive ambitions of modern developers.

Many people will recognize **Nyack** from the lyric of the song "Let's Get Away from It All," where it is made to rhyme with *kayak.* It is located on a tranquil, lakelike part of the Hudson, the Tappan Zee, and is a notable art and antiques center. It was the birthplace of Edward Hopper, a perennially popular artist whose treatment of sunlight on buildings made him one of the bright points in American Realism. His home, at 82 North Broadway, is now a gallery of his works.

As the road approaches the village of Sparkill, watch for the turnoff to **Tappan**. In this village, the attempted betrayal of West Point had its beginning and its end. DeWint House was Washington's headquarters in 1780, and here Arnold was given command of the Point. Arnold, nursing an assortment of grudges against the colonial command, contacted Sir Henry Clinton, the British commander in New York City. Clinton sent an aide, Maj. John André, to meet secretly with Arnold. On his way back to New York, André was captured near Tarrytown, and evidence implicating Arnold was found in his boot. Arnold fled to the British lines upon hearing of the capture, while André was taken across the

Hudson to Tappan and imprisoned in the Seventy-Six House. He was tried in the Reformed Dutch Church on September 27, 1780, and five days later taken from his prison and hanged on a site still known as André Hill. His remains were interred on the property, but in 1821 they were turned over to England, and he was buried with honors in Westminster Abbey.

DeWint House is now a Masonic shrine and museum containing memorabilia of Washington. The Seventy-Six House still stands in the center of town. It is now a restaurant. Tappan lies right on the New Jersey border, and the end of André's story is the end of this drive as well.

VISITING HOURS

NEW YORK

AuSable: AuSable Chasm, (518) 834-7454. On U.S. 9. Daily, 8–4:30, mid-May–mid October. Admission.

Catskill: Thomas Cole House, (518) 943-6533. Off U.S. 9, at 218 Spring St. Wednesday–Saturday, 10–5; Sunday, 1–5, July–August. Admission.

Chazy: Miner Institute, (518) 846-7121. West, on New York 191. Daily, 10–5, all year. Free.
   Alice Miner Collection, (518) 846-7336. On U.S. 9, in town. Tuesday–Saturday, 10–4, February–December. Donation.

Cornwall-on-Hudson: Hudson Highlands Museum, (914) 534-7781. East from U.S. 9W on Storm King Highway, then south on the Boulevard. Monday–Thursday, 11–5; Saturday, noon–5; Sunday, 1:30–5, mid-June–Labor Day. Monday–Thursday, 2–5, weekend hours unchanged, at other times. Donation.

Coxsackie: Bronck Farm, (518) 731-8862. Off U.S. 9W, on Pieter Bronck Road. Tuesday–Saturday, 10–noon and 1–5; Sunday, 2–6, late June–Labor Day. Admission.

Elizabethtown: Adirondack Center Museum, (518) 873-6466. On U.S. 9. Monday–Saturday, 9–5; Sunday, 1–5, mid-May–mid-October. Admission.

Glens Falls: Hyde Collection, (518) 792-1761. East of U.S. 9, at 161 Warren St. Tuesday–Sunday, noon–5. February–December. Admission.

Highland: Hudson Valley Wine Village, (914) 691-7296. On U.S. 9W. Daily, April–October, noon–5. Weekends only, at other times.

Cagnasso Winery, (914) 236-4630. On U.S. 9W, in Marlboro. Thursday–Tuesday, June–October, 10–4:30; noon–4:30, April, May, November, December.

Royal KEDEM Winery, (914) 795-2240. Off U.S. 9W, on the Hudson, at Dock Road, Milton. Sunday–Friday, 10–4, May–November.

Kingston: Senate House, (914) 338-2786. West of U.S. 9W, at 312 Fair St. Wednesday–Saturday, 10–5; Sunday, 1–5, April–December. Weekends only, at other times. Free.

Hudson River Maritime Center, (914) 338-0071. East of U.S. 9W, on the river, at Rondout Landing. Daily, 10–4, all year. Admission.

Lake George: Fort William Henry, (518) 668-5471. South, on U.S. 9. Daily, 9–9, July–August; 10–5, May, June, September, October. Admission.

Newburgh: Washington's Headquarters, (914) 562-1195. East of U.S. 9W on Broadway to Liberty St. Wednesday–Saturday, 10–5; Sunday, 1–5, April–December. Free.

New Windsor Cantonment, (914) 561-1765. West from U.S. 9W on New York 17K, then south on New York 207 to Temple Hill Road. Wednesday–Saturday, 10–5; Sunday, 1–5, late April–October. Free.

Nyack: Edward Hopper House, (914) 358-0774. Off U.S. 9W, at 82 N. Broadway. Weekends, 1–5, all year. Donation.

Plattsburgh: Kent-Delord House, (518) 561-1035. Overlooking Lake Champlain, off U.S. 9, at 17 Cumberland Ave. Guided tours at 10, 2, and 4, Tuesday–Saturday, all year. Admission.

Rockwell Kent Gallery, (518) 564-2288. Off U.S. 9W, on the S.U.N.Y.–Plattsburgh campus. Tuesday–Friday, noon–4, all year. Free.

Saratoga Springs: Casino, (518) 584-6920. On U.S. 9, in Congress Park. Daily, 9:30–4:30, July–August. Monday–Saturday, 10–4; Sunday, 1–4, May, June, September, October. Wednesday–Sunday, 1–4, at other times. Admission.

National Museum of Racing, (518) 584-0400. East from U.S. 9, on Union St. Daily, 9:30–7, August. Monday–Friday, 9:30–5; weekends, noon–5, mid-June–July. Closed Sunday, May–mid-June. Monday–Friday, 10–4, at other times. Free.

National Museum of Dance, (518) 584-2225. South, on U.S. 9. Tuesday–Saturday, 10–5; Sunday, noon–4, June–Labor Day. Thursday–Saturday, 10–5; Sunday, noon–4, until mid-December. Admission.

State Park Bathhouses, (518) 584-2010. West from U.S. 9, south of town. Roosevelt Bath, open all year. Lincoln Bath, summer only. Call for schedule and rates.

Saugerties: Quarryman's Museum and Opus 40, (914) 246-3400. West of U.S. 9W, at 7840 Fite Road. Wednesday–Monday, 10–4, May–October. Admission.

Stony Point: Battlefield and Museum, (914) 786-2521. North, off U.S. 9W on Park Road. Wednesday–Sunday, 9–5, April–October. Free.

Tappan: DeWint House, (914) 359-1359. West from U.S. 9W at Sparkill, on Washington St., to Livingston Ave. Daily, 10–4, all year. Free.

West Point: U.S. Military Academy, (914) 938-2638. East from U.S. 9W on Storm King Highway. Grounds open daily, 8:30–4:15, all year. Call for times of cadet parades.

Wilton: Grant Cottage, (518) 587-8277. Off U.S. 9, in town. Wednesday–Sunday, 1–5, Memorial Day–Labor Day. Donation.

THE LAND OF THE PATROONS

Albany to New York, N.Y.
* 155 miles

The road is not very long compared to some of the others we follow in this book. But in the sheer concentration of historic places, great homes and memorable scenery, there may be no other road quite like this run down the eastern bank of the Hudson River. Two presidents lived here, several artists, countless industrial barons who built their palaces on the Hudson cliffs. Washington Irving, who celebrated the Hudson's legends with his pen, knew this road, as did Frederic Church, who celebrated the Hudson's aspects with his brush. From the Dutch aristocrats to the heroic figures of the American Revolution, the names of this valley resonate through our national history. U.S. 9 frequently strays far from the river's side, but a number of cutoffs enable you to take in the high points of the drive rather easily. In its southern portion, several limited-access highways parallel the road, easing the congestion as you pass through New York's Westchester County suburbs and into the city.

* MILEPOSTS *

U.S. 9 splits from U.S. 9W shortly after entering **Albany**, then heads into the northeastern corner of the state capital. Henry Hudson reached this spot on his namesake river in 1609 on his voyage of discovery. Fifteen years later, a small party of Walloons, Protestant refugees from the Spanish Netherlands, made their way here and established the first settlement, on the enormous Van Rensselaer estate.

In order to encourage settlement on these vast empty lands, the Dutch West India Company had granted huge holdings to a few wealthy families, the patroons. In return for underwriting immigration costs to their lands, the patroons were given title and rental claims to them in perpetuity. The result was a semifeudal system of landholding that survived here for two hundred years. Families like the Van Rensselaers ran their grants as independent fiefdoms, cooperating with company agents when it served their purpose and ignoring them when it did not. Even after the British took over the colony in 1664 and renamed this settlement in honor of the Duke of York and Albany, the older titles and rights were not disturbed. The patroons were highly romanticized in the writings of Washington Irving, but far from being jolly country squires, they were ruthless businessmen, adept at squeezing the last possible penny from their hapless tenants. Class hatred ran high here long after the democratic tide had washed across most other parts of America.

Just a few blocks from U.S. 9 as it crosses Livingston Avenue is Arbour Hill, built in 1798 by the Ten Broeck family and occupied for more than a century by the Olcott family. It is noted for its period furnishings as well as its lawns and gardens. Nearby, on Pearl Street, is the First Dutch Reformed Church (sometimes referred to in Albany as the First Church). The building dates from 1797, but the congregation was organized here in 1642. It is the second oldest Protestant congregation in the country. Its pulpit was put in place fourteen years after the church was founded, making it the oldest on these shores. A plaque is affixed to the pew occupied by Theodore Roosevelt, who worshiped here when he was governor of New York. (For the attractions of Albany around the state government complex, see the chapter on U.S. 20.)

Albany was built on a hill above the river, and the road now descends to the water. It crosses the Parker Dunn Memorial Bridge, built in 1933 and named for a Congressional Medal of Honor winner in World War I. Now in the town of **Rensselaer**, it immediately turns south to begin its Hudson-side journey to Manhattan as the Albany Post Road. Almost at once you come upon Crailo, seat of the Van Rensselaers during their long holding of these lands. It was built as a combination home and fortress in 1704 by Hendrik Van Rensselaer and is now a museum of Dutch culture in the Hudson Valley.

According to local legend, this is the place where "Yankee Doodle" was written. A British surgeon, Dr. Richard Shuckburgh, was watching local militia drilling on the grounds in 1758, during the French and Indian War. Amused by what he saw, he penned a few satirical verses to show his friends. He never dreamed that in twenty more years they would be used as a marching song by the sons of these soldiers as they wrested their freedom from his country. How strange, too, that the national song "Yankee Doodle" and the national symbol Uncle Sam (see U.S. 4) should originate just a few miles from each other on this part of the Hudson.

Just beyond the intersection with U.S. 4 is East Greenbush, the final resting place of Edmond Charles Genet, one of the infant republic's most controversial citizens. Sent as an envoy to the United States in 1793 by the revolutionary government of France, he landed in Charleston, South Carolina, and immediately touched off a bitter partisan furor. President Washington had indicated that the nation would follow a course of strict neutrality between France and England. This appalled the followers of Thomas Jefferson, who sympathized with the aims of the French Revolution and loathed their recent British enemies. The division fell mainly along class lines, the propertied classes identifying with England and looking with horror at the excesses of the Parisian mobs. The new envoy was greeted enthusiastically by the less well-to-do, and in the revolutionary style was called Citizen Genet. He began making his way north in triumph, authorizing American privateers to attack British ships and proposing to raise troops in a campaign against Spanish outposts in Florida. Unaware of the intense antagonisms he was arousing Genet finally overplayed his hand. Jefferson was forced to renounce him and join the rest of Washington's cabinet in demanding his recall. Genet was stunned. Realizing that a return to the upheavals in France could mean his death, he pleaded to remain in America and the request was granted. He married the daughter of New York's Governor George Clinton and lived out his days quietly in this village. He died in 1834 and is buried at the Dutch Reformed Church.

Two years after Genet's death, one of his neighbors succeeded to Washington's office. Martin Van Buren was born in 1782, in **Kinderhook**, the son of a poor tavernkeeper, and grew up in the rough and tumble of upstate New York's Democratic Party politics. He was a poor cousin of the powerful Van Ness family, who built their great house 2 miles south of town in 1797. A few years later, that family hired a tutor who had the odd habit of taking notes on the people he met in the area. Those notes would become the basis of *The Legend of Sleepy Hollow,* after Washington Irving changed professions from tutor to writer. Van Buren later claimed that the Ichabod Crane character was modeled after his schoolteacher in Kinderhook.

Van Buren later purchased the Van Ness home, which he called Lindenwold, intending to retire there after serving two terms as president. His anticipations fell one term short, though. As vice president during Andrew Jackson's second term, he was thoroughly overshadowed by the popular, flamboyant Old Hickory, and he took office as a pale imitation of the outgoing president. Even his nickname, Old Kinderhook, was derivative—although the initials are said to have given the country its most enduring expression of approval, O.K. Van Buren inherited severe financial problems that would lead to the Panic of 1837 and was unable to hold his party together in the face of a challenge from the newly formed Whigs. So he retired to Lindenwold four years early, in 1841. He attempted a comeback as the candidate of the Free Soilers in 1848. Aside from that, he spent the last years of his life cut off from national politics. He died at Lindenwold in 1862. You can cut off U.S. 9 at Kinderhook on N.Y. 9H to reach the house, now a National Historic Site.

Nearby is the older Luykas Van Alen house, built in 1737 and now a small museum of typical domestic life in the Dutch days.

Continue along 9H to N.Y. 66, then turn west into the town of **Hudson** to rejoin the main road. Hudson was settled by natives of Nantucket, and although it seems unlikely, it was once a whaling port. Many of these old river towns engaged in the trade, and that lively chapter in Hudson's past is explored in the D.A.R. Museum on Warren Street, in an area of several attractive Federal-style homes. There are fine views of the Hudson town and river from Promenade Hill, but the town's red-hot attraction is the American Museum of Fire Fighting. This is the biggest collection of antique fire equipment in the country, some pieces dating back to 1725.

Follow the signs toward the Rip Van Winkle Bridge, then turn south along the river on N.Y. 9G. In about 5 miles you will come to an Arabian Nights fantasy called Olana, the most singular dwelling in a valley noted for distinctive homes. It was the estate of painter Frederic Edwin Church, who insisted that it was built in the Persian style. But this is Persia the way only an artist immersed in Romanticism ever saw it, full of turrets and domes and colorful imaginings.

Church was part of the Hudson River School, the group of artists dedicated to celebrating the beauty of the American landscape, and a disciple of its founder, Thomas Cole, who lived across the river in Catskill. But Cole merely lived in a house, not a fantasy. Church planned Olana as a unified work of art; house, paths, scenic lookouts, gardens were all of a piece. He spent four years building it, starting in 1870, and the last twenty-six years of a long life enjoying his role as Caliph of the Hudson. It is now a State Historic Site.

You have now entered the domain of the Livingstons, a Scottish family that intertwined with the old patroons and ended up with larger holdings than any of them. Robert Livingston arrived in Albany and became town clerk in 1674. According to legend, he was called to help draft a will for the ailing Nicolaes Van Rensselaer, but when the dying man saw Livingston he sat upright and cried, "Anyone but you, for you will marry my widow." He was right on the money. That is exactly what Livingston did fourteen months later. His new wife was also a Schuyler, so the marriage united what were to be the three major families of the upper Hudson.

Unlike the great landowners of the southern Hudson, these families supported the colonial cause. The great-grandson of the founder, Robert R. Livingston, helped draft the Declaration of Independence. In retaliation, the British torched his home south of **Germantown** on their raid up the Hudson in 1777. Livingston began to rebuild immediately and by 1782 had completed his new estate, which he called Clermont. From here he ran his affairs and was said to be the most powerful man in New York. As chancellor, the state's chief legal officer, he administered the first oath of office to Washington in 1789. He helped negotiate the Louisiana Purchase while serving as Jefferson's minister to France. He also sponsored the work of inventor Robert Fulton, who adapted the work of several predecessors to launch a steamboat in 1807. Livingston used his clout to get Fulton a monopoly grant for the use of steam power on the Hudson, and then married him into his family. Clermont is now a museum of the Livingston family and its 200-year occupancy of the site.

A bit further along the road is **Annadale-on-Hudson** and another Livingston estate. Montgomery Place was built by the chancellor's sister, Janet, the widow of Revolutionary War hero Gen. Richard Montgomery, in 1805. It was recently restored and contains several rooms of exquisite furnishings and memorabilia. Also in town is the Blum Art Institute of Bard College, with changing exhibitions.

The road now rejoins U.S. 9, but if you jog back just a little to the north, you'll come to the Old Aerodrome in **Rhinebeck**. This is not only a museum of antique aircraft, but also an ongoing barnstorming tour and air show. The old planes, dating from 1907 to 1937, are flown regularly throughout the summer months. If you've seen too many old Gary Cooper movies, you can take a ride in an open cockpit plane yourself, before or after the shows.

In Rhinebeck itself is the Beekman Arms, billed as the oldest hotel in continuous operation in the country. Actually, it's been operating ten years longer than the country has. The building dates from around 1700, but it became a hotel in 1766. It is right in the center of town, on a square named for itself, a certain indication of longevity.

It seems that all the illustrious families of this valley wind up related to each other. Morgan Lewis was governor of the state and a general in the War of 1812, distinguishing himself at the Battle of Sackets Harbor. He married into the Livingston family and built a home with his wife near **Staatsburg** in 1832. Their great-granddaughter Ruth married Ogden Mills, and in 1895 they expanded the old family home into a sixty-five-room mansion. Architect Stanford White oversaw the work, which turned the place into a Neoclassic French showcase, containing furniture and art objects from around the world. Their son, also named Ogden Mills, was a congressman, and although he was President Hoover's secretary of the treasury, he was still regarded as a leading financial expert. The mansion and its surrounding grounds are now part of a state park overlooking the Hudson.

FOCUS

* * *

To an entire generation of Americans, the name of the place means only one thing: **Hyde Park** is FDR. It is linked to him through a thousand datelines and photographs and newsreel memories. Those who remember Franklin D. Roosevelt as president approach his home as if on a pilgrimage.

A recent book about the modern presidency was called *In the Shadow of FDR.* It argued that his policies and personality so changed the office that his successors were still being influenced by him almost half a century after his death. His shadow also fell across the lives of millions of ordinary Americans, whom he influenced to a greater extent than any other man who ever held the office. So Hyde Park, a village on the east bank of the Hudson, has taken its place among the top attractions in the country.

But FDR's neighbors cast some pretty imposing shadows of their own. Before his election in 1932, in fact, most people would have identified Hyde Park with another family whose roots ran deep in the Hudson Valley, the Vanderbilts. By the late nineteenth century, the village had become a favored country retreat for wealthy New Yorkers. To the Roosevelts, Hyde Park was a year-round home, expansive but informal. To Frederick William Vanderbilt, who bought land just to the north, it was just a spring and fall residence. Nonetheless, the mansion he built here was a palazzo, an estate more than a home.

Vanderbilt came here in 1895 and quickly put up a pavilion, or temporary residence, to be inhabited while the existing house was torn down and a more suitable abode arranged. This took the best part of four years, and by May 1899, the fifty-four-room Beaux Arts palace, designed by McKim, Mead and White and built at a cost of $660,000 (a lot of money back then) was ready for its first gala. Louise Vanderbilt, a famous beauty, was a legendary hostess whose soirees defined the Gilded Age. But she also sponsored many activities for the needy in the area and helped establish a Red Cross chapter in Hyde Park. Frederick Vanderbilt enjoyed puttering around his garden and was an enthusiastic exhibitor at local horticulture shows. Most endearing of all, he was accustomed to excuse himself early from his wife's elaborate parties and retire to an upstairs bedroom to read. How can you resent a man like that?

The Vanderbilts had no children, and at Frederick's death in 1938 the estate was left to a niece. She talked to neighbor Roosevelt who arranged for the mansion to be accepted by the U.S. government as a bequest and declared a National Historic Site. An orientation center has exhibits on the house and the family, as well as on other great estates of the various Vanderbilt branches. There are guided tours to the mansion, or you can wander around on your own with a brochure. Standing in the living room or dining room, with their paneling of Circassian walnut, Italian fireplaces and Renaissance ceilings, you may well regret the deplorable failure of your great-great-grandparents to found a few railroads, too.

James Roosevelt, the future president's father, bought his estate, Crum Elbow, in 1866. The core of the Roosevelt house dated from about forty years before and was left essentially unchanged. FDR was born here in 1882 and educated at home before leaving for Groton and Harvard. He campaigned for his first elected position from this place, touring the Dutchess County countryside in a red Maxwell in 1910 to win a state senate seat from a normally Republican district. He returned following his unsuccessful vice presidential bid in 1920, and for the rest of his life split his time between Hyde Park; his cottage in Warm Springs, Georgia; and a large white mansion in Washington, which he occupied for twelve years. He is buried here.

Even before the end of his second term, FDR had established a library on the grounds of his estate. This facility is open only to researchers, who must apply in advance, but the adjoining museum is a fascinating showcase of the great events that marked the four Roosevelt administrations and the family's life in Hyde Park. Next door is the house itself, reflecting most, perhaps, the personality and taste of FDR's strong-willed mother, Sara Delano Roosevelt. Extensive remodeling of the original house was carried out under her supervision in 1916. The rivalry between Sara and her daughter-in-law was one of the ongoing pressures on the Roosevelt marriage. Both women and FDR are buried in the rose garden.

The final adjunct of the estate, opened in 1984, is Val-Kill, Eleanor Roosevelt's personal retreat 2 miles from the main house. It is linked only by shuttle bus during the summer, as if to underline the sense of separateness that its occupant treasured. After the death of her husband, she spent much of her time at Val-Kill and entertained guests, including many of the world's most prominent leaders, there. It is now designated the Eleanor Roosevelt National Historic Site.

* * *

Hyde Park has also become one of the country's more noted gastronomic destinations. Since 1946 it has been the home of the Culinary Institute of America, which moved into the handsome riverside facilities of the St. Andrews Novitiate. Chefs from around the world teach an enrollment of about 2,000 here in what has become the country's most prestigious cooking academy. Of the four restaurants operated by the school, three require reservations, far in advance in most cases. The St. Andrew's Cafe is informal, though, and raises the American coffee shop to its most exalted level. Closed on weekends, however.

South of Hyde Park, U.S. 9 becomes a four-lane divided highway, whooshing through Poughkeepsie on a rocky terrace above the river. (For the attractions of this city, see U.S. 44.)

One of the most wide-ranging intellects of the mid-nineteenth century was Samuel F. B. Morse. A portrait artist, candidate for mayor of New York, advocate of education for women and inventor of the telegraph, Morse was a man whose mind reached into all sorts of corners. His work with telegraphy won him not only fame but great wealth, since he controlled rights to the patent. He purchased a home on U.S. 9 just south of **Poughkeepsie**, remodeled it into a Tuscan villa, called it Locust Grove and lived there until his death in 1872. The home now displays Morse memorabilia, as well as artwork and furniture acquired by its subsequent owner, Martha Innis Young.

Cut off the main road once more on highway 9D to **Beacon**. Signal fires from the crest of the adjacent hilltop warned the colonial army in Newburgh across the river of any British troop movements in the area, giving the town its name. Long before that, Francis Rombout is supposed to have climbed to the top and closed a deal for all the land he could see. His granddaughter, Catharyna Brett, inherited many of his holdings and moved to the area in 1709. When her husband died seventeen years later, Madame Brett's vision proved to be just as expansive as her ancestor's. She ran the enormous estate alone, enlarged it and became the dominant economic force in the area. She died in 1764, and the home remained in the family's hands for almost another two hundred years. The period furnishings and formal gardens are the highlights of a visit to this museum-home.

Beacon was also the birthplace of a formidable political force in the country's early years. The Verplanck estate, Mount Gulian, was headquarters of the garrulous Prussian general and military aide to Washington, Baron Friedrich Wilhelm von Steuben. He was an accomplished storyteller (Martha Washington referred to him once as "another Munchausen") and genial host, and his home became a popular gathering place for colonial officers. As the war wound to its close, the officers met at Mount Gulian to establish the Society of Cincinnati. It was named for a Roman hero who twice left his farm to free Rome from a dictator and returned each time without seeking political office. Classical symbols were very powerful at the time, and although most of the American generals were professional men rather than farmers, the image appealed to them. The fraternal organization, founded in 1783, was a strong force for many years in national politics, even inspiring the name of a city in Ohio far to the west. Mount Gulian is located on Sterling Street in Beacon.

Almost directly opposite the river from West Point is the village of **Cold Spring**, where in 1818 Congress chartered a foundry to make weapons for the officers being trained across the water. It was the primary source of cannons for the Civil War. An old schoolhouse is now the Foundry School Museum on Chestnut Street.

Boscobel is one of the great surviving Federal-era mansions in the country. It almost didn't make it, though. Scheduled for demolition in 1955, it was rescued by a citizens' campaign headed by Mrs. DeWitt Wallace, whose husband owned the *Readers' Digest.* The mansion was transported to this site, south of Cold Spring, from its former location near the town of Crugers to the south. In many ways, this is a better spot, for the house now commands sweeping views of West Point. In addition, it was embellished with some features it lacked in its original setting (so the restoration was not as faithful to the house as to the period and style). It was built by States Morris Dyckman, a Loyalist, for his bride in 1806.

The road now runs above the river opposite Bear Mountain and rejoins U.S. 9 at Peekskill. It becomes a freeway here, but you should get off at Croton-on-Hudson and take highway 9A. During the 1920s, Croton-on-Hudson was a favored summer retreat for members of the Greenwich Village intellectual vanguard. Several writers and editors—Edna St. Vincent Millay, Max Eastman, John Reed—had homes here. The home to see, though, belonged to the Van Cortlandt family and was the manor house of their 86,000-acre estate.

In early days, the Van Cortlandts went against the prevailing tide in the neighborhood and were strong supporters of the colonial cause. As a reward, their home was burned down by the British in 1780. The rebuilt house is furnished as it would have appeared during the Revolutionary era. Stephanus Van Cortlandt was the first native-born mayor of New York, holding office in

1677, and he purchased this estate six years later. His grandson Pierre Van Cortlandt made this his full-time residence starting in 1749. On the property is the Ferry House, used to lodge travelers who crossed the Hudson at this point on the arduous trek between New York and Albany.

Ossining marks the northern edge of the Philipse family holdings, largest of all the land titles granted by the British at the end of the seventeenth century. The estates you have been traversing along the Hudson were a major impulse behind the great movement west that began after the Revolutionary War. Farmers were relegated to permanent tenancy on these lands and moved onward to find property of their own. The last of these estates wasn't broken up until 1846, and it took a bitter rent war and adoption of a new state constitution to do it. This is also the start of the later estate country, where New York merchants and industrialists sought to emulate the life-style of the patroons by building their own castles on the Hudson.

Ossining is where you went when you were sent "up the river." Sing Sing Prison was established here in 1824 and its location relative to New York became a slang expression that came to mean any prison sentence. The town changed its name from Sing Sing in 1901 to disassociate its newly fashionable surroundings from the stigma of durance vile.

On a cheerier note, the old Croton Aqueduct passes through town. It was built to carry water into New York in 1842, and the double-arched bridge to the west of U.S. 9 is one of its more spectacular vestiges. The aqueduct right-of-way has been preserved as a public walkway off and on from Croton to Manhattan.

The characters may have been drawn from Washington Irving's experiences as a tutor near Kinderhook, but the village he describes in *Legend of Sleepy Hollow* was unmistakably **North Tarrytown**. As the highway crosses the Pocantico River to enter the town, you are near the site of the bridge where schoolmaster Crane had his final encounter with the Headless Horseman and was never seen again.

Nearby is the Old Dutch Church, also described in the tale. The oldest in the Hudson Valley, the little stone building was erected in 1699. In its churchyard is the grave of Irving, as well as latter-day residents, such as Andrew Carnegie and William Rockefeller. The church was built by Frederick Philipse on the grounds of his 90,000-acre estate.

Philipse arrived in New York City as a carpenter but by 1683 had accumulated enough money to build Philipsburg Manor here, as well as Philipse Manor in Yonkers, a bit down the road. Tarrytown was named after the Dutch word for "wheat," *tarwe,* and Philipsburg Manor was primarily a milling and trade center for the surrounding tenant lands. The mill, which was the core of the complex, has been restored, and demonstrations are given on its operation. The era depicted in the restoration is the early eighteenth century, when Adolphus Philipse, son of the founder, lived here. The manor itself is a three-story stone farmhouse, a rather simple domicile considering the riches that flowed through these lands. But the family concentrated its wealth on the Yonkers estate. This was only its country headquarters.

The dividing line between North Tarrytown and Tarrytown is still called André Brook, for Maj. John André, who was captured on its banks after his meeting with Benedict Arnold at West Point. Patriots Park marks the approximate spot where André was apprehended by a group of local militia, led by John Paulding. André's figure tops the Captors Monument in the park. It may seem a bit odd to erect a monument to a man you hanged, but André was apparently regarded as a most gallant officer, and everyone seemed to regret having to kill him. There are more exhibits on André and his capture at the Historical Society.

The Pauldings figured prominently in the Tarrytown area for several generations. William Paulding, a former mayor of New York, chose to build a country home, Lyndhurst, here in 1838. It was built of marble quarried by convict labor at Sing Sing. (The prison was placed there because of the quarry. Reformers of the time believed in the therapeutic effects of hard labor.) Upon Paulding's death, the house was sold to George Merritt, a wealthy merchant, who promptly doubled its size and made it a mansion. Railroad tycoon and stock manipulator Jay Gould took it over in 1880 and filled it with artwork and Gothic interior embellishments. He also added the estate's enormous greenhouses, which were soon emulated by other monied squires around the country in a horticultural fad. The house is regarded as a model of Hudson River Gothic. Gould's daughter left the estate to the country as a museum of the era, and you'll find it to the west of U.S. 9 south of Tarrytown.

Tarrytown is also the place Washington Irving is most closely identified with, and his home, Sunnyside, is a literary shrine. His romanticized pictures of the old Dutch settlers often strayed a good distance from the truth. For example, he wrote that this town's name came from the practice of husbands to "tarry" in its taverns, whereas in fact the name was tied to commerce rather than recreation. No matter. His home, like his stories, is built around the kernel of a Dutch original. He expanded it, added a Romanesque tower, planted some ivy for the walls and soon put together an "elegant little snuggery." The rooms are filled with personal memorabilia, reflecting the tastes and eccentricities of the author, who was world famous in his lifetime. Irving lived here from 1835 until his death in 1859. At the entry gate is the Irving Memorial, sculpted by Daniel Chester French and peopled with Irving's literary inventions.

Turn off U.S. 9 just before you enter Hastings-on-Hudson, onto Warburton Road. For many years this town was the home of artist Jacques Lipchitz. As a token of his appreciation, he gave it an 11-foot bronze sculpture, *Between Heaven and Earth.* It is displayed on Maple Street, just west of Warburton.

Warburton continues into **Yonkers**, separated from the river by railroad tracks. The Hudson River Museum combines the Victorian mansion of James B. Trevor, built in 1876, with a contemporary addition to create a facility for regional art, history and planetarium shows.

Farther along Warburton is Philipse Manor. This was the Philipse family seat from the time they acquired the land in 1683 until it was confiscated by the colonial government in 1779 because of their Loyalist sympathies. The original landowner, Adriaen Van der Donck, was given the honorary Dutch title of Jonker, and that evolved into the name of the community that formed here. Philipse Manor, with its Georgian woodwork and elaborately decorated ceilings, was a city office building before being turned into a museum of its own history. It also houses the Cochran portrait collection.

Return north on Warburton to Ashburton Ave., then turn east to get back to U.S. 9, which now is called Broadway. It runs along the western edge of Van Cortlandt Park, the northern border of **New York City**. This part of the Bronx was also part of Van der Donck's grant. He took title to it in 1646, it passed into the hands of the Philipse family, and then, through marriage, to Jacobus Van Cortlandt, mayor of New York from 1710 to 1719. It became city land in 1899. The mansion at Broadway and 242nd Street was built by his son, Frederick, in 1748. It is now a museum of the Dutch-English period of the city's history.

The Harlem River was the southern border of the Philipse estate and now marks the entrance to Manhattan Island. At 204th Street you'll find the Dyckman House. The original was built about the same time as the Van Cortlandt mansion, but this northern tip of the island was bitterly contested in the early days of the Revolutionary War and the Dyckmans' home was burned. Rebuilt in 1783, it is the last surviving Dutch farmhouse in Manhattan.

Between Broadway and Riverside Drive, to the west, is the rocky ridge of Fort Tryon Park. It was named for a defensive outpost there, which was overrun by Hessians during the colonial retreat from Manhattan in 1776. Now the jewel of the Fort Tryon heights is the Cloisters, housing the medieval collections of the Metropolitan Museum of Art. You can reach it by leaving U.S. 9 at Dyckman Street and following the signs into the park. The period represented here is the ninth to fifteenth centuries, and the exhibits include parts of five monastery cloisters, their covered passages surrounding a central garden. Not only is the art wonderful, but many of the exhibits can be viewed against a backdrop of the Hudson and the Palisades on the opposite shore. From this height you can also make out the George Washington Bridge to the south, the route U.S. 9 takes into New Jersey. Fort Tryon Park and the Cloisters is the best place to speed it on its way.

VISITING HOURS

NEW YORK

Albany: Arbour Hill, (518) 436-9826. West of U.S. 9 on Livingston Ave., then south on Swan St. to Ten Broeck Place. Tuesday–Sunday, 1–4, all year. Free.
   First Dutch Reformed Church, (518) 463-4449. West of U.S. 9 on New York 32, at Pearl and Clinton Sts. Monday–Friday, 9–4, all year. Donation.

Annadale-on-Hudson: Montgomery Place, (914) 758-5461. Off New York 9G. Wednesday–Monday, 9–5, April–November; weekends only, at other times. Admission.
   Blum Art Institute at Bard College, (914) 758-6822. In town, off New York 9G. Tuesday–Sunday, noon–5, all year. Free.

Beacon: Madame Brett House, (914) 896-6897. Off New York 9D, at 50 Van Nydeck Ave. Friday–Sunday, 1–4, May–October. Admission.
   Mount Gulian, (914) 831-8172. Off New York 9D, at 145 Sterling St. Wednesday and Sunday, 1–5, May–December. Donation.

Cold Spring: Foundry School Museum, (914) 265-4010. On N.Y. 9D, at 63 Chestnut St. Wednesday, 9:30–4, and Sunday, 2–5, March–December. Free.
   Boscobel, (914) 265-3638. South, on New York 9D. Wednesday–Monday, 9:30–4:30, April–October. Closes at 3:30, March, November, December. Admission.

Croton-on-Hudson: Van Cortlandt Manor, (914) 631-8200. South, at Croton Point Ave. exit of U.S. 9. Daily, April–November, 10–5. Closed Monday at other times. Admission.

Germantown: Clermont, (518) 537-4240. South on New York 9G. Wednesday–Saturday, 10–5; Sunday, 1–5, Memorial Day–mid-October. Free.

Hudson: D.A.R. Museum, (518) 828-7288. Off U.S. 9, at 113 Warren St. Wednesday and Friday, 1–4; Sunday, 1–3, July–August. Admission.

American Museum of Fire Fighting, (518) 828-7695. Off U.S. 9, at Harry Howard Ave. Tuesday–Sunday, 9–4:30, April–October. Free.

Olana, (518) 828-0135. South, on New York 9G. Wednesday–Saturday, 10–4; Sunday, 1–4, Memorial Day–Labor Day. Wednesday–Saturday, noon–4, to mid-October. Admission.

Hyde Park: Roosevelt Home and Museum, (914) 229-8114. South, on U.S. 9. Home open daily, 9–5, April–October; Thursday–Monday, 9–5, at other times. Museum open daily, 9–5, all year. Combined admission.

Val-Kill, (914) 229-9115. Accessible from Roosevelt Museum. Daily, 9:30–5, April–October; weekends only, 9–4:30, March, November, December. Admission.

Vanderbilt Mansion, (914) 229-9115. North, on U.S. 9. Daily, 10–6, April–October; Thursday–Monday, 9–5, at other times. Admission.

Kinderhook: Lindenwold, (518) 758-9689. South on New York 9H. Daily, 9–4:30, Memorial Day–Labor Day. Free.

Van Alen House, (518) 758-9265. South on New York 9H. Tuesday–Saturday, 11–5; Sunday, 1–5, Memorial Day–Labor Day. Admission.

New York City: Van Cortlandt House, (212) 543-3344. On U.S. 9, Broadway at 246th St. (the Bronx). Tuesday–Sunday, 10–5, all year. Admission.

Dyckman House, (212) 397-3188. On U.S. 9, Broadway at 204th St. Tuesday–Sunday, 11–5, all year. Free.

The Cloisters, (212) 923-3700. West, off U.S. 9, at Fort Tryon Park. Tuesday–Sunday, 9:30–5, all year. Admission.

North Tarrytown: Old Dutch Church, no phone. North, on U.S. 9. Daily, noon–4, June–September. Donation.

Philipsburg Manor, (914) 631-8200. North, on U.S. 9.

Daily, 10–5, April–November; closed Tuesday, at other times. Admission.

Poughkeepsie: Morse Home, (914) 454-4500. South, on U.S. 9. Wednesday–Sunday, 10–4, Memorial Day–September. Admission.

Rensselaer: Crailo, (518) 463-8738. South, off U.S. 9, at 9½ Riverside Ave. Wednesday–Saturday, 10–5; Sunday, 1–5, April–December. Free.

Rhinebeck: Old Aerodrome, (914) 758-8610. North on U.S. 9, then east on Stone Church Road. Daily, 10–5, mid-May–October. Admission. Shows are scheduled for weekends at 2:30. Additional admission.

Staatsburg: Mills Mansion, (914) 889-4100. North, on U.S. 9. Wednesday–Saturday, 10–5; Sunday, 1–5, Memorial Day–Labor Day. Wednesday–Saturday, noon–5; Sunday, 1–5, to mid-October. Free.

Tarrytown: Historical Museum, (914) 631-8374. Off U.S. 9, on Grove St. Tuesday–Saturday, 1–5, all year. Donation.
Sunnyside, (914) 631-8200. South on U.S. 9. Daily, 10–5, April–November. Closed Tuesday, at other times. Admission.
Lyndhurst, (914) 631-0046. South, on U.S. 9. Tuesday–Sunday, 10–4, April–October. Weekends only, November–December. Admission.

Yonkers: Hudson Museum, (914) 963-4550. West of U.S. 9, on Warburton Ave., in Trevor Park. Wednesday–Saturday, 10–5:30; Sunday, noon–5:30, all year. Admission.
Philipse Manor, (914) 965-4027. West of U.S. 9, on Warburton Ave., south on Ashburton Ave. Wednesday–Saturday, noon–5; Sunday, 1–5, Memorial Day–October. Free.

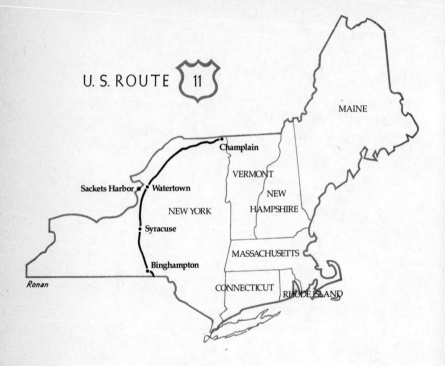

U. S. ROUTE 11

MAINE

Champlain

VERMONT

NEW
HAMPSHIRE

Sackets Harbor • Watertown

NEW YORK

Syracuse

Binghampton

MASSACHUSETTS

Ronan

CONNECTICUT

RHODE ISLAND

The Iroquois Trail

U.S. 11

Champlain to Binghamton, N.Y.
* 319 miles

You could call U.S. 11 the French Connection, I suppose, because it begins on the Quebec border and ends in New Orleans. It is a long, oblique journey between these Gallic outposts, angling steadily down the continent through the natural valleys of the Appalachians. Unfortunately, the route is so natural that almost its entire course is now hawked by Interstates. Only in this, its most northern portion in the St. Lawrence Valley, does it run unencumbered by an adjacent freeway. On this drive, you skirt the northwestern edge of the Adirondacks, then swing south to parallel the shore of Lake Ontario. After passing through the middle of Syracuse, the road begins a scenic descent of the Tioughnioga Valley, following the river to its junction with the Susquehanna at Binghamton.

* MILEPOSTS *

In its early stages, U.S. 11 follows the route of the old Iroquois Trail and Military Turnpike, built in 1826 to connect Lake Champlain with Lake Ontario. Overland routes between the Great Lakes and the rivers flowing to the Atlantic were of critical strategic importance in colonial times. The main road was farther to the south, running to the military base at Oswego. During the War of 1812, though, there were threats to American strongholds at both Sackets Harbor on Lake Ontario and Plattsburgh on Lake Champlain. Both were beaten back, but the idea of linking the two areas by military road took hold, and this route was the result.

It roughly follows the fall line between the Adirondack highlands and the St. Lawrence plain. You get some idea of that in **Chateaugay**, at High Falls Park. The Chateaugay River drops 120 feet in this glen, and hiking trails surround the tract. The town and river are named for the adjacent Quebec land grants awarded to Charles Lemoyne in 1796. Most of the little towns between the road's start at Champlain and Chateaugay were settled by French Canadians, many of whom came during the big lumbering boom of the early nineteenth century. The French influence is still strong, with Montreal just across the border and booming in clearly every night over the television.

A pair of local chaps who were pretty much relegated to second fiddle are the subjects of exhibits in the Franklin County Museum in **Malone**. William A. Wheeler was a lifelong resident of the town, unless you count the four years when he was vice president under Rutherford B. Hayes. In recent decades, the occupant of this office has been given a bit more power and media exposure. But in the nineteenth century, the vice president was truly an invisible man, and Wheeler was no exception. He came home after his term expired in 1881 and died six years later, his name forgotten almost everywhere but in Malone. On display with his mementoes are those of Alonzo Wilder. He was the husband of Laura Ingalls Wilder, whose "Little House" books are classics of children's literature and have been adapted as a popular television series.

Malone is quite a distance from the Kansas and Minnesota depicted in those books but not so far from Canada, which made Malone a favorite hangout of the Fenians. These were the Irish revolutionaries who, in the years after the Civil War, threatened to invade Canada in an effort to pry Ireland loose from Britain. They were enthusiastically supported by the mass of recent Irish immigrants to America but met with serious disapproval in Washington. Threats of federal action finally ended the border disturbances. An attractive corner of town now is Ballard Mill, a turn-of-the-century building turned into an arts center, with studios, shops and galleries.

Among the first groups to settle the **Potsdam** area was a utopian colony out of Massachusetts, which broke up when the indolent demanded an equal share of the proceeds. Utopias usually have that problem. Potsdam managed to attract a more industrious group in the Clarkson family. They received the original land grants for the area and endowed the town with several facilities throughout the nineteenth century. Clarkson University was established by the family in 1896 and has become a top engineering and technical institute. The Clarkson's land agent, Benjamin Raymond, was a bit of a go-getter himself. The academy he started here in 1816 eventually grew up to become part of the state university system, which absorbed it in 1949. The Rolland Gibson Gallery in Brainerd Hall on the campus presents changing art exhibits. The public museum in the Civic Center shows off an especially noteworthy collection of English pottery, dating from 1700 to 1870.

The town was once known for its sandstone quarries, from which the material for Canada's parliament buildings was taken. They closed down in the 1890s. Potsdam was even better known for being the royal residence of the Prussian monarchy. Of course that was the Potsdam in Germany, but that was the idea behind naming this town. A little reflected glory never hurts. Settlers would open a world atlas and pick out a name for their community that seemed likely to attract a good class of neighbors. So in the immediate vicinity you also have Madrid and Stockholm, and the next town along the road, **Canton**.

Canton's most famous native son looked west rather than east for inspiration. Frederic Remington captured the romance and beauty of the American West in his paintings and sculpture and helped shape our visual concept of that region. His father was editor of the newspaper in Canton. If you are a Remington admirer, it would be a shame to get this close and not see the largest collection of his works. **Ogdensburg** really isn't on our route, but it's just a 17-mile detour to the north on N.Y. 68. After Remington's death in 1909, his widow moved back to this area and recreated his studio in Ogdensburg, adding memorabilia from his travels. You can take that in, then return to U.S. 11 by way of N.Y. 812 and not really miss much. Before leaving Canton, though, you may want to see the campus of St. Lawrence University and the home of Silas Wright, a former governor and U.S. senator. The Greek Revival house has been restored to its appearance of the 1830–50 era.

The area around Gouverneur once was dotted with zinc and talc mines and they still attract rockhounds. But local legend says that more valuable treasure is buried somewhere in the area. The town is named for Gouverneur Morris, a member of the one of the great landholding families in New York. He helped administer the finances of the infant republic after the Revolution and was a shaping force at the Constitutional Convention. (One historian said of the Pennsylvania delegation to which he belonged, "Thomas Mifflin never opened his mouth and Gouverneur Morris never closed his.") He was a powerful figure in the Federalist party and was named minister to France by President Washington. Morris detested the revolutionary leaders in France and was accused of plotting with members of the imprisoned nobility to overthrow the new government. Recalled from Paris, Morris settled on his holdings in this part of New York and built a mansion here in 1809. His neighbors firmly believed that somewhere in the mansion he hid a treasure he had acquired for safekeeping from his titled French friends. None of it has ever turned up.

Another visitor from France lived for a time in the village of

Oxbow. Joseph Bonaparte was the older brother of Napoleon. As a token of fraternal regard, he was made King of Naples and later of Spain. He was not especially suited for either job, though, and managed to lose Spain to the Duke of Wellington in 1813, in a prelude to Waterloo. After Napoleon's defeat, Joseph came to America. He lived mostly in New Jersey for the next twenty-six years but came to upstate New York in 1838 for a brief stay. This part of New York had become something of a haven for politically displaced Frenchmen. Chaumont, on the nearby Lake Ontario shore, was founded by and named for a French nobleman whose father befriended Benjamin Franklin in Paris and loaned funds to the American Revolution. The younger Chaumont was reimbursed, and he established his colony for French émigrés in 1802. His plan was to make it a lake port to rival the Canadian city of Kingston. But when the Erie Canal was built, U.S. trade to the Great Lakes was diverted south to Lake Erie. Even with this failure, the area maintained a strong French identity for many years afterwards. So Bonaparte may have felt he was moving in among friends. But he stayed only a year before heading back to New Jersey and, eventually, to Italy. His American-born daughter, Caroline, also lived in Oxbow. She was later given royal privileges and rank during the Second Empire reign of her cousin, Louis Napoleon, and spent the rest of her life in France.

With all this folklore involving buried treasure and French nobility, it sounds like penny-ante stuff to talk about the five-and-dime. But Frank Woolworth probably built a greater fortune on those little coins than anything buried in Gouverneur Morris's basement. Woolworth started his career in **Watertown**. During a county fair in 1878 he was struck by the thought of offering to sell all items in one bin for a nickel. The response cleaned out his stock. Woolworth had made a discovery that would change merchandising: if the price is low enough, people will buy anything. The price itself is the product for sale. Woolworth had been a flop as a salesman, so unsuccessful that his salary had been lowered from $10 to $8.50 a week. But his new way of selling did not require a salesperson. It was based on a fixed low price and appealing display, the attention-getting red and gold background colors he had admired while working in a local dry goods store. Within a year of that fair in Watertown he had opened his first store in Utica. In seven years he had seven stores, and by 1900 he was the biggest merchandiser in America. The Jefferson County Historical Society, housed in an Italianate villa on Washington Street, recounts this and other chapters from the city's past.

It would hardly be right to pass this close to Lake Ontario and not get a look at it. U.S. 11 runs inland, out of sight of the lake, so from Watertown, take a side trip west on N.Y. 3 to **Sackets Harbor**. This is now a resort town on a deep inlet of the island-studded northeastern corner of the lake. But its military past is long, impressive and a little bizarre. As you enter the town, you pass the Madison Barracks. Built in the 1840s, during a time of border tension with Canada, the barracks were used for a century, and some of the most illustrious names in the army, including Ulysses S. Grant and John Pershing, passed through. The post is being restored and an interpretive program installed. A visitor's center is currently open.

Sackets Harbor was the target of two British assaults in the War of 1812. The first came as a complete surprise, just a month after the formal declaration of war, when a British fleet swooped down on what they thought was an undefended shipyard. They were right, but the handful of workers there managed to load the biggest cannon they could find, nicknamed the Old Sow, and sent a shot whistling through the mast of one of the ships. Not prepared for resistance, the British withdrew, but the following May they returned and landed some troops. This time a small militia unit arrived, and the British, under the impression that it was the vanguard of a major force, retreated once more.

That sort of reluctance marked the entire conflict, or lack of a conflict, on Lake Ontario. The war turned into a shipbuilding contest between the two adversaries. No major engagements were fought because neither commander ever felt he had a large enough numerical advantage in ships. The real battle was in the Sackets Harbor shipyard, which had to keep turning out vessels to keep pace with British production. Occasional shots were exchanged, and each side accused the other of a deplorable lack of spirit, but nothing much ever came of it, which is probably just as well. The former Union Hotel, built in 1817, is now a museum of the battlefield and the era. Nearby is the Pickering-Beach Museum, with further displays on local history, including a U. S. Grant exhibit.

The road turns south and passes some lovely vistas of the lake. Westcott Beach State Park is right on the way, if you care to stop for a swim. At Henderson Harbor, pick up N.Y. 178 and head east to rejoin U.S. 11.

The town of **Adams** was a starting point, or a brief stopover, in several brilliant careers. Joseph Smith brought his band of Mormons here from Palmyra, New York, and stayed a year before moving west to Ohio. Charles G. Finney switched careers from attorney to minister while living here and became a prominent religious leader of the 1850s. He founded the Broadway Tabernacle in New York and also moved on to Ohio to become president of Oberlin College. J. Sterling Morton headed west from Adams, too, but he kept going all the way to Nebraska. The empty plains of that state made a vivid impression that lasted the rest of his life. He fostered the idea of planting trees to bring some green to the barren plains, and Nebraska, in 1872, became the first state to designate an official Arbor Day. The idea caught on in the Midwest, and when Morton went to Washington, as secretary of agriculture in Grover Cleveland's cabinet, he used his position to have Arbor Day recognized on a national scale. It is usually observed on the last Friday in April, but not many places make much of a fuss about it anymore. There is a local historical association and museum on Church Street if you care to delve into these matters further.

During the height of the Ku Klux Klan's national influence in the 1920s, it ran a home for orphans near Mannsville. An odd sidelight, since the organization was usually more concerned with creating orphans than caring for them.

Between Central Square and Syracuse, we are on the route of the first plank road in America. These roads were built in lumbering areas during the 1840s and were regarded as an improvement over the old corduroy roads, which were made of logs set side by side. Planks gave a smoother ride, but as the wood started to rot and split they weren't really much of an improvement. The first paved highway, which would be put in place near Detroit, was still seventy years in the future.

Near Brewerton and the shore of Lake Oneida are the ruins of Fort Brewerton, built during the French and Indian War.

FOCUS

*   *   *

A reporter from *Godey's Lady's Book* arrived in **Syracuse** in 1845 and declared that the city reminded her of Venice. The one in Italy. Not many people have made that comparison lately, but to her eyes the sights along the Erie Canal were every bit as grand as those along the Grand Canal. "There are fine bridges," she wrote, "and a wide street built so directly on the canal that you step out from the door into a boat."

It is hard for us, sitting comfortably in our speeding cars, to imagine what an incredible impact the Erie Canal had on travel in the America of its time. Comparisons to Venice may sound a bit forced today, but to the generation that saw this marvel take shape before their eyes, the comparisons were quite apt.

This wasn't the first canal project undertaken in the United States. There had been a few along the Connecticut River (see U.S. 5), but they were built primarily as diversions around rapids rather than as longer transportation links. After the War of 1812, when peace was restored to what was then the northwest frontier, a group of visionaries in New York began to grasp the benefits of a barge canal connecting the Hudson River with the Great Lakes.

Earlier efforts had been made along this line, using the Mohawk River and the chain of lakes that began just northeast of

Syracuse, to reach the Lake Ontario outlet at Oswego. But it was an arduous journey, and the Mohawk was an unpredictable stream. The new project called for constructing a separate canal along the Mohawk plain. According to its promoters, it would provide an inexpensive way of moving goods to the northwest. More than that, it would steer all this trade into New York. Unlike other river routes to the west, this one didn't pass through mountainous terrain. There were some major obstacles to overcome in the Genesee Valley and Niagara Escarpment, but the engineering technology of the time was equal to it. The federal government refused to help out, though, and so did the western states that stood to benefit. So New York decided to go it alone.

Eight years later, in October 1825, the governor of New York, DeWitt Clinton, and a small army of dignitaries pulled out of the boat basin in Buffalo Harbor on their way to deliver a bottle of Lake Erie water to the Hudson and the sea. Cannons boomed all along the way. The canal was open and the history of American transportation altered forever.

True to the word of its promoters, the canal opened up the empty lands of Michigan and Wisconsin to settlement. It encouraged Illinois farmers to grow wheat on a large scale, because they now had an economical way to get it to the markets of the East. Buffalo, Detroit and Chicago grew into major ports. More than that, New York City started a spiral of growth that would eclipse all other eastern commercial competitors. It became the unchallenged economic and financial center of the country because of the interior trade coming through. Just slightly larger than Boston, Baltimore and Philadelphia in 1820, it grew within thirty years to be three times the size of the next largest city in the country.

In relative terms, the impact was even greater on Syracuse. The canal went right through the heart of town and transformed the little salt-mining settlement into a city of 22,000 people in that same thirty-year span. Salt deposits on Onondaga Lake had brought settlers into the area for hundreds of years, and a salt-works was set along the shoreline as early as 1788. The main north-south street in town is still called Salina. Clinton Square, where Salina intersects the canal, is still the center of town, filled with splashing fountains and surrounded by office towers. A block to the east is Hanover Square, the oldest surviving part of the city, with several historic buildings. And one more block over is the Erie Canal Museum, the last visible reminder of what the waterway meant to the city.

The area between Water Street and Erie Boulevard was the original canal bed, paved over in 1920 when the canal was relocated. The old weighmaster's office is now the museum. Once there were seven such buildings along the canal, designed to weigh 100-foot-long barges and assess the appropriate toll. This is the only one left, and it has been restored to its appearance of the 1850s. You can board a reconstructed canal boat here and experience through imaginative exhibits what life was like for those who traveled and worked along the great waterway west. By tracking the adventures of actual passengers who went west on the canal, the museum brings the era to dramatic life.

If this stirs your fancy, there are other places to recapture the romance of canal life around Syracuse. From the junction of N.Y. 92 and N.Y. 5 in the eastern suburb of Dewitt, head north on Lyndon Road. This leads to Cedar Bay Road, which runs along the southern bank of the original canal. The entire route through this area is now a state park, with interpretive displays, hiking trails and several old bridges along the way. For an even closer look, the Mid-Lakes Navigation Co. operates three-day and seven-day cruises along the new barge canal to Albany and Buffalo. They leave from Liverpool, a suburb northwest of Syracuse.

*　*　*

The highway runs through downtown Syracuse as State Street, along the eastern edge of the Civic Center, past the courthouse, county offices and War Memorial Auditorium. Just to the east, at

Harrison Street, is the Everson Museum of Art, a stunning structure designed by I. M. Pei and opened in 1968. It contains the country's largest collection of American ceramics, in the Syracuse China Center, as well as a fine permanent collection of American paintings. In another few blocks, the campus of Syracuse University is visible across the Interstate to the east. It is dominated by the white balloon of the Carrier dome, over the country's largest indoor athletic facility.

South of Syracuse, U.S. 11 leaves the route of the Great Western Road, taken by pioneers heading for the Susquehanna Valley, and runs through the lovely Tioughnioga Valley. The drive south through Tully is a nice scenic route.

David Harum was one of turn-of-the-century America's most beloved fictional characters. He appeared in a book by small-town banker Edward Noyes Westcott. The author's portrait of the shrewd Yankee trader struck a nostalgic chord in a country that was rapidly leaving that small-town world behind as it accelerated into a new, urban century. Will Rogers later played Harum in the movies and made the role an extension of his personality. The model for Westcott's book, though, was a resident of Homer, named David Hannum, and as far as this town is concerned, it was the ideal community depicted in the book. Another of Homer's favorite sons was Francis B. Carpenter, who painted *Lincoln Reading the Emancipation Proclamation* for the U.S. Capitol.

According to David Harum, "the truest statement in the Bible is them that has, gets." He would have approved of the 1890 House in **Cortland**, built by industrial tycoon Chester Wickwire, who certainly had. Outfitted with the finest woodwork, stained glass and parquet floors, the house, built in the year of its name, is a great example of Victorian Chateau.

Near Whitney Point, the road passes a dam at the head of a hill-rimmed reservoir. A roadside park opens out on the overlook.

You may not guess it when you drive into the place, but when you reach **Binghamton** you have entered the Twilight Zone. It's where writer Rod Serling, who created the series on television, grew up, and an exhibit is devoted to him in the Forum Theatre, on Washington Street. For more scientifically verifiable phenomena, try the Roberson Center for the Arts and Sciences, located in an old mansion on Front Street.

Philadelphia financier William Bingham bought the tract on which the town is located in 1786, sensing the importance of the site at the junction of the Susquehanna and Chenango rivers. A major bridge was built there, and that stimulated growth of the city, which was first called Chenango, then renamed for the farsighted Bingham.

The Susquehanna winds south from here, reentering Pennsylvania for a bit before doubling back to its source in New York's Catskills. U.S. 11 winds along with it on the eastern bank. But it never comes back to New York. It just keeps rolling along, into Pennsylvania and out of this book.

VISITING HOURS

NEW YORK

Adams: Historical Association, (315) 232-2616. Off U.S. 11, at 9 E. Church St. Monday–Friday, 8–11:30 and 1–4, all year. Admission.

Binghamton: Forum Theatre, (607) 772-2480. Off U.S. 11, at 228 Washington St. Monday–Friday, 8–4, all year. Donation.
   Roberson Center, (607) 772-0660. South of U.S. 11 from the east end of the Susquehanna River bridge, at 30 Front St. Tuesday–Saturday, 10–6; Sunday, noon–5, all year. Donation.

Canton: St. Lawrence County Museum, (315) 386-8133. On U.S. 11, at 3 E. Main St. Monday–Friday, 9–5; Saturday, 1–5, all year. Free.

Chateaugay: High Falls Park, (518) 497-3156. West, on U.S. 11. Daily, 8–8, mid-May–mid-October. Admission.

Cortland: 1890 House, (607) 756-7551. West from U.S. 11, on New York 13, at 37 Tompkins St. Tuesday–Sunday, 1–4, all year. Admission.

Malone: Franklin County Historical Museum, (518) 483-2750. Off U.S. 11, at 51 Milwaukee St. Tuesday–Saturday, 1–5, mid-June–Labor Day. Donation.

Ballard Mill, (518) 483-0909. Off U.S. 11, on S. Williams St., at Salmon River. Daily, 10–4, all year. Free.

Ogdensburg: Remington Museum, (315) 393-2425. North from U.S. 11 on New York 68, to Washington St. Monday–Saturday, 10–5; Sunday, 1–5, May–October. Closed Sunday and Monday, at other times. Admission.

Potsdam: Public Museum, (315) 265-6910. On U.S. 11, in Civic Center, at Elm and Park Sts. Tuesday–Saturday, 2–5, all year. Free.

Gibson Gallery, (315) 267-2254. Off U.S. 11, on New York 56, in Brainerd Hall, S.U.N.Y.-Potsdam. Daily, noon–4, all year. Free.

Sackets Harbor: Battlefield and Museum, (315) 646-3634. West from U.S. 11, on New York 3, to Washington St. Wednesday–Saturday, 10–5; Sunday, 1–5, Memorial Day–Labor Day. Admission to museum. Grounds are free.

Pickering-Beach Museum, (315) 646-2052. Adjacent to battlefield. Daily, 10–5, Memorial Day–Labor Day. Admission.

Madison Barracks, no phone. Off New York 3, at eastern edge of town, on Pike St. Information center open daily, 9–5, all year. Free.

Syracuse: Erie Canal Museum, (315) 471-0593. West of U.S. 11, on Erie Blvd. E. Tuesday–Sunday, 10–5, all year. Admission.

Erie Canal Cruises, through the Mid-Lakes Navigation Co. (315) 685-5722. Depart from Liverpool, west from U.S. 11 on New York 370, at Lake Onondaga marina.

June–October. Call for schedule and rates.

Everson Museum, (315) 474-6064. On U.S. 11, at S. State and Harrison Sts. Tuesday–Friday and Sunday, noon–5; Saturday, 10–5, all year. Donation.

Watertown: Historical Museum, (315) 782-3491. Off U.S. 11, at 228 Washington St. Tuesday–Saturday, 10–5, all year. Free.

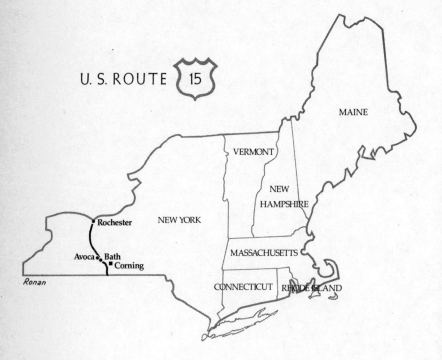

U. S. ROUTE 15

MAINE

VERMONT

NEW
HAMPSHIRE

NEW YORK

Rochester

Avoca • Bath
■ Corning

Ronan

MASSACHUSETTS

CONNECTICUT RHODE ISLAND

Genesee Valley

U.S. 15

Rochester to Painted Post, N.Y.
*   *102 miles*

This old road suffered the ultimate indignity. It disappeared. U.S.
15 used to begin in downtown Rochester, embarking on a scenic
journey through the Middle Atlantic states to Walterboro, South
Carolina. For most of the route, it still carries that number. But
U.S. 15 doesn't make an appearance in New York now until just
10 miles north of the Pennsylvania border. Its former path has
been usurped by Interstate 390 and N.Y. 17, both freeways. The
old road is still there, though, if you go poking around to find it.
Part of the way, from its start in Rochester to around Wayland,
it goes by the name of N.Y. 15. Easy enough. But once beyond
there, it is called N.Y. 415, as it plays peek-a-boo with the freeway, ducking in and out of sight of that road. Beyond Painted
Post, it becomes U.S. 15 once more. It isn't too difficult to stay on
course, and the countryside is unfailingly pleasant. For most of
the way, you'll pretty much have the road to yourself, too.

* MILESTONES *

The core of downtown **Rochester** is surrounded by the Inner Loop, a beltway that gives access to all directions from the middle of town. You'll start this drive in the middle of that loop, the corner of Clinton and Broad, at Midtown Plaza. This two-story indoor mall has a 28-foot-high clock at its center, which features dancing puppets every hour. It makes for a cheery send-off. Before revving your engine, though, walk over to Manhattan Square, a block east on Chestnut Street. Here you'll find the Strong Museum, an enormous collection that tracks popular taste in the nineteenth century and examines how it was influenced by the coming of the Industrial Revolution. It has a superb doll collection, as well as exhibits charting the changes in glassware, silver and other branches of the decorative arts. Most of it comes from the collection of Margaret Woodbury Strong, who endowed the facility.

All right, now you can roll. South of the Inner Loop, N.Y. 15 becomes Mt. Hope Avenue, named for the site of the city's largest cemetery. The graves of Frederick Douglass and Susan B. Anthony, both Rochester residents, are contained within, and there are lots of spectacular Victorian sculptures on the peaceful grounds. Anthony and Douglass were close in life, as well. Douglass edited his abolitionist newspaper, *North Star,* in Rochester for seventeen years. Anthony carried on her battle for woman's suffrage for forty years from her home in the city. She campaigned with Douglass in the emancipation movement and many other causes. (Her house, just west of the Inner Loop, is now a memorial to her.) She died fourteen years before she could see the triumph of her life's work in 1920.

Across the road from the cemetery is Highland Park, noted for its botanical gardens, conservatory and lilacs. In mid-May, the city celebrates Lilac Festival and the park becomes a blooming wonderland. Rochester has a long association with blooms, by the way. It started off as a milling center along the falls of the Genesee River and was known as the Flour City. But when grain production moved further west, Rochester turned to plant nurseries to bolster its economy and took to calling itself the Flower City. This is probably the most unusual case of motto modification in American urban history.

The highway splits into east and west Henrietta Road beyond the park. I'd suggest following East Henrietta, N.Y. 15A. It's a bit less crowded and passes through some very nice old towns on the way. Lima, especially, is a pleasant place to stop for a stroll. The road continues through Livonia Center and along the eastern shore of Hemlock Lake, before rejoining highway 15 at Springwater. Starting at Cohocton, the road, now numbered N.Y. 415, runs alongside the Cohocton River for several miles through enjoyable hilly country.

FOCUS
* * *

One of the major advances made thanks to the old roads was the motel. Drive right up to the door, carry the bags a few feet, and you're home. No long corridors to negotiate, no bellhop to tip, no elevator to wait for. It was a noble victory for convenience.

By the 1960s, however, a certain sameness had crept into the enterprise. National franchises took over the motel industry and began to yank it upscale. The plain, honest motel evolved into the motor hotel. This was simply the return of the old hotel, with a big parking lot attached. The term motel began to have unpleasant class overtones. It was regarded as the lower end of the accommodations scale.

But there is still a place for style and imagination in the motel world, and as you approach **Avoca** on N.Y. 415, you will come upon one such place. It is the Goodrich Motel, the special achievement of Jack McBride. It may be the only place in the country that permits you to bunk down in a caboose.

McBride grew up in nearby Hammondsport and worked as a bank manager. Upon reaching the age of fifty, though, he was seized with a certain restlessness. "I saw too many men die at their desks," he says. "If I was going to go, I wanted it to happen in a more interesting place than a bank. My wife was coordinating tours down at the Corning Glass Center, and that struck me as a lot more entertaining than running a bank. So I quit and we bought this motel."

There were just two problems with the place. Most of the traffic that once used old U.S. 15 now ran on the Interstate. A lot of potato trucks passed by on their way to the processing plant in Avoca, but that didn't do McBride a lot of good. The other problem was that his place looked just like a few thousand other motels around the country.

"I drove out to Kansas to see my son right after we bought this place," he says. "I went through lots of country. Some of it was flat, some of it was hilly, but all the motels looked the same. I decided that if I wanted to make this go, we had to have something different, something no one else had. And to tell the truth, I was sick of cutting all the lawn we had here. We had the room to expand, so the answer was to put something into that space that people could sleep in. That's when it came to me. Cabooses."

Actually, it was sleeping cars that came to him first. But he found cabooses easier to find. He located six of them sitting in a freight yard in Reading, Pennsylvania. They all dated from the World War I era and all had become useless as the railroads phased them out. The little red cars at the end of the train had served many purposes in their time. They were offices, tool sheds and kitchens. According to McBride, they originated on the Auburn and Syracuse line, just a whistle away from here, in the 1840s, when conductors began storing equipment on the last boxcar of freights. Soon they started using a flatcar instead and put a little shanty on it. By the 1870s, the car had evolved into its familiar shape. But now all the functions once carried on in the caboose are done electronically. The tag-end cars have become anachronisms.

McBride managed to get the six cars as far as Wallace by train. There they were loaded onto flatbed trucks and ferried to Avoca. One was set up across the road as a diner, and five became motel units at the Goodrich. The cars are 33 feet long and can sleep five. McBride, with the aid of his father-in-law, took about four months to restore each car, retaining as much of the original as possible. Old tables, grab bars, stenciled messages have been left in place. Newer plexiglass windows were replaced with real glass. But modern bathrooms and beds were added.

The cabooses opened for business in 1986, and within a year McBride had an attraction that drew customers on its own. During the summer, reservations are usually filled weeks in advance.

"We're real popular with honeymooners," says McBride. "On their twenty-fifth anniversary, they probably wouldn't remember if they stayed in a Hilton or a Sheraton on their wedding night. But they'll sure remember where they were if they spend it in a caboose."

* * *

Great land schemes flourished in this part of New York in the eighteenth century. Sir William Pulteney headed a group called the London Associates, which purchased the land between the Genesee River and the line traced today by N.Y. 14. Capt. Charles Williamson, the land agent for the associates, envisioned Bath as the capital of this inland empire. He laid out an expansive community in 1793, promoted it throughout the country and within eight years had managed to lose $1 million. That earned him his dismissal, and Bath never quite became the major city of his dreams. But its main square still bears Pulteney's name, and a farmer's market is held there each Saturday morning in summer.

During the summer of 1779, Gen. John Sullivan brought terror to England's allies in the Iroquois Confederacy as his New England troops raged through this area, burning all the Indian lands they could reach. The expedition didn't accomplish its primary objective, the capture of Fort Niagara, but it resulted in something even more dangerous for the shattered Iroquois. It gave Sullivan's land-hungry soldiers a look at the fertile area, and after the war they could hardly wait to return.

Painted Post is on the site of a village wiped out by Sullivan's force. The name comes from an oak post found in the ruins. The Indian Heritage Museum tried to preserve remnants of that culture.

A short jog 2 miles east along N.Y. 17 brings you to **Corning**.

Although it isn't right on your route, you can cheat a little bit to take it in. After all, why miss nice things because of a technicality?

Glass companies began moving into this area right after the Civil War. The Chemung Canal connected Corning to the coal fields of northern Pennsylvania and cut down substantially on transportation costs of raw materials. But the great impetus to growth came with development of Thomas Edison's incandescent light. If the invention were to have a practical application, glass bulbs would have to be made in unprecedented quantities. The Corning ribbon machine solved that problem by impressing the shape of the bulb on the glass as it was being drawn out by rollers. Puffs of compressed air were then injected into this mold, and light bulbs rolled off the line to illuminate the nation. The glassworks here also cast the 200-inch mirror disk on the Mount Palomar Observatory telescope.

The Corning Glass Center contains one of the most extensive collections of antique glassware in the world, and there are demonstrations on everything from the making of Steuben crystal and industrial glass to the latest advances in optical fibers.

More Steuben is displayed at the Rockwell Museum, on N.Y. 17 at Cedar Street, in the former City Hall. More than 2,000 pieces are exhibited, but the top attraction is the collection of Western art, one of the greatest in the East. Market Street, the core of the old business district, has been restored to its turn-of-the-century appearance, making it an unusually pleasant place to wander and browse. The Gates-Rockwell Department Store carries copies of many of the items you'll see on display at the Rockwell Museum. Nearby, on West Pulteney Street, is the Patterson Inn, built in 1796 to attract settlers to the area and restored to its appearance of that era.

Returning to Painted Post and heading west, you at last pick up the start of the real U.S. 15. The meeting is brief. The road rushes into Pennsylvania through mountain scenery along the Tioga River, and we leave it there.

VISITING HOURS

NEW YORK

Avoca: Goodrich Center Motel, (607) 566-2216. North, on New York 415. Reserve caboose rooms well in advance.

Corning: Glass Center, (607) 974-8271. East from New York 415, on New York 17. Daily, 9–5, all year. Admission.
Rockwell Museum, (607) 937-5386. On New York 17 at Cedar St. Monday–Saturday, 9–5; Sunday, noon–5, all year. Admission.
Patterson Inn, (607) 937-5281. Off New York 17, at 59 W. Pulteney St. Monday–Friday, 10–noon and 1–4, all year. Admission.

Painted Post: Indian Heritage Museum, (607) 962-1382. East of New York 415, on W. Water St. Monday–Friday, 1–4, July–August. Tuesday and Thursday, 1–4, March–June and September–November. Admission.

Rochester: Margaret Strong Museum, (716) 263-2700. One block east of New York 15 (Clinton Ave.), on Manhattan Square. Tuesday–Saturday, 10–5; Sunday, 1–5, all year. Admission.
Mt. Hope Cemetery, (716) 461-3494. South, on New York 15. Dawn to dusk, all year. Free.
Highland Park Conservatory, (716) 244-4640. South, on New York 15, opposite Mt. Hope Cemetery. Daily, 10–5, all year. Free.

U. S. ROUTE 20

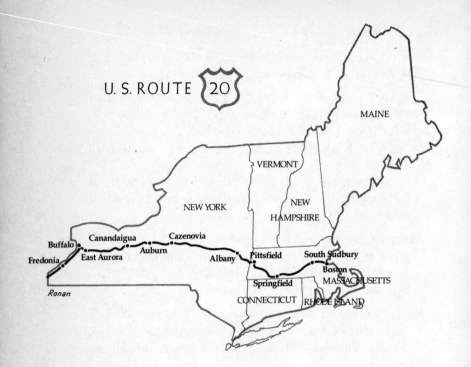

The Longest Road of All

U.S. 20

THE GREAT WESTERN ROAD

Boston, Mass., to Cardiff, N.Y.
* *312 miles*

This is the big one, America's longest highway, one of the two remaining bicoastal old roads. U.S. 20 starts in Boston, and by the time it reaches Newport, on the Pacific coast of Oregon, it will have traversed 3,000 miles, eleven states and four time zones. If it didn't break off for a few miles around Yellowstone National Park, its total mileage figure would be even longer. U.S. 30 also makes the coast-to-coast trip to an Oregon destination, but it starts significantly further west, in Atlantic City, New Jersey, so its final mileage figure is less. All the other old roads that once completed the transcontinental trek now falter, their routes co-opted in the West by the Interstates. Some of them barely make it across the Rockies, let alone to the Pacific.

All right, maybe I fudge a little bit when I call U.S. 20 bicoastal. It never gets within sight of the Atlantic, starting up on the western edge of Boston. Call me a liar. I think that's close enough. This first segment of the road runs across the Connecticut River Valley and the Berkshire Mountains of Massachusetts, then crosses the Hudson at the New York capital of Albany. From there it becomes the Great Western Road, the major overland route to the new western lands after the American Revolution. It weaves in and out with the Massachusetts Turnpike for part of the way, but mostly it is fast, uncluttered and very scenic.

* MILEPOSTS *

Numbers tend to change over the years, and U.S. 20 starts today in an outlying part of **Boston**. Historically, though, the roads that carried its number were Commonwealth Avenue and Beacon Street, running right to the heart of the city. That is the only conceivable place to begin a journey on such a fine old road. The drive begins, then, at the western edge of the Boston Public Garden, which is itself the western extension of Boston Common. The Garden took shape about two hundred years later, though. It was part of the mid-nineteenth-century urban engineering project that reclaimed the fens and turned Back Bay into a gracious, prestigious part of the city. Take a turn around the Garden, earnestly reading the labels on the rare trees to improve yourself. If the morning is nice, you may want to take a cruise on the city's beloved swan boats. Pay your respects to George Washington, whose mounted statue stands at the head of Commonwealth. Then let's get going.

Commonwealth is the main street of Victorian Boston, a wide boulevard lined with distinguished nineteenth-century buildings. It is a rarity in this city of narrow lanes that twist about with a fine disregard for logic or geometry. If you look at a map of Boston, you can see how unusual the grid pattern is in this part of the city. Five streets run east to west here, paralleling the Charles River: Beacon Street, on the north, to Boylston Street, which is the major commercial thoroughfare, on the south. Commonwealth was intended as a residential showcase, a grand boulevard in the European manner with a landscaped center mall, running from the Garden to Kenmore Square. It remains one of the country's stateliest urban vistas. At its western end, you are just two blocks from the country's coziest baseball stadium, Fenway Park. You may want to pay a call, if for no other reason than to stand on Landsdowne Street and gaze up at the backside of the most famous wall in sports.

Returning to Commonwealth, you pass through the midst of the Boston University campus in the blocks west of Kenmore Square. This city is famed as a center for higher education, and B.U. is not only an excellent school but also the largest in town, with an enrollment of 28,000 students. As you pass the university on the north, the border of the city of **Brookline** is to the south. Boston has tried to annex this suburb on six separate occasions and each time Brookline has fended it off. When Allston and Brighton succumbed and became part of Boston in 1874, Brookline alone remained independent, a slab of suburb that almost cuts Boston in half. Only a one-block strip of territory, between Commonwealth and the Charles, links the Brighton section of Boston with the rest of the city, east of Brookline.

Brookline was known as the Town of Millionaires around 1900 but has since built a reputation as a base for unapologetically liberal politicians, including the 1988 Democratic presidential nominee, Michael Dukakis. Brookline's most visited site is the birthplace of a man who combined both of the hallmark civic attributes. John F. Kennedy was born here in 1917, and the family home on Beals Street is now a National Historic Site. It has been restored to its appearance of that time and contains many family furnishings. Watch for the turnoff to the south, just past the B.U. campus. (The much larger museum and library devoted to the administration of the thirty-fifth president is in another part of Boston, south of the business district and off Interstate 93.)

Commonwealth dips to the south beyond Brookline, and U.S. 20 runs west along Brighton Avenue. The road swings across the Charles to enter Watertown. This was the first interior settlement of the Boston Colony, situated at the falls of the river. The U.S. Arsenal here has been in operation since 1816 and supplied much of the ammunition for the Union Army. Just beyond that is the

Perkins School for the Blind. Its first director was Dr. Samuel G. Howe, whose wife, Julia, wrote the words to the "Battle Hymn of the Republic." The martial images in her poem were inspired, no doubt, by the activities of her neighbors down the road. Helen Keller was a student at this school.

Just over the border in **Waltham** is Gore Place, a splendid Federal-period mansion. Built by Gov. Christopher Gore in 1805, the home is now a museum concentrating on artwork of that era. It is surrounded by a 40-acre park, which is also a museum of sorts, with rare farm animals wandering the cultivated fields. A bit farther along, at Lyman Street, is another of the town's historic homes, the Vale. The house was begun in 1793 and enlarged a century later, but it is the grounds that are most memorable. The greenhouses are classic nineteenth-century constructions, stocked with unusual tropical growths and grapevines transplanted from Hampton Court near London.

In an earlier era, this town was known for the making of Waltham watches, the best-selling brand in the country. The Charles River Museum of Industry, on Moody Street south of the highway, has exhibits on this and other products once manufactured in the area. Waltham is best known today as the seat of Brandeis University, a Jewish-founded nonsectarian school. The Rose Art Museum, on South Street, specializes in works of the twentieth century.

Let us be ecumenical. In **Weston**, the next town along the road, is Regis College, which houses the enormous stamp collection of the late Francis Cardinal Spellman. Its two galleries feature changing exhibits drawn from the 300,000-item collection. Regis is located on Wellesley Street, south of U.S. 20. Weston was also the home of the Rev. Edmund H. Sears (going all the way with the ecumenical angle) who wrote the carol "It Came Upon a Midnight Clear."

FOCUS

* * *

Henry Ford was a man of many obsessions, but one of his strongest was to recreate the world his motor car helped destroy. In his later years, his fortune assured and his company administered by others, this was his prime driving force. Near his birthplace in Dearborn, Michigan, just west of Detroit and a few miles from his gigantic Rouge manufacturing complex, he put together Greenfield Village. There he gathered historic structures and homes associated with the idols of his childhood and placed them in the setting of an idyllic, nineteenth-century town.

Near the village of **South Sudbury**, on this old road, Ford had another crack at doing that. But this time he was working with the original location of the Wayside Inn. This section of U.S. 20 is part of the northern cutoff of the Boston Post Road (see U.S. 1), the colonial lifeline between New York City and Boston. Near the town of Sturbridge, Massachusetts, the Post Road joined the future path of U.S. 20, and it is still identified by that numerical designation all the way into Boston. But in some places the original Post Road has become a quiet lane, several yards removed from the current highway. It is a case of an old road being shadowed by an even older road. This is what happens at South Sudbury. Just east of town, a turnoff (called Wayside Inn Road) is marked to the north. While U.S. 20 speeds on, this back road dives behind a grove of trees and in about a quarter of a mile comes to the Wayside Inn.

The full title is Longfellow's Wayside Inn. This seals the connection with the poet who stayed there, wrote about it, immortalized it and must share equal billing with Ford for preserving it. In Longfellow's time it was known as the Red Horse, and before that it was the How Hotel. The original was built in 1702 as a private home, but when David How added two rooms it became a lodging place for travelers on the Post Road.

How was a colonel in the local militia and led his men to Concord, which is just 7 miles north of here, for the big fight on the Nineteenth of April in '75. The date comes easily to mind, without resort to reference book, because of Longfellow's poem: "Listen, my children, and you shall hear/Of the midnight ride of Paul Revere,/On the Eighteenth of April in '75;/Hardly a man is now alive/Who remembers that famous day and year. . . ." The battle at Concord Bridge, of course, took place the day after the ride.

The poem first appeared in *Tales of a Wayside Inn,* published in 1863, which became an immediate best-seller. The poems were set in the form of stories told by travelers spending a night in the old inn. "The Midnight Ride of Paul Revere" quickly became the best known. Longfellow's poem explains why Revere's companion, Charles Dawes, who also rode that night to alert the countryside to British troop movements, is almost forgotten: his name just didn't have the right meter.

While Ford was attending grammar school in Dearborn, Longfellow's poem was a staple of classroom recitation. Half a century later, in the 1920s, when he heard the inn was in need of restoration, he decided to take on the job. He even turned the surrounding area into a mini-sized Greenfield Village. Just to the west of the inn is the Redstone School, moved to the site from the town of Sterling, about 10 miles west of here. Built in 1798, the school supposedly was the educational facility to which the little lamb followed Mary in another poem of note, by Sarah Josepha Hale. Historians dispute this, but it's well known what Ford thought about them. The school was used for classes here until 1952.

Ford also erected a reproduction of an eighteenth-century gristmill and a typical New England church on the grounds. But the Wayside Inn is the centerpiece. Even the best of restorations can run into problems, though. The inn did when it burned down in 1956. It was rebuilt, by the Ford Foundation, and it still calls itself America's Oldest Inn, but that year-long shutdown after the fire enables the Beekman Arms in Rhinebeck, N.Y. (see U.S. 9) to call itself America's Oldest Continuously Operating Inn. On such slight differences are reputations based.

Many of the rooms in the old inn are now open as a museum, including the original bar room operated by How, and the parlor, with many Longfellow mementoes. The Wayside also continues to operate as a full-service inn, with ten rooms for overnight guests and a restaurant open for lunch and dinner.

∗　∗　∗

The road angles southwest, as the suburbs of Boston merge imperceptibly with the suburbs of Worcester, the state's second-largest city. The dividing line is probably Interstate 495, which makes an enormous arc around the Boston area. Just past the next Interstate connection, which is I-395, is the cutoff south on Mass. 12 to **North Oxford**. This was the birthplace of Clara Barton, founder of the American Red Cross. Her experience as a nurse in military hospitals during the Civil War led her on a tireless campaign for better medical facilities during times of emergency. She organized the American National Committee in 1877, and four years later it grew into the American chapter of the International Red Cross, which had been founded in Switzerland in 1864. She headed the organization for the next twenty-three years, oversaw its effective use during the Spanish-American War and was lauded as the Angel of the Battlefield. She was born in North Oxford in 1821 and the home contains memorabilia of her life.

Henry Ford would have felt right at home in Old **Sturbridge** Village. Just a few miles along U.S. 20 from his restoration of the Wayside Inn is an entire New England town of the early nineteenth century, brought back to life with many of the same concepts Ford used in Greenfield Village. Structures from around New England were brought here and reassembled in the setting of a working community. Craftspeople go about their business just as they would in an actual town of the 1830s. There is a small farm on the premises, as well as shops, inns, tradespeople and other elements of small-town life of the time. The village opened in 1946 and is now the largest such living museum in the East.

Ford may also have felt a pang of recognition in **Springfield**, the state's third-largest city. This was the home of the Duryea Wagon Company, among the first American makers of automobiles with internal combustion engines. The work of the Duryea brothers was a goad to Ford's own experiments in Detroit. The Duryeas produced their first working vehicle here in 1895. That was one year before Ford's first successful model, four years before the first Olds plant opened in Detroit and eight years before the start-up of the first large-scale Ford plant. The automotive game was not destined to be in Springfield's future, though. Instead, another game, developed at about the same time as the Duryeas' car, left its mark.

Dr. James Naismith was a physical education instructor at the local YMCA Training School in 1891. He was asked by the head of his department to come up with a new activity to replace the tedium of calisthenics and marching drills. It had to take place in a gym, involve little physical contact and give everyone a chance to get into the action. So Naismith invented basketball. Nine players to a side and the first team to score was the winner. The sport has changed somewhat since then—especially the physical contact part—but it comes home to Springfield for its Hall of Fame. The basketball museum has a replica of Naismith's first court and items associated with the game's most famous players. It is located on Columbus Avenue, just a few blocks south of the historic route of U.S. 20 through the city along State Street.

U.S. 20 sweeps through town as a freeway now, but where it turns north, you should continue straight ahead on Boston Road to reach the middle of Springfield on the former route. Longfellow's poetry also touched this part of the highway; in "The Arsenal at Springfield" he drew musical images from the stacks of weapons he saw there. He compared them to a mighty organ, and the "organ of rifles" remains on display. This was the first federally commissioned armory in the country, started by direction of President Washington in 1794. From the flintlock to the M-14 of the Vietnam War, the Springfield rifles were known for quality. The armory closed in 1968 and is now a historic site, a museum of the guns that were made here. It is just east of downtown, on Federal Street, running north from State.

A bit farther down the road is the Quadrangle, composed of four museums, the city library and Christ Church Episcopal Cathedral. Arranged about this vast green square, which borders State on the north, are the Museum of Fine Arts, Springfield Science Museum, Connecticut Valley Historical Museum and

George Walter Vincent Smith Art Museum. You can easily spend a couple of days on this block alone. For a quick visit, though, the Smith Museum, which is housed in a beautiful Italian Renaissance–style chateau, is just the right size to make a relaxing respite from the road. The historical museum has many exhibits dealing with just the sorts of things you've been seeing on this road (and on U.S. 5, which passes through this area in another chapter). If you're with kids, I'd recommend the science museum.

Just a block north of State, on Main Street, is Court Square, which is the heart of the city's reborn downtown. Many of Springfield's public buildings front the square, and a campanile modeled on the one in St. Mark's Square in Venice is located here as well. The streets here are drier, though.

Across the Connecticut River, the highway becomes Westfield Street and leads to the town of that name. This was the westernmost settlement of the Massachusetts Bay Colony, the very edge of the frontier in 1669. Past here, U.S. 20 was the Western Road and led to the great unsettled beyond. Before you push beyond Westfield, though, stop at Stanley Park, just west of town. This is an especially pleasant place, with fine rose gardens, a Japanese garden, old bridges and waterwheels and a huge map of the United States and Canada made of inlaid slate.

Once past Huntington, the road starts to climb into the Berkshires, ascending to the pass at Jacob's Ladder at 2,300 feet. Nearby, in the town of **Becket**, is Jacob's Pillow, site of the country's oldest dance festival, founded by Ted Shawn. It runs from mid-June through Labor Day.

As the road approaches **Lee**, you'll find great views north toward October Mountain. Scenic train trips through the Berkshires to Great Barrington leave the depot here from Memorial Day through October. Once Lee was the leading manufacturer of cigarette paper in the country. Some papermaking still goes on here, as it has for almost two centuries. But it is primarily a tourist center.

From Lenox to Pittsfield, this road joins U.S. 7 and the attractions of the area can be found in that chapter.

The road turns due west again at Pittsfield and enters the heart of Shaker Country. Within a few miles of one another are the museum villages of **Hancock**, Massachusetts, and **New Lebanon**, New York. Just to the south, in **Old Chatham**, New York, is the largest collection of Shaker artifacts in the world.

The Shakers got their name from their belief that the gift of prophecy came from bodily agitation. Originating in France, they moved to England in the eighteenth century and combined with more radical elements of the Quakers. The major figure in their growth was a Manchester woman, Mother Ann Lee, who was also the greatest contributor to their decline. She became a Shaker in 1758 and in a few years proclaimed herself God the Mother. She also declared that henceforth sex would be unnecessary, because the world was coming to an end and further propagation of the human species was a waste of time. "A consummated marriage is a covenant with death and an agreement with hell," she said. Despite this, she managed to convert many people, including entire Baptist congregations. She moved to America in 1774, bringing most of her followers with her, and settled near Watervliet, New York. After her death ten years later, the Shakers decided to move into colonies, separated from the rest of the world. New Lebanon was the first in 1787, followed by Hancock in 1790.

The Shakers were tremendously industrious and inventive, and their villages thrived for a while. Shaker workmanship, especially in home furniture, was prized as early as the mid-nineteenth century, and Shaker antiques are extremely valuable today. The Shakers also introduced the idea of packaged seeds to America's gardeners, along with a host of farming innovations. But Mother Ann's teachings on celibacy made it impossible to sustain themselves and converts were increasingly hard to find. They even resorted to newspaper ads at one point. One by one, the settlements died out. Hancock Village, one of the last, survived until 1960.

Today Hancock Village is the best developed of the Shaker sites. There are twenty restored buildings, including an unusual round barn, and guides demonstrate Shaker crafts around the property. The New Lebanon settlement is undergoing development and will eventually contain twenty-five buildings, a few to open each year. The North Family Washroom is now open as a visitor's center. The Shaker Museum on N.Y. 66 in Old Chatham has twenty-three galleries devoted to original objects made by the Shaker communities in the region.

The road descends from the Shaker country in the Taconic Mountains to the valley of the Hudson River. It joins U.S. 9 near the town of East Greenbush, and the two highways cross the river on the Parker Dunn Bridge.

There have been many Gateways to the West in American history, but Albany is one of the oldest. It was where the Great Western Turnpike began, which the land-hungry and the dispossessed traveled in droves from the 1780s to the 1820s. Veterans of the great Sullivan-Clinton campaign against the Iroquois in western New York had seen that fertile land, and as soon as the war was over, made plans to pack up and move there. Tenants of the great Hudson Valley estates, locked into a semifeudal land-holding system, concluded that there was no hope of getting ahead until they moved west to find land of their own. Albany became a staging area for the Erie Canal when it opened in 1825, but the waterway diverted most of the traffic and development away from the overland route. The big cities grew up along the canal, so many of the towns along U.S. 20 retain the appearance of earlier times. Commerce took the canal, while charm meandered along the old road.

Albany itself grew up along a bluff on the Hudson's western bank. Although the town was settled under the auspices of the Dutch West India Company, there was always friction with the company agents in Manhattan. Even under the Dutch, the battle between New York City and upstate had begun, a struggle that shows no signs of abating three centuries later.

The city was the site of the Albany Convention of 1754, the first meeting to discuss colonial unity. Nothing would come of that for another twenty years or so, but it planted an irresistible idea in the minds of many participants, among them Benjamin Franklin. After the Revolution, the city's location at the transportation crossroads of the state won it the designation as state capital. That presence dominates the life of today's Albany.

The great government complex, Empire State Plaza, project of Gov. Nelson Rockefeller, changed the face of the city. U.S. 20 runs along its southern edge as Madison Avenue. Starting at Eagle Street, on the crest of the Hudson bluff, the Plaza spreads across 96 acres. It includes the New York State Museum, with a historical overview of the state's development; the contemporary art collection of the State of New York, displayed along concourse walls within the Plaza; the Institute for the Performing Arts, known as the Egg because of its distinctive shape; and the Corning Tower, with its forty-second-floor observation deck. The state capitol, at the northern edge of the Plaza, offers a startling contrast to the Plaza's modernist style. Built in the style of a high Victorian French chateau, it is noted for its spectacular interior staircase.

Turn south on Eagle Street and you'll see the Gothic revival Cathedral of the Immaculate Conception, built in 1852, with a lovely carved pulpit and stained glass. Just down the block is the Executive Mansion, residence of New York's governors.

The finest house in Albany, though, is a few blocks further south. The Schuyler Mansion was built in 1762 by Philip Schuyler, who would figure prominently in the British defeat at Saratoga fifteen years later. This Georgian house was at the center of Albany life in this period. Most of the great figures of the time visited. Washington was a guest, and so was John Burgoyne, the British general, after he surrendered at Saratoga and became a prisoner of war. Schuyler's daughter, Betsy, married Alexander Hamilton in this home. The house is now a State Historic Site and a museum of the Schuylers, whose holdings north of Albany made them one of the most influential of the patroon families.

U.S. 20 now continues west, past Washington Park and the wealth of Victorian homes built along its margin. Visible at the park's main gate is the imposing King Fountain, placed there in 1879. West of Albany, the highway runs along a ridge between Schoharie Creek and the Mohawk River, with the peaks of the Adirondacks and Catskills visible to the north and south.

Duanesburg was named for James Duane, mayor of Manhattan from 1789 to 1793, who managed to shift from Tory to patriot just in time to take advantage of the shifting fortunes of the war. His occupation as a land speculator furnished good training for this political high-wire act. Christ Episcopal Church was built by Duane and is one of the state's oldest unaltered religious structures.

At **Sharon Springs**, you enter a part of New York that was controlled by Tories and used as a base for raids throughout the war. The worst of these came on November 11, 1778, when Loyalist leader Walter Butler and his Iroquois allies, headed by Joseph Brant, fell upon the settlement of Cherry Valley. The town was wiped out, with forty-eight settlers massacred on the spot and more dying in captivity. The Tory threat didn't end until the summer of 1781 when the base at Sharon Springs was destroyed. There is now a museum at Cherry Valley, just south of the highway, with displays relating to the massacre. Victims of the raid are buried in the adjacent graveyard.

Both Sharon Springs and Richfield Springs developed as spas in the 1820s because of the white sulphur springs in the area. Richfield remains an especially pleasant spot, near the head of Canadango Lake, with an illuminated fountain in the town park.

The towns of Madison and Bouckville are nicely preserved communities, noted for their wealth of antique shops. But they are just a prelude to **Cazenovia**, a town that has won several awards for the excellence of its restoration efforts. This is probably the most atmospheric of the old towns along U.S. 20, and people come here just to stay in its old inns and walk its unspoiled, nineteenth-century streets.

The town was settled by John Lincklaen, land agent for the Holland Land Company. This organization controlled 3.3 million acres in western New York and was the chief dispenser of property to those who came across the Great Western Turnpike. The main sales office was much farther west, in the town of Batavia, but Lincklaen set up shop here, at the eastern edge of its holdings, to grab the travelers early. He arrived in 1793 and named the town in honor of the company's general agent, Theophile Cazenovia. Lincklaen was a cultivated man, deeply influenced by the art of the Italian Renaissance. He named his own home Lorenzo, in honor of the Medici, and in his off hours dreamed of turning Cazenovia into a new Florence. That never quite happened, but it's a nice town all the same. Lorenzo, built in 1807, is now a State Historic Site. It overlooks Cazenovia Lake and contains many original furnishings.

As the traffic of the turnpike ran past his front door in the town of Pompey, William G. Fargo concluded that a delivery service over this road between Albany and Buffalo would have a fair chance of success. The company he set up along that predecessor of U.S. 20 became the basis of the national express delivery system Wells-Fargo.

Pompey was also the site of a noted hoax, involving spurious Spanish stones dated 1589, but that was nothing compared to the fraud that originated in the nearby village of Cardiff. There a farmer named William Newell discovered mysterious remains buried on his property in 1869. The body was petrified. Not only that, it was 10 feet tall. Soon people were recalling Indian legends of a race of giants who once inhabited the land, and the curious flocked to Newell's farm to get a glimpse of this marvel. He started charging admission.

After a few months, a Syracuse businessman bought the giant, carted it home and syndicated shares in it, at $25,000 per eighth. Unfortunately, when the big money started flowing in, someone started asking for proof. So an examination was made, and the giant turned out to be made of gypsum. Moreover, the Chicago sculptor who had carved it for Newell turned up.

Oddly enough, the Cardiff Giant remained a popular attraction for years. People would pay good money to see a hoax, if the hoax was big enough. At the ultimate level, phony reproductions of this phony giant toured the hinterlands for years, taking in the gullible with a sort of double whammy of a gyp.

The real hoax now rests in the Farmer's Museum in Cooperstown, New York. You may want to double back along this road to Richfield Springs, then go south on N.Y. 28, to see it as well as the Baseball Hall of Fame and Museum. Or you can press onward to the second leg of this drive along U.S. 20.

VISITING HOURS

MASSACHUSETTS

Becket: Jacob's Pillow Festival, (413) 243-0745. North of U.S. 20, on Massachusetts 8. Tuesday–Sunday, late June–August. Call for schedule.

Boston: Public Gardens, (617) 323-2700. Head of Commonwealth Ave. Swan boats operate daily, April 19–late September, dawn–dusk. Admission.

Brookline: John F. Kennedy National Historic Site, (617) 566-7937. South of Commonwealth Ave., at 83 Beals St. Daily, 10–4:30, all year. Free.

Hancock: Shaker Village, (413) 443-0188. On U.S. 20. Daily, 9:30–5, Memorial Day–October. Admission.

Lee: Berkshire Scenic Railway, (413) 273-2872. Depot is off U.S. 20, at 41 Canal St. Weekends, June–October. Call for schedule and rates.

North Oxford: Clara Barton Birthplace, (508) 987-5375. South of U.S. 20, on Massachusetts 12. Friday–Sunday, noon–5, June–mid-October. Admission.

South Sudbury: Wayside Inn, (508) 443-8846. West on U.S. 20, then north on Wayside Inn Road. Museum area of inn open daily, 9–6, all year. Admission.

Springfield: Basketball Hall of Fame, (413) 781-6500. South of State St., at the Connecticut River, at 1150 W. Columbus Ave. Daily, 9–6, July–Labor Day; 10–5, at other times. Admission.

Federal Armory, (413) 734-8551. North of State St., on Federal St. Daily, 8–4:30, all year. Free.

Quadrangle Museums: Smith Art Museum, (413) 733-4214. Connecticut Valley Historical Museum, (413) 732-3080. Museum of Fine Arts, (413) 732-6092. Science Museum, (413) 733-1194. North of State St., between Elliot and Chestnut Sts. All buildings open, Tuesday–Sunday, noon–5, all year. Donation.

Sturbridge: Old Sturbridge Village, (508) 347-3362. West, on U.S. 20. Daily, 9–5, April–October; 10–4, November; closed Monday, at other times. Admission.

Waltham: Gore Place, (617) 894-2798. Off U.S. 20, just west of the Watertown town line, at 52 Gore St. Tuesday–Saturday, 10–5; Sunday, 2–5, mid-April–mid-November. Admission.

   The Vale, (617) 891-7095. North of U.S. 20, at 185 Lyman St. Thursday–Sunday, 10–4, all year. Admission.

   Charles River Museum of Industry, (617) 893-5410. South of U.S. 20, at the river, at 154 Moody St. Daily, 10–5; Sunday, 1–5, all year. Admission.

   Rose Art Museum of Brandeis University, (617) 736-2000. South of U.S. 20, on South St. Tuesday–Sunday, 1–5, September–June. Tuesday, Thursday, and weekends, 1–5, at other times. Free.

Weston: Cardinal Spellman Philatelic Museum, (617) 894-6753. South of U.S. 20, on Wellesley St., at Regis College. Tuesday–Thursday, 10–4; Sunday, 1–5, all year. Donation.

NEW YORK

Albany: Empire State Plaza, (518) 474-2418. North of U.S. 20, between Eagle and Swan Sts. Daily, 9–4, all year. Free.

   New York State Museum, (518) 474-5877. In Empire State Plaza. Daily, 10–5, all year. Free.

   State Capitol, (518) 474-2418. North side of Empire State Plaza. Daily, 9–4, all year. Free.

   Cathedral of the Immaculate Conception, (518) 464-4447. On U.S. 20 at Eagle St. Monday–Friday, 6–4; weekends, 8–6, all year.

   Schuyler Mansion, (518) 474-3953. South of U.S. 20 and west of New York 32, at 32 Catherine St.

Wednesday–Saturday, 10–5; Sunday, 1–5, April–December. Weekends only, at other times. Free.

Cazenovia: Lorenzo, (315) 655-3200. South, on New York 13. Wednesday–Saturday, 10–5; Sunday, 1–5, mid-May–mid-October. Free.

New Lebanon: Shaker Village, (518) 794-9500. On U.S. 20. Daily, 9:30–5, Memorial Day–Labor Day. Weekends only, September–October. Admission.

Old Chatham: Shaker Museum, (518) 794-9100. South of U.S. 20, on New York 66. Daily, 10–5, May–October. Admission.

Sharon Springs: Cherry Valley Museum, (518) 264-3303. West on U.S. 20, then south to Cherry Valley, at 49 Main St. Daily, 10–5, Memorial Day–mid-October. Admission.

THE FINGER LAKES

Cardiff to Ripley, N.Y.
* *232 miles*

As the course of empire made its way westward over this road, it carried with it many of the big ideas that stirred Americans in the nineteenth century. Abolitionism. Women's suffrage. Temperance. Utopia. You'll find them all, still rooted in the places to which the settlers carried them, on this drive through western New York. The road runs along the northern shore of the Finger Lakes, those five long and narrow bodies of water that look so much like the imprint of a gigantic hand upon the map. After ducking around Buffalo, the highway comes into view of Lake Erie. The last ridges of the Alleghenies come almost to the lakeshore here, and the highway runs along a ridge between hills and water. Shielded from the worst of winter's blasts by the hills, the shore turned out to be a fine place for cultivating grapes, and that crop still plays a big part in the area's economy.

* MILESTONES *

When the glaciers began their long retreat northward after the last Ice Age, they left mounds of debris behind that dammed up the outlets to a number of rivers. This trapped water became the five finger-shaped lakes that are the distinguishing feature of this part of New York. That's how the geographers explain it anyway. I prefer to believe the story that they're the hand of the Great Spirit, but I always was weak in science.

The Finger Lakes country begins at **Skaneateles**. In its early years, it was a well-known stop on the Underground Railroad, through which escaped slaves were shuttled to safety in Canada. In the 1840s, it was also the site of a utopian community led by John Anderson Collins, who believed in communism, vegetarianism and no-fault divorce, not necessarily in that order. This is an odd combination in any age and may explain why the community lasted just three years.

By the end of the century Skaneateles was established as a prime resort, and for many years Krebs Restaurant, established here in 1899, was accorded an almost mystic reverence as the best eating place in the state outside Manhattan. Many wealthy New Yorkers built summer estates around the lake and helped magnify its reputation, in the time-honored manner of vacationing New Yorkers everywhere. The Krebs is still in business, although the area draws most of its business now from upstate New York. Mid-Lakes Navigation Company offers cruises around this scenic body of water during the summer.

The great frozen north was very much on the minds of two **Auburn** residents in the nineteenth century. William Seward, the man who arranged the purchase of Alaska, was born here in 1816. He was secretary of state in the cabinets of Abraham Lincoln and Andrew Johnson, after serving two terms in the U.S. Senate. His purchase of Alaska from Russia in 1867 was not highly regarded at the time and for many years afterwards was referred to as Seward's Folly. He never seemed to suffer buyer's remorse, though, even if he didn't live long enough to see his judgment vindicated in spades. His house, now a museum, is filled with personal and political memorabilia, including a portrait of him signing the Alaskan papers. A bit further along South Street is the home of another northward-looking individual, Harriet Tubman. An escaped slave who repeatedly returned to life-threatening danger in the South to lead other slaves to freedom in Canada, her story is one of the most courageous in the Abolitionist struggle.

Also concerned with getting to and from Canada are the wild-fowl who flock to Montezuma National Wildlife Refuge, near the head of Cayuga Lake. The refuge is situated on the major East Coast flyway for migratory birds. There are observation towers and a self-guiding auto loop. Peak times for watching the flocks are March and November.

Harriet Tubman was one of several remarkable, strong-willed women who came to this part of New York around the same time. In fact, the town of **Seneca Falls** is considered the birthplace of the women's rights movement, whose first convention was held here in 1848. The town is now the home of the National Women's Hall of Fame. Amelia Jenks Bloomer was the first to arrive here, followed closely by Elizabeth Cady Stanton and Susan B. Anthony. Bloomer is remembered for many things, including her pioneering efforts to establish a uniform for suffragettes. The knee-length skirt worn over trousers was not original with her, having been traced back to much earlier utopian communities in Oneida, New York, and New Harmony, Indiana. But through her editorship of *The Lily,* the feminist newspaper, Bloomer became such a strong advocate of the outfit, as a symbolic casting off of dress restrictions placed on women by men, that her name became attached to the garb.

Stanton and Anthony were more dogged in their approach. Allies for better than fifty years, they sought to broaden the political base of feminism by allying it with the causes of abolition and temperance. (It's interesting to note, however, that slaves were freed and liquor stopped flowing before women got the vote.) Anthony lived in Rochester (see U.S. 15) but was a frequent guest at the Stanton home here. Stanton lived here from 1847 to 1862, and the house has been restored as a museum. Nearby is the Womens' Rights National Historical Center, with exhibits commemorating the landmark 1848 convention and other milestones on the way to sexual equality.

The State Barge Canal runs right through Seneca Falls and you can observe the operation of the hydraulic locks, near Bayard and Seneca.

When farmer James W. Johnson left **Waterloo** for the Civil War, he plunged his scythe into a poplar sapling and said, "Let it hang there 'til I get back." Johnson was killed in 1864 and the blade is still visible in the grown tree's trunk. That may have been the impetus behind observance of the first Memorial Day, honoring the Civil War dead, held here in 1865. There are some disputants to the title; both Columbus, Mississippi, and Boalsburg, Pennsylvania, claim to have held earlier tributes. But Waterloo's claim comes by presidential proclamation, which gives it a ring of authority, if not authenticity. The home in which the initial Memorial Day was planned is now a museum with exhibits relating to the holiday.

Many early land promoters turned to Europe for inspiration when they named their towns. Most of the time, the name had absolutely nothing to do with the setting of the new community. But when land agent Charles Williamson planned a town at the head of Seneca Lake for the Pulteney Company of London, he knew exactly what he was about when he called it **Geneva**. Built on a terrace above the water, Geneva may be the prettiest of the lakeside towns along this route. Comparing it to its Swiss namesake isn't that much of a stretch. The stateliest of its many stately homes is Rose Hill, built in 1839 in the Greek Revival style by Robert S. Rose. In keeping with the feminist theme that runs so strongly along this route, Hobart College, in Geneva, was the first school to grant a medical degree to a woman. That distinction went to Elizabeth Blackwell in 1849.

The countryside around the Finger Lakes is especially lovely in spring, when its acres of fruit orchards come into bloom. This part of the drive is amply endowed with them.

The Granger family of **Canandaigua** had a lock on the office of postmaster general. Gideon Granger, who built his handsome Federal-style home here in 1816, held the job under Thomas

Jefferson and James Madison. His son, Francis, who twice ran for president as the anti-Mason candidate, contented himself instead with dad's old post under William Henry Harrison. He distinguished himself chiefly by cleaning out every Democrat he could find in the nation's post offices. Things like that are what gave the spoils system a bad name. The Granger Homestead is a museum of four generations of the family and also includes a collection of horse-drawn wagons. Just north of town, on N.Y. 21, are the Sonnenberg Gardens, a country estate surrounded by nine Victorian formal gardens.

You now have a choice. Just west of here, the road splits. U.S. 20 continues due west, through flat country, all the way to the outskirts of Buffalo. Highway 20A bends to the south, through a much hillier landscape. It winds around a bit and also does a good deal of climbing and descending, a roller coaster style of road. It is by far the more interesting choice. If you want to ignore my advice, though, I can tell you that on U.S. 20, East Bloomfield was the original home of the Northern Spy apple, so named by an orchardman with distinct Abolitionist sympathies.

On 20A, you will soon come to the northern edge of Honeoye Lake, one of the four Little Finger Lakes, which carry on the digit configuration to the west. (Another one is Conesus Lake, which you'll pass in a few miles more in Lakeville.) There are some geodesic domes along the road near **Center Honeoye**, under which are exhibits of pottery and its making.

Geneseo looks down from a ridge upon the scenic Genesee Valley. This is where the Seneca ceded what remained of their lands in the Big Tree Treaty of 1797. There is a small historical museum in Geneseo, containing the only intact Shaker prayer stone in existence. The museum is housed in a former cobblestone school. Just west of town is the place where the Iroquois got in their best licks during the Sullivan raid. The Boyd-Parker Shrine commemorates two colonial scouts who were captured and put to death here. Cuylerville, the next village along the road, marks the western limit of the expedition's advance.

The road rolls up and down, through the town of **Warsaw**, with its museum in the home of Abolitionist Congressman Seth Gates.

It descends Buffalo Hill past Varysburg, crosses Tonawanda Creek and heads through the dairy country around Wales Center. Look for the farm with the plastic cows out front, a case of a dairyman who simply couldn't get enough of his favorite animal.

FOCUS

* * *

Horatio Alger was alive and well in turn-of-the-century America, a time when it was widely believed that determination, straight dealing and a measure of pluck could accomplish anything. Moral exhortations were a common part of public discourse. Private behavior in business and politics may have fallen a bit short of the most elevated standards, but for popular consumption the ideal of right behavior was celebrated as the norm.

That may explain why a short tract by a writer named Elbert Hubbard, "A Message to Garcia," sold 42 million copies in the few years after it was written in 1899. The New York Central Railroad distributed it on all passenger trains. Hubbard was hired to lecture on the Orpheum Circuit and became a nationally syndicated columnist with the Hearst newspapers. The article had appeared in a small paper Hubbard published, *The Philistine,* and it managed to hit all the right gongs and buzzers as a moral sermon, a celebration of American manhood and a paean to the recently concluded Spanish-American War.

It told how an American officer overcame incredible hardships to get a vital bit of intelligence to Cuban rebel leader Calixto Garcia. Hubbard concluded that if all Americans did likewise in their daily tasks, we would be unstoppable. Later a movie was based on this article, and almost a century later the article was still being reprinted and distributed as a model for emulation.

"A Message to Garcia" made Hubbard rich and famous, and it was to the village of **East Aurora** that much of this wealth and celebrity flowed. Hubbard is best described as a self-styled eccentric, and he was indeed an individual with strong ideas and a flair for getting them across. He grew up in Illinois, but came to Buffalo as a teenager to work in the soap business, where his knack for promotion and advertising made him a top executive. But during a trip to England in 1892, when he was thirty-six years old, he met William Morris. A strange mix of artist, philosopher and socialist theorist, Morris had founded the arts and crafts movement as a reaction to industrialization and set out to introduce medieval crafts techniques into contemporary art and furniture. Hubbard was won over by his ideas and determined to introduce them to America.

He quit his job and set up *The Philistine* as an arts and crafts organ. The magazine was a small success, and soon Hubbard had the funds to open a print shop in East Aurora. Quality printing was one of Morris's top priorities, and for the next few years Hubbard's Roycroft Press turned out a variety of well-made books and magazines. But after "Garcia," Hubbard became a wealthy man, and his wealth enabled him to carry out the rest of the project. He built an entire Roycroft campus in this village. Furniture, leather and copper shops were installed alongside the press, and craftsmen were encouraged to move in and teach their skills. An inn was built for visitors, and guest lecturers were brought to speak at the Roycroft Chapel. For several years, the Roycroft products enjoyed a vogue in America, and the movement became a significant force in domestic furnishings and architecture.

While on his way to Europe in 1915 to report on World War I, Hubbard and his wife went down on the Lusitania. His son, Elbert Hubbard II, tried to carry on his father's work but was eventually forced out of business by the Depression in 1938.

For almost forty years, the campus in the heart of this Buffalo suburb was deserted. Then a reexamination of Hubbard's ideas blossomed into a Roycroft renaissance, and in 1976 restoration of the old campus and its techniques began. Its fourteen buildings became a National Historic Site, and several of the crafts shops were reopened. The Roycroft Inn, built in 1903, has also been restored, and the chapel is now the East Aurora Town Hall, with a museum on the ground floor. Another museum dedicated to Hubbard's work with the Roycrofters is located two blocks east in the village hall.

East Aurora is also the home of Fisher-Price Toy Company, which moved into town just about when the original Roycrofters were moving out. Vidlers, an old-fashioned five and dime store on Main Street, stocks a large assortment of their toys, and East Aurora celebrates a Toy Festival on the last Sunday of August.

As if all this weren't enough, East Aurora was also the home of Millard Fillmore. The future president moved into a small brick cottage on Shearer Street with his bride, Abagail Powers, in 1826. He was twenty-six at the time, just starting a career that would take him to Congress and, eventually, to one of the more obscure presidencies. He was president number thirteen, serving from the death of Zachary Taylor in 1850 until he failed to retain the Whig party nomination in 1852. He ended his career as a Know-Nothing candidate in 1856. But this green-shuttered little house was his honeymoon cottage, secluded from the turmoil of his times and the jeers of posterity.

* * *

Now called Quaker Road, U.S. 20A heads into the suburb of Orchard Park. Close readers of the sports pages will recognize the name as the location of Rich Stadium, home of professional football's Buffalo Bills. This road is one of the stadium's main access routes, so it would be best to avoid passing through immediately before or after a home game.

You finally rejoin U.S. 20 south of Buffalo and drive on a ridge above Lake Erie with a succession of lakeside suburbs below. The highway passes through the Cattaraugus Indian reservation, near Irving and dips briefly down to the lakeside near the town of Silver Creek. This is the start of the Concord grape belt, a crop introduced to the area in 1824. In the 1890s, when a local dentist began experimenting with unfermented grapes to produce a non-alcoholic beverage, growth really took off. The inventive dentist was Thomas B. Welch, and you'll encounter the grape juice empire he founded in a few more miles.

Welch was strongly encouraged in his work by activities in **Fredonia**. This is yet another of those towns that seemed to get swept up in the great crusades of the nineteenth century. Here was the first chapter of the Grange, the national organization dedicated to improving the lot of farmers. Officially known as the Patrons of Husbandry, the Grange grew up after the Civil War as a social and insurance organization, but its growth coincided with concerns over monopolistic practices by the railroads and food processors. Soon the Grange had become a major political force set in opposition to those groups. The idea originated in Minnesota, but the first chapter was chartered in Fredonia in 1868.

Five years after that Dio Lewis came to town and really shook things up. He was a temperance lecturer, and when he hit Fredonia in 1873 he found an eager audience. His plea to women to shut down the local saloon produced dramatic immediate action, and by the end of the day the local pharmacist had been convinced to cut off the sale of alcohol for medicinal purposes. The shutdowns sparked a series of imitations all over the country, in the first major direct action temperance crusade. As a result, the Women's Christian Temperance Union was founded here to lead the battle against drink. It emerged victorious forty-five years later with Prohibition and all the good works that accomplished. The WCTU was a major influence on Welch, who was working just down the road in Westfield. The Darwin R. Barker Museum in Fredonia contains exhibits about all these colorful chapters of the town's past. Fredonia was the first town to be lit by natural gas, coming from fields opened here in 1821.

As if to spite the WCTU, some vineyard owners continue to ignore Dr. Welch's work and use the local grapes to make wine. Vetter Vineyards is just east of **Westfield**, and Johnson Estate Wines is to the west. Both have tasting rooms. The McClurg mansion, built in 1820 on Main Street in town, is a museum of the area with exhibits on local history. Nearby is a monument to the Concord grape, and some of Welch's earliest production plants are also in the vicinity.

From Westfield, there are two short side trips that make a fitting close to this drive. For the first, head north to Barcelona on New York 394. Its harbor has one of the most secluded and picturesque lighthouses on the Great Lakes. The Barcelona Light was also the first in the world to be lit by natural gas, pumping it from the fields in Fredonia in 1828.

The other side trip is the perfect culmination to all the idealism and social uplift that symbolize this stretch of U.S. 20. A drive of 10 miles south on N.Y. 394 from Westfield brings you to **Chautauqua**. The Institution here, founded in 1874, was one of the great forces for carrying cultural and educational programs around the country in the days before anyone ever heard of mass media. The traveling Chautauqua shows were a major attraction in rural America until the 1930s.

It no longer takes to the road, but the Institution still holds annual summer programs here, on the shores of Lake Chautauqua. The surrounding colony of Victorian cottages on the lakeside grounds is worth a visit even if you don't feel a particular need to be educated or uplifted. There is no entrance fee to the grounds if you sign up for a boat ride aboard the Gadfly III, which leaves from the landing near the bell tower.

VISITING HOURS

NEW YORK

Auburn: Seward House, (315) 252-1283. South of U.S. 20, on New York 34, at 33 South St. Tuesday–Saturday, 1–5, April–December. Admission.

Harriet Tubman House, (315) 253-2621. South of U.S. 20, at 180 South St. Call for appointment.

Montezuma National Wildlife Refuge, (315) 568-5987. West, on U.S. 20. Daily, dawn–dusk, all year. Free.

Canandaigua: Granger Homestead, (716) 394-1472. North of U.S. 20, at 295 N. Main. Tuesday–Saturday, 10–5; Sunday, 1–5, April–December. Closed Sunday in May, September–October. Admission.

Sonnenberg Gardens, (716) 394-4922. North, on New York 21. Daily, 9:30–5:30, mid-May–mid-October. Admission.

Center Honeoye: Geodesic Pottery Domes, (716) 229-2980. On U.S. 20A. Daily, 9–5, all year. Free.

Chautauqua: Chautauqua Institution, (716) 357-6200. South of U.S. 20 from Westfield, on New York 394. July–August. Call for schedule of events. Lake cruises leave from grounds, every day but Monday. Call (716) 753-2753 for schedule.

East Aurora: Elbert Hubbard Museum, (716) 652-5362. On U.S. 20A, at Main and Paine Sts. Wednesday and weekends, 2–4, June–October. Donation.
  Millard Fillmore House, (716) 652-1252. North of U.S. 20A, at 24 Shearer Ave. Wednesday and weekends, 1–5, June–mid-October. Free.

Fredonia: Barker Museum, (716) 672-2114. On U.S. 20, at 20 E. Main St. Tuesday and Thursday–Saturday, 2:30–4:30, all year. Free.

Geneseo: Historical Museum, (716) 226-6894. On U.S. 20A, at 30 Center St. Thursday and Sunday, 2–5, May–October. Donation.

Geneva: Rose Hill, (315) 789-3848. East on U.S. 20, and south on New York 96A. Monday–Saturday, 10–4; Sunday, 1–5, May–October. Admission.

Seneca Falls: Women's Rights Historical Park, (315) 568-2936. Off U.S. 20, at 116 Fall St. Daily, 9–5, June–September. Closed weekends at other times. Donation.
  Women's Hall of Fame, (315) 568-2991. At 76 Fall St. Monday–Saturday, 9–5; Sunday, noon–5, April–November. Closed Sunday, at other times. Admission.
  Elizabeth Stanton House, (315) 568-2991. Adjacent to historical park, at 32 Washington St. Daily, 9–5, June–September. Donation.

Skaneateles: Lake Cruises, (315) 685-5722. Leave from U.S. 20, on the lakefront in town. Mid-May–mid-September. Call for schedule and rates.

Warsaw: Gates House Museum, (716) 786-3515. Off U.S. 20A, on Perry Ave. Sunday, 2–5, July–August. Donation.

Waterloo: Memorial Day Museum, (315) 539-9611. On U.S. 20, at 35 E. Main St. Tuesday–Friday, 10–5, Memorial Day–Labor Day. Free.

Westfield: McClurg House, (716) 326-2977. On U.S. 20 (Main St.). Tuesday–Saturday, 10–noon and 1–4; Sunday, 2–5, July–August. Closed Sunday, mid-April–June, September, October. Admission.

Vetter Vineyards, (716) 326-3100. East on U.S. 20. Daily, 10–8, May–October; 10–6, November–January.

Johnson Estate Winery, (716) 326-2191. West on U.S. 20. Tours, daily, 10–5:30, July–August. Tasting, daily, 10–6, all year. Free.

U. S. ROUTE 44

MAINE

VERMONT

NEW
HAMPSHIRE

NEW YORK

MASSACHUSETTS

Plymouth

Norfolk   Conventry

Ronan   Poughkeepsie

Providence

Ellenville   Hartford   RHODE ISLAND

CONNECTICUT

West from Plymouth Rock

U.S. 44

Plymouth, Mass., to Kerhonkson, N.Y.
* *242 miles*

This road was built as a sort of back street alternative to the major highways of U.S. 6 and 20 connecting the Massachusetts coast to the New York highlands. It touches highway 6 briefly in the cities of Providence and Hartford but mostly sticks to the less traveled way. It crosses an especially scenic portion of northern Connecticut, then heads into the Catskills of New York. It also follows the route of the first road west from the Plymouth colony, the King's Highway, which gives it a special place in the story of the American frontier.

The road begins as Samoset Street in Plymouth, one block away from the ocean and a few hundred yards northwest of Plymouth Rock.

FOCUS

* * *

When we talk about **Plymouth**, we must inevitably talk about beginnings. There were European settlements before Plymouth in what would become the United States: in Virginia, in Florida, in the southwestern deserts. But it is from Plymouth that the stream of national identity flows. English-speaking people were living in Jamestown eleven years before the Pilgrims hit the beach here. But Virginia never developed a literary tradition to celebrate its beginnings, nor did it have a Thanksgiving to provide a divine link to our national history. Thanksgiving was first proclaimed a national holiday by Abraham Lincoln during the Civil War. It was done, quite obviously, to establish the Massachusetts experience as the legitimate foundation of America, giving it primacy above that of Virginia and the South as the more genuine national root.

So the Pilgrims have entered a mythic realm in our history. Everything about them is so colored by legend that it is hard to think of them as actual human beings. From the rock they first stepped on to the hill they first climbed, their every activity in Plymouth is tied to the distant dawn of our history. That's why it is such a shock to walk into Pilgrim Hall and see their belongings, the things they owned and used. Pilgrim Hall itself dates back to the bicentennial of their landing, 1820, and is now the oldest public museum in America. It is located just one block south of U.S. 44 as the road begins its journey west.

Here is William Brewster's chair; there is Miles Standish's sword; over here, the battle ax belonging to his intended go-between, John Alden. The Bible of William Bradford, elected governor of the colony thirty times, is here. Even the tiny cradle used to rock Peregrine White, the first American-born child to survive into adulthood, has found its way into a display case.

It is the very plainness of these articles that makes the impact. Because here is evidence of the ordinary, everyday life carried on by men and women who would become legends. The boast that one's ancestors came over on the Mayflower has become an American synonym for snobbery. The heroic paintings of the

Pilgrims, also part of Pilgrim Hall, give them a larger than life quality. (Since many of these paintings were commissioned by their descendants, that is understandable.) But as your gaze comes down from the stern figures in the paintings and rests on the homely implements in the display cases, a balance is restored.

That balance is all the more important when contrasted to the tourist circus that Plymouth becomes in season. Even the local guidebooks point out that the big boulder under the portico on the waterfront is only the "traditional" landing place of the Pilgrims. There is no possible way of knowing for sure. It looks the part, though. The rock was first identified in 1741 by a ninety-five-year-old man who said his father had pointed it out to him. But his father had arrived in Plymouth in 1623 and received his information secondhand. In 1834, the rock was moved to Pilgrim Hall, then into a warehouse and finally, in 1921, back here, near what is thought to be its original site. If for nothing else, the length of time for which this rock has been identified as Plymouth Rock gives it some interest.

Around the rock are the usual collection of wax museums, souvenir stands and restaurants bearing the names of prominent members of the first landing party. The tour buses disgorge passengers. Signs for Cranberry World warn that the attraction "will boggle your mind." After all this, Pilgrim Hall is a restorative.

Plimouth Plantation is an authentic recreation of the first settlement, but it is a bit off our route. However, it is assuredly worthwhile to make the 3-mile drive south on Mass. 3A to see the costumed interpreters going about their daily lives in the Plymouth of 1627. The Plantation also administers the full-scale reproduction of the *Mayflower* anchored back near Plymouth rock. There are more costumed guides aboard, portraying members of the crew and passengers of the original. The replica was built in England and sailed to America in 1957.

Coles Hill, an affecting place to visit, is just across Water Street from the rock. This is where the Pilgrims secretly buried their dead during the first terrible winter, so the Indians would not know how many had perished. A sarcophagus contains many of the remains. On this hill, as well, is a statue of Massasoit, the

Indian leader who befriended the Pilgrims and, with his people, attended the first Thanksgiving. It was one of his sons who led the last futile resistance to the tide of European settlement across New England, half a century later, in King Philip's War. But by then the land was no longer theirs.

* * *

William Bradford may have held the office thirty times, but the first governor of Plymouth Colony was John Carver, and the first town inland along U.S. 44 was named for him.

Another small museum of Pilgrim belongings is nearby in **Middleboro**. The Eddy Homestead is north of the highway on Mass. 105 and contains the possessions of the brothers John and Samuel Eddy, who came over on the *Mayflower*.

Taunton had an ironworks as early as 1652. The town was also among the first to honor an actual (as opposed to mythical) woman on its seal. Elizabeth Poole traded with the Indians here in the settlement's early days. She was depicted on the seal with the inscription, "A woman was the leader of the things accomplished." The Old Colony Museum shows off a variety of historical items, including a cannon used to disperse rioters during Shay's Rebellion of 1786. "Away with your whining," said the judge whose court was threatened with disruption at the time. "I will hold this court if I hold it in blood. I will sit as a judge or die as a general." This statement seemed to have the desired effect. (For more on Shay's Rebellion and its impact, see U.S. 202.)

The highway crosses the state line into Rhode Island and enters East Providence as Taunton Avenue. Roger Williams, the founder of Rhode Island, was banished from Massachusetts in 1635 for disputing the right of civil authorities to punish religious infractions or to dispense land that belonged to Indians. Warned that he was about to be seized and sent back to England, Williams instead escaped to the south, to the eastern bank of the Seekonk River in what is now East Providence. Told that the Plymouth colony claimed that land, Williams and four fellow dissenters obligingly paddled up the river to find a likely spot on the opposite bank. Seeing an Indian standing on the shore, they greeted him with a hearty "What cheer, friend," and made for the spot, taking it as a divine sign. They named their settlement for "God's merciful providence" and obtained the grant for it in 1638. A monument on Gano Street, just north of the U.S. 44 bridge across the Seekonk, marks the spot of this first landing. The road is an expressway at this point, but just as it reaches the Providence River U.S. 44 turns off to become South Main Street.

This core of historic **Providence** is a wonderful walking area. You can easily spend days strolling through the history and fine commercial restoration along South Main and the adjoining streets, Water and Benefit. Watch for the Bayard Ewing Building at 231 South Main, restored in 1977 as a project of the Rhode Island School of Design architecture department.

Leave the car as close to the corner of South Main and College as you can manage. Just west of here is Market Square, centered as it has been since 1773 by Market House, the great meeting place of colonial Providence. You will find two historical markers as you walk around here. One commemorates the Providence Tea Party, which, though important, was not as dramatic as the one in Boston. (No disguised Indians whooping as they dropped the cargo into the waves. The bags were simply piled in the square, tarred and set afire.) The other marker recalls the Great Gale of 1815, one of the worst New England hurricanes on record, when the entire square was under water.

To the east on College is the museum of the Rhode Island School of Design. As one of the top art schools in the country, its museum is among the more important smaller collections. Market House is the headquarters of its graphic design department. Especially noteworthy in the museum is the Pendleton House wing, with its outstanding collection of colonial furniture. The entrance is on Benefit at College.

Back on Main and one block up, at Waterman, is the First Baptist Church, built in 1775. Almost flawless in the simplicity and execution of its design, it is the prototype of every picture postcard colonial church you've ever seen. This Baptist congregation is the oldest in the country, established by Roger Williams in 1638. The building was the masterpiece of architect Joseph

Brown. Among the interior features, pay special notice to the Waterford chandelier, just seventeen years younger than the building.

At South Court Street you'll come to the rear of the Old State House, meeting place of the Rhode Island legislature from 1762 to 1900. Rhode Island always went its own way, and independence from Britain was declared here in May 1776, two months to the day before the rest of the colonies got around to it in Philadelphia. On the far side of Main is the Roger Williams National Memorial, marking the core of the original Providence settlement. A visitor's center runs a brief slide show on Williams's life and work.

At Smith Street, U.S. 44 turns west to cross the river. Here is the Cathedral of St. John, the oldest Episcopal congregation in the state, built in 1810 and renovated in 1967. The adjacent graveyard is worth exploring. The road now continues west on Smith Street through the Providence suburbs and past the Waterman reservoir, near Greenville.

In the area around **Chepachet**, the abortive Dorr's Rebellion was played out. It was a comic opera affair, made serious only by the principle that propelled it. Thomas W. Dorr, reacting to a property requirement in the Rhode Island constitution that disenfranchised about half the state's population, formed the People's Party in 1841 to demand universal male suffrage. Dorr declared the elected government illegal and had himself inaugurated governor in May 1842. He then organized a march on Providence to seize the state armory, but that fizzled out when it was discovered that the artillery pieces accompanying the marchers didn't work. The state government then decided the rebellion had gone far enough and dispatched militia to Chepachet. Dorr sent out a rallying cry for troops, but only fifty men showed up. The militia fired a few volleys, killed a cow and arrested Dorr. He was tried for treason and imprisoned for a year, but during his incarceration universal male suffrage was approved by the state. The Dorr Monument is just south of town, near the battlefield site. The biggest draw in Chepachet now is the Brown and Hopkins Country Store. It has operated here since 1809 and claims to be the country's oldest country store. The Glocester Town Historical Society is located next door in the former Job Armstrong Store.

The country gets a bit hilly as you near the Connecticut line, although hilly may be too strong a word. Durfee Hill, just south of the highway near the border, was once thought to be the highest point in Rhode Island at 806 feet above sea level. But closer observations gave that distinction instead to Jerimoth Hill, 6 feet higher and 4 miles south.

The northwestern corner of Connecticut was the home turf of Israel Putnam, the state's foremost leader in the Revolution. The first town in the state along this route was named for him. Cargill Falls powered industrial growth in Putnam and you can catch a glimpse of them from the bridge across the Quinebaug River.

Putnam lived in Brooklyn (see U.S. 6) as an adult, but he spent his boyhood around **Pomfret**. And an eventful boyhood it was. At Mashamoquet Brook State Park, southwest of town, you can still see the wolf den into which Putnam was lowered by rope to battle a marauding wolf to the death. Putnam won. Also in this park is the Brayton Mill and Marcy Blacksmith Museum, the last mill standing in Pomfret. It now houses the tools of three generations of Marcy smiths.

The road heads west through lightly populated forest, some of the most open territory in this thickly populated state. At Mansfield Depot, take a swing south on Conn. 32 to Eagleville, then west on Conn. 275 to **Coventry**. There is a statue of Nathan Hale in New London, where he worked as a schoolteacher until the Revolution called him away from class. It is a duplicate of the one that stands in front of City Hall in New York, where he was hanged as a spy by the British in September 1776. His home, though, was in Coventry. At least, it is called the Nathan Hale Homestead, although he only lived there for a matter of weeks. It was built by his father, Richard, the year of his son's death, and it is believed Nathan helped to build the wall and flagstone court. His family lived there for sixty more years, but Hale is buried in an unmarked grave in Manhattan. The house contains many family belongings.

If you are more fond of herbs than history, Coventry has an

even more arresting stop for you. Caprilands Herb Farm consists of a colonial farmhouse surrounded by thirty gardens containing more than three hundred varieties of herbs. Think of it as the Herb Hall of Fame. A bookstore stocks information on everything you ever wanted to know about the topic. Luncheons with guided tours of the gardens are available by advance reservation only.

Conn. 31 will return you to the main road, which joins U.S. 6 at Bolton Notch. As it climbs the notch, watch for Squaw Cave, named in memory of an Indian woman who was shot for chopping firewood on the Sabbath. This happened quite a while ago, of course. Such energetic activity on any day of the week now would merit a gubernatorial commendation.

Beyond Manchester (see U.S. 6) the roads divide, and U.S. 44 continues past Wickham Park, an exceptionally pleasant spot, containing many gardens and walking trails, on the former estate of a local industrialist.

The road now heads through the middle of **East Hartford**, an industrial suburb of the state capital. This was an early center of the airline industry, and the Pratt and Whitney division of United Technologies Corp. still has a large engine plant here. North of town is the remnant of the state's tobacco-raising region in the Connecticut Valley. The Edward E. King Museum on Main Street has exhibits that trace the impact of these two local products on the world.

There are fine views of the Hartford skyline as the road approaches the Connecticut River and the Bulkeley Bridge. After a short run as a freeway, it turns off and runs northwest through the city as Albany Avenue into pleasant residential areas of West Hartford. Soon it ascends Talcott Mountain, the ridge that closes in the capital area on the west, where you'll find views back to Hartford from the crest.

Avon foresaw explosive industrial growth for itself when the Farmington Canal was completed in the 1820s, linking it to the Connecticut River. But landslides kept closing the canal and it was finally abandoned. So Avon became an exclusive residential suburb instead. The only explosiveness in the picture now is in a factory that once made them and has been converted into the

Farmington Valley Arts Center. Several studios and galleries are located in the center, just west of town on the highway.

This stretch of road is haunted by a headless horseman, although he is not nearly as celebrated as the decapitated ghost who galloped through Sleepy Hollow (see U.S. 9). This rider is a French paymaster who was on his way from Hartford to Saratoga to deliver money to his country's troops during the Revolution when he was murdered at an inn near **Canton**. He now comes riding out of the darkness at odd intervals looking for the purloined payroll. This could be disconcerting, but I wouldn't let it stop you from making a stop at Roaring Brook Nature Center, north of Canton on Conn. 179. It has several miles of trails, natural and historical exhibits and lookout towers.

Now you are entering the Litchfield Hills, Connecticut's corner of content. **Winsted** is noted for the beauty of its mountain laurel and holds a festival to show it off on the third week in June. The town of Riverton, where the famed Hitchcock chairs have been made since 1826, is a bit north of our route, but the Solomon Rockwell House in Winsted has several examples of Hitchcock artistry, as well as other furniture made in the surrounding area.

The road continues through beautiful hill country to **Norfolk**, one of the state's highest towns, at 1,230 feet. Haystack Mountain is just north of town, on Connecticut 272, and a state park road leads to the summit, with vistas across the entire northern half of Connecticut. On clear days, you can see all the way to Long Island Sound. Dennis Hill is just south of town on Connecticut 272, and you'll find another lookout there, in slightly more exalted surroundings (it was the pavilion of a former country estate). Norfolk itself has an especially pleasant Green with a small museum housed in a former boys' academy built in 1840. During the summer months, chamber music concerts are a staple of Norfolk life, as they have been since 1899, when they were founded by the Stoeckel family. They were moved to a music shed on the family estate seven years later, which is still their setting today. It is an easy drive from here to the Tanglewood festival in Lenox in the Massachusetts Berkshires, and many people choose to combine both musical experiences by basing themselves in this more secluded town.

Now U.S. 44 runs along the Blackberry River to Canaan in a drive of great charm. (For more on Canaan, see U.S. 7.) After crossing the Housatonic River, the road dips south to Salisbury on the slopes of Mount Riga. Iron was discovered here in 1732, and Salisbury and its neighboring town, Lakeville, became major production centers. Many cannon used by the Continental Army of the Revolution were forged here. Remember that the U.S.S. *Constitution* was nicknamed "Old Ironsides"? This is where the iron for her guns came from. One of the first forges in the area was run by Ethan Allen, who was born in Connecticut before his fateful move to Vermont. Many of the Green Mountain Boys also came out of these ironworks, a life experience of which Allen heartily approved. "Put iron in the blood to whet resolve," he said. "They make as good a regiment of marksmen and scalpers as America can afford." Allen must have been loads of fun at a dinner party.

Lakeville, named for adjacent Wononscopomuc Lake, is the home of Hotchkiss, the well-known prep school. It is also the site of the country's first pocketknife factory, although there is surely no connection. The Holley-Williams House on Main Street was the residence of the plant's ironmaster, John M. Holley. It overlooks the site of the forge and is virtually unchanged from the time of his ownership in 1808. The iron industry is just a memory in both of these towns, which are primarily resort centers.

As the road enters New York, it retraces the route of the Dutchess Turnpike. This was once the breadbasket for New York City, and products grown here were taken to Poughkeepsie by wagon along this road for shipment down the Hudson. The vein of iron that ran through northwestern Connecticut crossed into New York, as well. Amenia was also an iron-working center during the Revolution.

The highway now climbs the ridges of the Taconic Mountains to the town of **Millbrook**. This has become a noted center for gardening. As you might guess from its title, the Mary Flagler Cary Institute of Ecosystems Study takes a very serious look at plants and their environment. It is located on the bypass south of town. Nearby, on Tyrrel Road near South Millbrook, is Innisfree, dedicated to the study of Oriental design principles on gardens.

When the all-female enrollment of Elmira College succeeded in mastering the standard curriculum for males, impetus began building for new schools devoted to the highest levels of education for women. One of the leading advocates for such a school was the inventor of the telegraph, Samuel F. B. Morse, who lived on an estate near Poughkeepsie (see U.S. 9). He persuaded a friend who had made a fortune as a brewer, Matthew Vassar, to endow such a school. Vassar, a **Poughkeepsie** resident, tossed in $800,000, and the school opened there in 1865. (Good thing it was Vassar who decided to endow the school. Another top Poughkeepsie business at the time was the cough drop firm run by the Smith Brothers. There would have been terrible confusion between women's colleges if it had been named for them.)

A few patrician members of the first class dropped out, complaining that the school was attracting the wrong sort—daughters of millionaires whose money was too new. Nonetheless, Vassar flourished, even with a 6 A.M. wake-up for morning prayer and two more hours of silent prayer after breakfast. Vassar has become, arguably, the best-known symbol of women's education, accented by the 1960s best-seller *The Group,* which traced the lives of several fictional graduates. It is now a coeducational school. The campus is just south of U.S. 44, on Raymond Avenue, and the grounds are well worth a stroll. You can also drop in at the Vassar College Art Gallery, in Taylor Hall.

Poughkeepsie became the state capital in 1777 after the burning of Kingston, so it was here that New York's delegates came eleven years later to debate and ratify the U.S. Constitution. The home of George Clinton, first governor of the state, is the historical museum of Dutchess County.

Once across the Mid-Hudson Bridge, swing north for a bit on U.S. 9W, then west on N.Y. 299. This side trip into the Catskills leads to **New Paltz**, a settlement founded in 1678 by Huguenots, French Protestant refugees from religious oppression. Another group of Huguenots settled in New Rochelle shortly afterward (see U.S. 1), but the New Paltz community is much better preserved. Six of the stone houses they built here still stand along Huguenot Street. There is also a church and the imposing house put up by Jean Hasbrouck in 1694. It looks like a little slice of rural Europe.

The Hasbrouck family did quite well in this area, and as you head south from New Paltz on N.Y. 32 you'll come to Locust Lawn, the Federal-era estate built by Josiah Hasbrouck in 1814. The furnishings are authentic to the period and the estate also contains many of the original farm outbuildings.

The road rejoins U.S. 44 near Gardiner and begins to climb into the Catskills. There are great mountain views in the Lake Minnewaska area. The highway hits U.S. 209 near Kerhankson and comes to an end there.

VISITING HOURS

MASSACHUSETTS

Middleboro: Eddy Homestead, (508) 947-3615. East on U.S. 44, then north on Massachusetts 105 to Plympton St. Weekends, noon–6, July–August. Free.

Plymouth: Pilgrim Hall, (508) 746-1620. South of U.S. 44, on Court at Chilton St. Daily, 9:30–4:30, all year. Admission. Plimouth Plantation, (508) 746-1622. South, on Massachusetts 3A. Daily, 9–5, April–November. Admission. Mayflower II, (508) 746-1622. South of U.S. 44, at State Pier, on Water St. Daily, 9–5, April–November. Admission.

Taunton: Old Colony Museum, (508) 822-1622. Off U.S. 44, at 66 Church Green. Tuesday–Saturday, 10–4, all year. Admission.

RHODE ISLAND

Chepachet: Brown and Hopkins Country Store, (401) 568-4830. On U.S. 44. Wednesday–Sunday, 10–5, all year. Free.

Providence: First Baptist Church, (401) 751-2266. On U.S. 44, at 75 N. Main St. Monday–Friday, 10–3, all year. Saturday, 10–noon, April–October.

Rhode Island School of Design Museum, (401) 331-3511. One block east of U.S. 44, at College and Benefit Sts. Tuesday, Wednesday, Friday, and Saturday, 10:30–5; Thursday, noon–5; Sunday, 2–5, September–mid-June. Wednesday–Saturday, noon–5, at other times. Admission.

Old State House, (401) 277-2678. On U.S. 44 (N. Main St.) between North Court and South Court Sts. Monday–Friday, 8:30–4:30, all year. Free.

Roger Williams Memorial, (401) 528-5385. On U.S. 44, at 282 N. Main St. Daily, 9–5, May–October; closed weekends, at other times. Free.

Cathedral of St. John, (401) 331-4622. On U.S. 44 (N. Main St.) at Smith St. Monday–Friday, 8:30–4, all year.

CONNECTICUT

Avon: Farmington Valley Arts Center, (203) 678-1867. West, on U.S. 44, then north at Avon Park North. Wednesday–Saturday, 11–4, all year. Free.

Canton: Roaring Brook Nature Center, (203) 693-0263. East on U.S. 44, then north on Lawton Road. Monday–Saturday, 10–5; Sunday, 1–5, mid-June–Labor Day. Closed Monday, at other times. Admission.

Coventry: Nathan Hale Homestead, (203) 742-6917. South of U.S. 44, on Connecticut 31. Daily, 1–5, June–mid-October. Admission.

Caprilands Herb Farm, (203) 742-7244. South of U.S. 44, on Silver St. Daily, 9–5. Call for reservation for special herb luncheons and lectures.

East Hartford: Edward E. King Museum, (203) 289-6429. Just south of U.S. 44, at 840 Main St., in the Public Library. Monday–Friday, 9–9; Saturday, 9–5, all year. Free.

Lakeville: Holley-Williams House, (203) 435-2878. On U.S. 44 (Main St.). Thursday and Saturday, 1–5, July–mid-October. Admission.

Norfolk: Chamber Music Festival, (203) 542-5537. On the Stoeckel Estate, U.S. 44 at Connecticut 272. Friday–Saturday, July–August. Call for schedule.
   Historical Museum, (203) 868-2214. On the Town Green. Weekends, 10–4, mid-June–mid-September. Free.

Pomfret: Brayton Grist Mill, no phone. South, on U.S. 44, in Mashamoquet Brook State Park. Thursday and weekends, 2–5, May–September. Free.

Winsted: Solomon Rockwell House, (203) 379-8433. Off U.S. 44, on Prospect St. Thursday–Sunday, 2–4:30, mid-June–mid-September. Admission.

NEW YORK

Millbrook: Innisfree Gardens, (914) 677-8000. South of U.S. 44, on Tyrrel Road, in South Millbrook. Wednesday–Friday, 10–4; weekends, 11–5, May–September. Admission on weekends.
   Cary Arboretum, (914) 677-5343. West, on U.S. 44A. Monday–Saturday, 9–4; Sunday, 1–4, all year. Free.

New Paltz: Huguenot Houses, (914) 255-1660. North of U.S. 44, from Highland, on U.S. 9W and New York 299. Tours are given Wednesday–Sunday, 10:30 and 1:30, Memorial Day–September. Admission.
   Hasbrouck House, (914) 255-1660. North of U.S. 44, on New York 32. Wednesday–Sunday, 10–4, June–September. Admission.

Poughkeepsie: Vassar College Museum, (914) 452-7000. East on U.S. 44, then south on Raymond Ave. Monday–Friday, 9–4:30; weekends, 1–4:30, during school term. Free.
   Clinton House, (914) 471-1630. Off U.S. 44, on Main and N. White Sts. Monday–Friday, 9:30–2:30, all year. Free.

U. S. ROUTE 62

MAINE

VERMONT

NEW HAMPSHIRE

Ronan

NEW YORK

Niagara Falls
Buffalo

Conewango

Frewsburg

MASSACHUSETTS

CONNECTICUT   RHODE ISLAND

The Roar of Niagara

U.S. 62

Niagara Falls to Frewsburg, N.Y.
** 99 miles*

This is one of the more individualistic of the old roads, running in a long, lonely diagonal across the country, from the Canadian border of New York to the Mexican border at El Paso, Texas. It makes its way through the Alleghenies, the Bluegrass country of Kentucky, the Ozarks and the Great Plains. It offers one of the most varied national itineraries of any of these highways and is rarely within sight of an Interstate. In our brief meeting in these pages, it takes a turn from Niagara Falls into the outer neighborhoods of Buffalo and then twists through the beautiful foothills of the Alleghenies before moving on to Pennsylvania. The whole thing is done in under 100 miles, but they are eventful miles.

FOCUS

* * *

From the corner of Ferry and Main in the city of **Niagara Falls**, where this road begins, all you can see is the mist. It rises in a thick sheet, hovering above the end of the street like some localized squall. You are still too far away to hear the sound. The traffic noises are too loud on most days, as the tourists circle in search of parking places or ride to another nearby attraction. But if you come in the middle of the night, when all the tourists are safely tucked in their motel beds, you will hear it: the roar of several tons of water plunging over a 182-foot-high precipice to crash on the rocks below. Then maybe you can recapture some of the awe and wonder that must have been felt by the first Europeans to see Niagara Falls.

There are many higher waterfalls in this country. Throughout the West, they plummet from greater heights. Here height isn't the point. It is the sheer volume, the violent onrush of power battering itself into spray, that is the spectacle. Maybe this mist is the first thing that Fr. Louis Hennepin saw. The peripatetic French Franciscan, who made his way around the Great Lakes and upper Mississippi Valley on exploring trips, reached this area in 1678. He had heard from the local Indians of the great falls that blocked the lake passage west and asked to be taken to them. He must have been impressed, because in his written account of the journey he describes them as being 600 feet high. All travelers exaggerate a little, but this was better than a threefold mistake. Nonetheless, as you watch that surging power you can understand how the good father could have overshot the mark a little.

The falls became a virtual synonym for honeymooners by the late nineteenth century, and you will still encounter a few places that cater to that trade. But most honeymooners travel elsewhere these days. Today the best synonym for the falls is frightening. (Or am I being redundant?) They are a scary thing to see. That much power and violence concentrated in such a small place seems to bring out some deep-seated terror within us. Thus the barrel trips over the brink and the tightrope walkers who strutted across the Niagara Gorge, defying instant death in the churning waters, become more precarious. If you cross over to Canada, you'll find an entire block of strange attractions on a street called Clifton Hill, all of them having a theme based on horror movies or supernatural creatures. I don't think that's accidental. The falls bring it out.

The most violence done by the falls is to themselves, though. They have so eroded the underlying rock that they have already retreated a sixth of a mile upriver from where Hennepin first saw them. In a few thousand years, all that will be left of them is a big whirlpool at the mouth of Lake Erie. So say the geologists. The Niagara Escarpment, the ridge over which the falls drop, runs from the middle of New York State to Manitoulin Island in northern Lake Huron. At the start of U.S. 62, you are at the crest of this ridge.

Niagara Reservation State Park is right across the street from the falls. It was established in 1869 in an effort to eliminate the cluster of privately owned viewing towers and commercial ventures that intruded upon the majesty of the falls. You are just a few blocks north of Prospect Point, the best viewing area on the American side of the falls. From there you can take an elevator down to the docks of the Maid of the Mist, those little boats that bob to the fall's base. You can also take the bridge over to Goat Island, the piece of land that divides the American and Canadian falls. This is the best vantage point of all. You can wander near the river's edge here or take an elevator ride down and visit the Cave of the Winds beneath the falls. This is a bit of an adventure because you get to put on a raincoat and boots. Any trip requiring a special costume definitely falls under the heading of adventure.

But before you do any of that, just stand for a few moments at the start of U.S. 62 and look at that mist.

* * *

The road heads west through the residential areas of this highly industrialized town. It then becomes Niagara Falls Boulevard, a divided highway that gradually swings south toward Buffalo. Past the intersection of 87th Street you'll find a twentieth-century landmark of sorts. The land to the south backs up to Love Canal. Almost depopulated now, the area is the most vivid symbol of the price of industrial pollution that the country has to offer.

The highway runs past the airport and Oppenheim Zoo and

into the industrial suburb of **North Tonawanda**. Industrial . . . but musical. North Tonawanda calls itself the Carousel City, because it was here that the Herschell Company began building merry-go-rounds in 1883. It produced the first steam-driven model and set off the amusement park craze for these rides, which have now entered the realm of nostalgia. For many, the barrel organ music that they produce is still the defining sound of an amusement park. The old Herschell plant is now a museum of the carousel industry. There was also a major Wurlitzer plant in North Tonawanda, adding to the music in the air.

At Sheridan Road, among the vast shopping malls of Buffalo's affluent suburb of Amherst, the road jogs slightly east and then turns south once more as Bailey Avenue, the main commercial thoroughfare of Buffalo's east side. As you enter **Buffalo**, the Main Street campus of the State University of New York is to the west. The larger campus in Amherst is a few miles northeast. On the east side of the road here is Grover Cleveland Park, named for the twenty-second president, whose first big political post was mayor of Buffalo in 1881–82. You are several miles from the center of this manufacturing city, and Bailey Avenue runs through one blue-collar neighborhood after another, giving you a cross-section of the Buffalo experience. Nothing outstanding, though, unless you're intrigued by the workaday side of big cities.

After twisting around Interstate 190, with the downtown skyline visible on the west, the road becomes South Park Avenue. It heads into yet another industrial suburb, Lackawanna, named for the Scranton-based steel firm headquartered there. Just on the right as you enter town is South Park Botanical Gardens, with its twelve greenhouses of tropical plants. Buffalo is among the snowiest big cities in America, and the warm, luxuriantly overgrown greenhouses must come as a relief to those afflicted with cabin fever during the endless Buffalo winters.

A few blocks down, at South Park and Ridge Road, is the huge dome of Our Lady of Victory Basilica. This ornate church, with a dome 251 feet in circumference, was the crowning achievement of Monsignor Nelson Baker. The Buffalo-born priest managed to establish an entire colony of charitable institutions along Ridge

Road in Lackawanna. The basilica, the focal point of this community, was dedicated in 1926. It was elevated to the status of minor
basilica by Pope Pius XI that same year. The incredible interior
decor is worth a stop.

The highway continues through the town of Hamburg and
almost immediately afterward enters hill country. At **Eden**, that
industrial music we heard back in North Tonawanda rises again.
This is headquarters of the American Kazoo Company, and the
plant contains a collection of oddities related to this virtuoso
instrument. Eden, incidentally, calls itself the Garden Spot of
New York State. But you probably knew it would.

Across the gorge of Cattaraugus Creek, the highway enters a
small patch of Amish country. Beyond Dayton and south to
Conewango Creek, you will see several of the plain black buggies
and immaculate farms that are symbols of this religious sect.
Many families offer homemade quilts and furniture for sale—
watch for signs along the road. In Leon, you'll pass the Valley
View Swiss Cheese plant, a facility with a lot of holes in it. From
here U.S. 62 winds through hilltop settlements on the western
edge of the Allegheny River Valley, with the higher peaks of
Allegany State Park to the east. Past the town of Frewsburg, the
road bends sharply south and crosses the state line into Pennsylvania.

VISITING HOURS

NEW YORK

Buffalo: South Park Botanical Gardens, (716) 828-1040. On
U.S. 62, at McKinley Parkway. Daily, 9–4, all year. Free.

Eden: American Kazoo Factory and Museum, (716) 992-3690.
On U.S. 62, at 8703 S. Main St. Tuesday–Saturday, 10–5, all
year. Free.

Lackawanna: Our Lady of Victory Basilica, (716) 823-2490.
On U.S. 62, at Ridge Road. Daily, 7–7, all year.

Niagara Falls: Maid of the Mist cruises, (716) 284-4233. Boats leave from the base of Prospect Point, south of U.S. 62, at the end of Main St. Daily, mid-May–October, 9:15–8. Admission.

Cave of the Winds, (716) 282-8979. On Goat Island, accessible by both footbridge and auto bridge from Prospect Point. Daily, 9–9, Memorial Day–mid-October. Admission.

North Tonawanda: Herschell Carousel Museum, (716) 693-1885. West of U.S. 62, at 180 N. Thompson St. Monday, Wednesday, Friday, and Saturday, noon–8; Sunday, noon–6, July–August; Wednesday–Sunday, 1–5, June, September–October. Free.

U. S. ROUTE 104

MAINE

VERMONT

NEW
HAMPSHIRE

Oswego

Niagara Falls

Rochester

NEW YORK

MASSACHUSETTS

Ronan

CONNECTICUT   RHODE ISLAND

New York's Ridge Road

U.S. 104

Kasoag to Niagara Falls, N.Y.
*   *179 miles*

We now enter the realm of the metaphysical. Highway 104 was
a federal highway . . . once. Now it is designated a state road along
its entire route. But if you travel in some of its more rural portions,
you will still see the old shield-shaped signs marking it as U.S.
104. Even though it is now officially N.Y. 104, it is very much one
of our old roads. It is known as the Ridge Road, riding along the
crest of a moraine left by the retreating glaciers of the Ice Age. It
retraces the route of a far older road, the Iroquois Trail, another
of the earliest ways to the west. The drive parallels the Lake
Ontario shoreline for most of the route, but it comes within sight
of the big lake infrequently. In some portions, however, it weaves
in and out with the Seaway Trail, and this route makes a pleasant
side trip to the lakeshore. You'll pass through the rich fruit belt
on the lake's southern littoral and through the city of Rochester.
Finally, at the Niagara River, the road turns south for the run to
Niagara Falls. This ride could easily be combined with that in the

previous chapter, U.S. 62, since highway 104 ends about a block from where the other road begins.

The road starts in a lake-speckled farming area north of Syracuse. It heads directly west and hits the Lake Ontario shore near the village of New Haven. For the next several miles, it carries the Seaway Trail marker. This is a designation used by New York for the road that most nearly follows the lakeshore. It was a brave attempt to plot a continuous scenic drive, but sometimes the road is several miles removed from the water. You'll catch a few looks at Lake Ontario, however, as we go along.

FOCUS

* * *

Oswego doesn't look much like a battleground. It is a rather pleasant lakeside town of some 20,000 inhabitants. There is a branch of the New York State University system here. A town Green, just east of the business district, is surrounded by some impressive houses of worship. It is a tranquil sort of place. But for a century, this Lake Ontario port was regarded as a place of the highest military importance. It was the closest Great Lakes outlet to the eastern seaboard, the terminus of the long-established portage route along the Mohawk River, Oneida Lake and Oswego River. Like Pittsburgh far to the south, it controlled water access to the West. It also pointed at the soft underbelly of Canada to the north. So in three different wars, invasion forces swarmed ashore to battle here, and the place was heavily fortified to prepare for a fourth invasion that never came.

The history of the place goes back to 1727, when the British built Fort Oswego on the western bank of the Oswego River where it emptied into the lake. As fears about French ambitions in the area grew, a second fort was built on the eastern bank. This was Fort Ontario. It would become the most important installation in the area, and its successor is the fort that stands today.

As it turned out, the British were quite right about French intentions. At the outbreak of the French and Indian Wars, the brilliant general Louis Joseph de Montcalm landed here and leveled both forts after a short siege. This was the first blow of a campaign that nearly succeeded in detaching northern New York from British rule. But in 1759, a new prime minister, William Pitt, imbued the British war effort with more vigor. The British returned to the destroyed fortification and built it up once more. It became the base for the campaign against Fort Niagara to the west and for Lord Jeffrey Amherst's successful assault on Montreal.

It was here in 1776 that the alliance between the British and Iroquois forces under Joseph Brant was approved and signed, and the fort became a base for Loyalist raids throughout New York during the Revolution. In 1777, as part of the overall strategy for Gen. John Burgoyne's invasion of the Hudson Valley, a British force from Fort Ontario was supposed to head east to link up with him north of Albany. But this force was held up and then battered into uselessness by the colonials under Gen. Nicholas Herkimer at Oriskany. That enabled the Americans on the Hudson to build up a numerical advantage and destroy Burgoyne at Saratoga. After this disappointment, Fort Ontario was abandoned once again and the British retreated into Canada.

Five years later, realizing its continuing importance, they came back. An American attack was repulsed, and for thirteen years after the Treaty of Paris had ceded it to the United States, the British refused to give it up. They finally left in 1796, but when the War of 1812 began, back they came one more time. The American fort was captured but the British landing force was so badly mauled that it could not hold the place. So they leveled it instead.

That was the last battle fought here, but there were always apprehensions. During the Civil War, the fort was expanded and strengthened in case a feared British intervention on the side of the Confederacy materialized. The fort was restored in 1949, and Fort Ontario today is intended to give the sense of a military outpost of the 1860s. Costumed guards hold drills through the summer months. Even at other times, though, this gray bastion above the lake is an impressive sight, almost medieval in its appearance of bristling might.

Oswego's military history quieted after the War of 1812, and its commercial fortunes took a downturn, too. The town expected to be the Great Lakes outlet of what came to be known as the Erie Canal. It would have been the shortest and least expensive route. But there were fears that in making the canal outlet this far east, much of the anticipated trade would be siphoned off to Canadian ports on Lake Ontario. Besides, the well-connected Holland Land Company wanted the canal to pass through its holdings to the west, which would enhance their value immeasurably. When it kicked in with a 100,000-acre gift to the state, the matter was settled. Buffalo would become the canal outlet on Lake Erie. Oswego would remain a quiet town on Lake Ontario. A canal cutoff from Syracuse was eventually added, but the city never regained a primary position.

The H. Lee White Marine Museum, at the foot of First Street, contains exhibits on the history of Oswego's relationship with Great Lakes history.

*   *   *

Just west of Oswego, follow the Seaway Trail signs and turn off on highway 104A. This is a delightful little lane, running past well-shaded old farmhouses and serene country villages. Stop in Fair Haven, an especially pleasant lakeside village, with a state park beach nearby and another waterfront park right in town. This is a perfect spot to walk around and explore a bit, the sort of old town on an old road that usually yields the unexpected.

Now the Seaway Trail plays highway tag with old 104. The main road is a high-speed thoroughfare that avoids the towns, while the Seaway Trail winds all over the lot and cuts through every town around. It's a far more entertaining alternative. I'd especially suggest the cutoff that heads north from 104 at Alton, on New York 14, running up to Sodus Point and then west through Pultneyville, another real charmer of a lakeside town. Return to the main road along N.Y. 21 and get ready for **Rochester**.

A few miles east of this city, the road turns into a freeway. As you shoot through Webster, you can catch a glimpse of the Xerox plant, one of Rochester's big home-grown businesses. It sounds like a word that was wholly invented, the way George Eastman made up the word *Kodak* because he thought the letter *k* crackled with kinetic action. *Xerox,* though, comes from a Greek compound meaning "dry writing." It was coined by inventor Chester Carlson in 1938 as he worked on the concept of copying images through photoconductivity. His experiments came to the attention of a pair of Rochester businessmen who owned a photocopying equipment firm called Haloid. They committed themselves to Carlson's process, renamed their own company Xerox and away they went. But it was that other punchy little word, *Kodak,* that brought companies like Haloid to Rochester in the first place. And it is to Kodak Central that this road is headed.

As the road crosses Irondequoit Bay, you can see the lakeshore and the old amusement grounds at Seabreeze Park to the north. Still running as a freeway, it sweeps across the east side of the city, crosses the Genesee and then resumes its identity as Ridge Road, a surface street, on the west side of the river. The freeway has thus deposited you in the midst of Kodak Park. Eastman purchased 16 acres of open land in this area in 1891 for his first factory. It has grown into a self-contained industrial city that employs 28,000 workers in 170 buildings, all along Ridge Road. Tours of the plant leave from 200 West Ridge Road (you can leave your car in a parking lot opposite the entrance). By the way, no cameras are permitted on the Kodak tour.

A few blocks south of here, on Lake Avenue, is Maplewood Park, with extensive rose gardens. A drive north on Lake Avenue will take you to the mouth of the Genesee and the Charlotte-Genesee Lighthouse, with a small museum of old Great Lakes ships and lights.

Back on highway 104, the road narrows down to two lanes after its run through Rochester's western suburbs. It now enters the heart of the lakeside fruit belt. Rich orchards line the highway and you'll see produce stands every few miles. The towns are small and not terribly interesting, although Clarkson contains some nice old homes. It was there, by the way, that George Selden first successfully applied the internal combustion engine to a wheeled vehicle in 1877. Toot the horn for Selden as you pass. On second thought, let the town enjoy its peace and quiet.

A position atop this ridge of glacial debris gave the early settlers of **Childs** an abundance of building material. So it became a cobblestone town. In the heart of Childs is a cobblestone church dating from 1834, as well as a school, blacksmith shop, print shop and homes. All are built of these stones—the tiny ones known as baby's tears—and they form a museum complex.

Turn south at N.Y. 63 to Medina and a little side trip along the Erie Canal. There is a turning basin for canal boats here and the adjacent park is the site of various events during the year, including a Canal Festival in early July.

Head west on N.Y. 31 to **Lockport**. This is where the canal crosses the divide separating the Genesee and Niagara valleys. The locks built to get the canal across this 66-foot rise gave the town its name. You'll get a view of the locks from the Cottage Street bridge, one of the widest single-span structures in the world. The original locks, dating from 1847, can be seen from the Pine Street Bridge. There are also cruises through the locks and canal, leaving from the marina at Market Street.

Now return to highway 104 by way of N.Y. 78 and head west again. Take the turnoff into **Lewiston**, a charming old town on the Niagara River and the start of the old portage trail around Niagara Falls. Lewiston has lots of interesting shops and restaurants but is best known today for Art Park, a state-run cultural facility just south of town along the river. All summer long, a full slate of concerts, plays and art exhibits is held here.

The road now parallels the Niagara River as Lewiston Road, but the more scenic alternative is the Niagara Parkway. Part of the falls' flow has been diverted for power usage for more than a century, but never quite as awesomely as at the Niagara Power Project Visitor Center. The Power Vista, south of Lewiston, looks right into the maw of these works and gives a historical overview of the attempts to harness the force of the falls for energy.

Beyond this is Devils Hole State Park, overlooking a narrow portion of the Niagara Gorge. It was given its name after a supply train from Fort Niagara was ambushed and wiped out here during Pontiac's Rebellion of 1763. Just a bit further along is Whirlpool State Park. The river bends 90 degrees here and sends the waters into a frothing torrent. A trail is cut into the side of the gorge, enabling you to walk down to the water's edge for a closeup view. Remember, though, you'll also have to climb back up.

Just before it ends in the city of **Niagara Falls**, the parkway passes the Schoellkopf Geological Museum, which explains as lucidly as possible how Niagara Falls works from a geological standpoint. Over the last 30,000 years, the falls have moved backward along the road we have just traveled, their original location being at the head of the gorge, near Lewiston. With that thought in mind, let's end the drive here, within sight of the falls' current location and the start of U.S. 62.

VISITING HOURS

NEW YORK

Childs: Cobblestone Museum, (716) 589-9013. On New York 104. Tuesday–Saturday, 11–5; Sunday, 1–5, July–Labor Day. Sunday only, September–October. Admission.

Lewiston: Art Park, (716) 754-3377. South, along Niagara River, west of the Robert Moses Parkway. Daily, Memorial Day–Labor Day. Parking fee. Call for schedule of events.
   Niagara Power Project Vista, (716) 285-3211. South on Robert Moses Parkway. Daily, 10–7:30, July–Labor Day; 10–5, at other times. Free.

Lockport: Erie Canal Cruises, (716) 693-3260. South of New York 104. Boats leave from Market St. marina, June–Labor Day. Call for schedule and fares.

Niagara Falls: Schoellkopf Geological Museum, (716) 278-1780. On N.Y. 104, at the end of Walnut St. Daily,

9:30–7, Memorial Day–Labor Day; 10–5, through October;
Wednesday–Sunday, 10–5, at other times. Admission.

Oswego: Fort Ontario, (315) 343-4711. North of New York
104 on E. Seventh St. Wednesday–Saturday, 10–5; Sunday,
1–5, Memorial Day–Labor Day. Grounds open through
September. Free.

H. Lee White Marine Museum, (315) 341-2140. North of
New York 104 on W. First St., at the lakefront. Daily, 10–5,
Memorial Day–Labor Day. Admission.

Rochester: Kodak Park Tours, (716) 722-2465. On N.Y. 104, at
200 Ridge Road W. Monday–Friday, 9:30–1:30,
mid-May–mid-September. Free.

Charlotte-Genesee Lighthouse, (716) 621-6179. North of
New York 104 on Lake Ave. to Lighthouse St. Saturday,
noon–4; Sunday, 1–5, Memorial Day–Labor Day. Admission.
Grounds are free.

U. S. ROUTE 201

MAINE

Jackman

VERMONT

Waterville
Augusta

NEW
HAMPSHIRE

Brunswick

NEW YORK

Ronan

MASSACHUSETTS

CONNECTICUT

RHODE ISLAND

The Kennebec Valley

U.S. 201

Quebec Border to Brunswick, Maine
* 172 miles

This was the old trail from the Maine coast to Quebec City, followed by generations of Indians, fur traders and the forces of Benedict Arnold on his failed Canadian invasion of 1775. Today this highway penetrates a part of Maine in which it is the only paved road, sometimes the only road of any kind, for miles around. So close to the major population centers of the country, this section of the state remains almost as wild as it was when Arnold marched through. For much of the way the road runs beside the Kennebec River and is designated a scenic route. It follows the river through Augusta, the state capital, before cutting away to its terminus in the old college town of Brunswick. Although the total distance is short, in terms of scenery, cultural attractions, history and even shopping, this is an old road with everything. And not a freeway in sight.

* **MILEPOSTS** *

One of the more overworked phrases in the literature of the tourist brochure is "sportsman's paradise." Everytime I see it I come up with a vision of a fisherman with wings on his back, sitting placidly in a canoe while large trout jump into it. But if the words can ever be used with a degree of accuracy, it is probably at the head of U.S. 201.

Jackman, a storied name in sporting circles, is 16 miles south of the Quebec line. It is the commercial center of the area, most of which is private land owned by lumber companies. They permit access on their gravel roads, as long as you don't interfere with logging operations. What that means, I suppose, is try not to let the roof of your car blemish a falling tree. The town is built around Wood Pond, and you'll find several other good-sized lakes in the vicinity. You'll also find trout and salmon fishing, deer and bear hunting in fall, canoeing, hiking—if they stock the gear in the L. L. Bean store in Freeport, chances are you can do it in Jackman. Some local resort owners call the area the Switzerland of America. I wouldn't go that far. But there is some lovely lake and mountain scenery around Jackman, so even if your sporting activity consists of just driving through, it is worth the effort.

White-water rafting has become one of the growth segments of Maine tourism since its introduction here in 1976. The most intense concentration of such tours is in the village of The Forks. A whole lineup of companies offers trips along the Kennebec and Dead rivers from here. (The rivers join at this crossroads, hence the name.) The trip to the wilderness area of Kennebec Gorge is the most popular short excursion.

Among the first to raft these waters were the colonials under Benedict Arnold's command, and they were none too happy about it. Arnold's campaign against Quebec, which headed west on the Dead River from The Forks after ascending the Kennebec, was a gallant but totally misconceived operation. Geographical ignorance of this part of Maine was almost total in 1775. The colonials thought they had about half as far to travel as the 350 miles they actually had to go. The white water along the Dead

River was not anticipated. The expedition also started too late in the year to avoid the killing northern winter. Part of the plan, to be sure, was that with the waterways frozen, the British would be unable to reinforce Quebec. Nonetheless, it also meant terrible hardship and danger for the army that had to march through it.

By the time Arnold reached Quebec City, he had lost nearly one-third of his 1,000-man force. Some were dead, others had turned back, and many more were too weak to fight. Arnold could do little else but camp across from the city and wait. By late December, the forces of Gen. Richard Montgomery, who had come north from New York and captured Montreal, joined Arnold. On the last day of the year, the combined armies began an assault on Quebec in a driving snowstorm. But the defenders had dug in too well and anticipated exactly where the attack would come. Arnold was wounded, Montgomery killed and the attack disintegrated. The remnant of the American forces retreated through Montreal and didn't threaten Canada again for the rest of the war. The remains of Montgomery, by the way, were traded years later for those of Maj. John André, hanged after conspiring to seize West Point with Montgomery's old comrade-in-arms Benedict Arnold. Two miles east of The Forks on a paved road is Moxie Falls, a lovely cascade in a backwoods setting.

The road heads through Caratunk, a village noted for being the place where the Appalachian Trail crosses the Kennebec. A bit beyond that, on dam-formed Wyman Lake, is the town of Bingham. It was named for William Bingham, who won the lottery. No, not one of these paltry modern affairs, in which the winner walks away with a scant few million dollars. Bingham's win came in 1786 and he won 2 million acres of the surrounding land.

When the Arnold expedition reached Solon on August 7, spirits were still running high. You'll see a historical marker here, just below Caratunk Falls, where they camped before making a portage around the cataract. This portage point had long been the site of a permanent Indian encampment, and petroglyphs were recently discovered on the rocks here. Just past the town, watch for the signs to the South Solon Meeting House, built in 1842 and decorated by a group of Maine artists more than a century later.

The road splits at Solon. Highway 201 heads straight into Skowhegan, while 201A meanders with the Kennebec through a few more riverside towns. I'd go with 201A, by way of Norridgewock, named for the Indians who once inhabited the area.

The Kennebec Valley was a prize jealously guarded by the British, and they were especially sensitive to any evidence of French influence seeping down from Quebec. So the mission of Fr. Sebastian Rasle, a French Jesuit, was looked on with suspicion. Established near Norridgewock in 1695, the mission built up great loyalty among the tribes. The British struck in 1723, raiding the village and carrying off many of Fr. Rasle's educational innovations, including an Indian-language dictionary. Not content, they returned a year later, burned the mission and killed the priest. There is a marker over his grave on the road from Madison to Norridgewock. The mission bell is in the State Museum in Augusta, farther down the road.

The road swings back east to Skowhegan (see U.S. 2) to rejoin the main highway and then continues south. Hinckley is the home of Good Will Farm, established as a home for children by the Rev. George Hinckley in 1889. There is a museum of natural history and antique farm implements on the grounds.

Although Colby College in **Waterville** dates back to 1813, its hilltop campus is of much more recent vintage. It was moved from the middle of town to Mayflower Hill, overlooking Waterville, in the 1930s. Lorimer Chapel, built in 1937, has an organ designed by Albert Schweitzer, and the museum in Bixler Center contains several works by Maine artist Winslow Homer.

Waterville grew up around the Ticonic Falls of the Kennebec, a district now occupied by several manufacturing plants, including Hathaway Shirts, which operates an outlet store here. There is a footbridge over the rapids. Until a few years ago, this was the last toll footbridge in the country, with a 2-cent tariff collected for the crossing. The tollhouse remains, but there is no longer any need to put your 2 cents in.

On the opposite bank is the town of Winslow, which split off from Waterville in 1802. Or maybe it was the other way around. The settlement actually began in Winslow, at Fort Halifax, and the blockhouse, dating from 1754, is still standing on U.S. 201. By the way, if you've ever mulled over the words to "My Country, 'Tis of Thee," trying to puzzle out their meaning, you have F. Samuel Smith to blame. He was the minister of the First Baptist Church in Waterville when he wrote them.

Maine did not separate from Massachusetts until 1819, one year before statehood, and its history is bound up with that of its parent state to the south. Fur traders from Plymouth Colony reached the Kennebec only eight years after landing at Plymouth and established an outpost at **Augusta** in 1628. Business was so good that they were able to repay a large portion of their debt to London sponsors with the profits. John Alden was a regular visitor here and so was Miles Standish. The post was eventually abandoned, but the site, at the head of navigation on the river, kept drawing people. Fort Western was built in 1754, not far from the Pilgrims' post. Benedict Arnold's party rendezvoused there for their journey up the Kennebec, and it was the hub around which the settlement grew. The fort has been restored, and even though it is called Fort Western, it is on the eastern bank of the river, on Bowman Street near the Kennebec bridge.

The same central location and easy access that attracted the Pilgrims made Augusta the logical choice for state capital in 1827. The State House, on the western bank of the river, was designed by Charles Bullfinch. It was enlarged early in the twentieth century but remains essentially true to the original plan of 1829. It dominates the city from its position on State Street at the crest of a bluff rising from the Kennebec. Between the State House and the river is Capitol Park, filled with native trees and shrubs. A strong Made-in-Maine theme runs through the State Museum, another part of the capitol complex. Among the displays are various products manufactured in the state during the nineteenth century.

The state's best-known product of that era may have been James G. Blaine, the Republican candidate for president in 1884. He was referred to as either "the plumed knight" or "the continental liar from the State of Maine," depending on outlook. Blaine began his career as a state legislator after editing the local newspaper. He became speaker of the U.S. House in 1869, then a senator and finally secretary of state before winning the GOP nomination. Then he became the first Republican to lose a presidential race in twenty-four years. An admiring New York minister undid him by describing the Democrats as the party of "rum, Romanism and rebellion." Blaine bought a home near the State House here before leaving for Congress in 1862, and his daughter gave it to the state in 1918. Called Blaine House, it is now the governor's mansion.

Augusta, by the way, was named for the daughter of Gen. Henry Dearborn, U.S. marshal for the area, in 1797. Dearborn gave his own name to the Detroit suburb that is the headquarters of the Ford Motor Company.

Hallowell has a handsomely restored business district along the river and is known as an antiques center. Granite for the State House in Augusta was quarried here.

Edward Arlington Robinson, who wrote elegantly ironic poems that examine defeat and failure, grew up in Gardiner. The fictional setting of his poems, Tilbury Town, is largely based on this place, and there is a monument to him on the town Green. In his first volume of poetry he wrote, "We lack the courage to be where we are: /We love too much to travel on old roads,/ To triumph on old fields." We will nod to a kindred soul as we pass through his hometown on this old road.

FOCUS

* * *

Bowdoin College did not get off to the most auspicious of starts. Its organizers, angling for financial assistance from a wealthy and prominent family, named it after a recently deceased governor of Massachusetts, James Bowdoin. But his successor, the always feisty John Hancock, disliked the man so much he refused to grant a charter to any school named after him. Not until Hancock passed away in 1794 did the incorporation go through.

Over the intervening two centuries, life in **Brunswick** has come to center around the Bowdoin campus. This may well be the quintessential New England college town, with handsome old streets surrounding the cultural core. Bowdoin is a small place, with an enrollment of only 1,400, but its campus is a jewel and the list of its alumni and faculty long and distinguished.

In 1824, the future president Franklin Pierce graduated, and the following year the class included both Henry Wadsworth Longfellow and Nathaniel Hawthorne. From 1850 to 1852, while Dr. Calvin Stowe taught here, his wife sat at home a few blocks away and wrote *Uncle Tom's Cabin*. In the 1870s, the school became involved with pioneering Arctic exploration, a connection that would lead another Bowdoin man, Adm. Robert E. Peary, to reach the North Pole for the first time in 1909—a claim that remains in hot dispute.

U.S. 201 enters town from the north as Maine Street. With a width of 198 feet, this is among the broadest thoroughfares in America. The original name was Twelve Rod Road. That old unit of measurement was 16.5 feet, and 12 rods was thought to be a suitable width for a stately road. Bowdoin lies at the end of this street, a few blocks south of the end of U.S. 201.

At the head of the campus is the First Parish Church. The original opened on the site in 1717, and this restored version dates from 1846. Longfellow spoke from its pulpit, as did Eleanor Roosevelt and Dr. Martin Luther King, Jr., but perhaps the most powerful sermon ever given here was delivered by Dr. Stowe. Harriet Beecher Stowe said she was struck by the inspiration that would lead her to write her celebrated book while listening to her husband speak from her seat in Pew 23. Later, she amended that to say that God dictated the book to her and she simply wrote it down.

The Stowes had moved to Brunswick from Cincinnati, across the river from the slave-owning state of Kentucky. It was Ohio and safety that the fleeing slave, Eliza, was trying to gain in the book as she picked her way across the ice floes. (Years later, an escaped slave named Josiah Henson who ran a vocational school for former slaves near Dresden, Ontario, said that much of Mrs. Stowe's narrative paralleled his own biography. His school opened in 1841 and the story of his life was widely disseminated by Abolitionists. So it may well be that Mrs. Stowe was hearing Henson's voice as well as God's.)

The Stowe house is just a few blocks east, on Federal Street, and is now a restaurant. Federal Street is the most atmospheric area in town, a delight to stroll, with a large number of appealing homes in the architectural style of the street's name.

After a turn around the well-shaded campus, you may want to examine the school's art museum, in the domed Walker Art Building. It features an excellent collection of American and British portraits, as well as Greek antiquities. Next to it is Hubbard Hall, the library, which houses the Peary-McMillan Arctic Museum. The museum details the activities of these two men, who together led the 1909 run for the pole. Peary, a Bowdoin graduate, was deeply touched by the spirit of the Arctic quest, devoting his life to it. He had tried for the pole and failed repeatedly when he set out on one final expedition in the summer of 1908 aboard his ship, the *Roosevelt.* He was aware that this was probably the last time for him. He was fifty-two years old, well past the age when men walked over frozen seas to reach this sort of goal. Maybe that explained what happened on this expedition, a voyage that has been a source of controversy ever since.

Peary emerged from the Arctic months later and reported attaining the pole. He found, however, that a Brooklyn physician, Dr. Frederick Cook—whose life, ironically, he had saved on a previous expedition—had come out months before and claimed to have beaten him to the prize. Cook won acceptance in the press, and Peary, a rather frosty man even in temperate climes, was ridiculed. But as more documentation came in, the prestigious National Geographic Society backed Peary and clinched the case for him. Peary never got over the bitter controversy, however, and for the last eleven years of his life was almost a recluse.

Then in 1988, as part of its centennial observance, the National Geographic Society released evidence that raised serious questions about whether Peary had reached the pole after all. An exhaustive inquiry into his journal and the corroborative evidence led the Society to conclude that he had fallen several miles short and had fudged the data to make it come out right. To its credit, the Peary-McMillan museum does not back off from any of this controversy and presents it all as part of an engrossing look at the great age of Arctic exploration. It even includes displays on the admiral's Arctic descendants whom he reportedly fathered by an Eskimo wife.

One other spot to stop in Brunswick is the Joshua Chamberlain Home, which is also a Civil War museum. Chamberlain was a governor of Maine and the general who led the defense of the critical Little Round Top position at the Battle of Gettysburg. He was chosen by U. S. Grant to accept the Confederate surrender at Appomattox.

VISITING HOURS

MAINE

Augusta: State House and Blaine Home, (207) 289-2301. On U.S. 201 (State St.) at Capitol St. Monday–Friday, 9–4, all year. Free.

Maine State Museum, (207) 289-2301. Adjoins the State House. Monday–Friday, 9–5; Saturday, 10–4; Sunday, 1–4, all year. Free.

Fort Western, (207) 622-1234. Off U.S. 201, at the eastern end of the Kennebec River bridge. Monday–Saturday, 10–4; Sunday, 1–5, July–August. Admission.

Brunswick: Bowdoin College Museums, (207) 725-3000. South of U.S. 201, at the end of Maine St. Tuesday–Saturday, 10–8; Sunday, 2–5, July–Labor Day. Tuesday–Saturday, 10–4; Sunday, 2–5, at other times. Free.

First Parish Church, (207) 729-7331. Adjacent to Bowdoin campus. Open by appointment.

Chamberlain Museum, (207) 729-6606. Off U.S. 201, at 226 Maine St. Monday–Friday, 10–3, July–mid-October, Admission.

Waterville: Colby College Museums, (207) 872-3000. West of U.S. 201, on Mayflower Hill. Monday–Saturday, 10–noon and 1–4:30; Sunday, 2–4:30, all year. Free.

Winslow: Fort Halifax, (207) 872-2706. On U.S. 201, at Bay St. Daily, 10–4, Memorial Day–Labor Day. Free.

U. S. ROUTE 202

MAINE

Bangor

Augusta

Lewiston

VERMONT

NEW HAMPSHIRE

Concord

NEW YORK

Peterborough

MASSACHUSETTS

Holyoke · Belchertown

Litchfield · Simsbury

Peekskill · CONNECTICUT

Danbury RHODE ISLAND

Ronan

New England's Back Door

U.S. 202

Bangor, Maine, to Suffern, N.Y.
*   *478 miles*

This is New England's backdoor road, an early attempt by high-way planners to bypass the congestion developing along U.S. 1 in the large coastal cities. U.S. 202 is an inland shadow of the route of U.S. 1. It avoids the big towns, sticking to the medium-sized places and the less traveled paths from Maine to Connecticut. It approaches the coast on a few occasions, only to dart away quickly and resume its course through the interior. This also allows it to remain aloof from the Interstates. In that regard it is almost a perfect old road, leading the way to the sort of travel experiences that the freeways shun.

*   MILEPOSTS   *

The road starts at the western edge of Bangor, and after running with U.S. 1A for a while along the Penobscot River, splits off to begin life on its own at Hampden. This was the birthplace of

Dorothea Dix, a tireless nineteenth-century crusader on behalf of the pauperized insane. Today these people swell the ranks of the homeless. Then they were incarcerated in conditions of hideous squalor and forgotten by the rest of the world, condemned to lives offering neither treatment nor human comfort. Ms. Dix managed to improve conditions while working in Boston, and by 1847 she had taken her campaign to eighteen states. She was superintendent of nursing for the Union Army during the Civil War and afterward carried her crusade on behalf of the insane to most industrialized nations. There is a plaque to honor her in Hampden, just south of town.

In Newburgh Center you'll find the Jabez Knowlton Museum, an old country store with antique fixtures and display cases, looking just as it did when open for business in its heyday in the 1840s.

The road then crosses the gentle Dixmont Hills and, after skirting marshy country around Unity Pond, arrives in China. This is a lovely town, with a main street on a ridge overlooking hill-rimmed China Lake. You can visit a small museum here, the Albert Church Brown Memorial House, but the town is mostly a fine place for strolling and enjoying the surroundings. The road then heads along the lake's eastern shore to South China.

The highway joins U.S. 201 on the east bank of the Kennebec and runs with it on the bridge into Augusta, passing just a few blocks north of the State House (see U.S. 201). West of the capital, the road crosses another scenic area, the Winthrop Lakes. There are wonderful views near Manchester on the shore of Cobboseecontee Lake.

Just south of the road, by way of Maine 132, is **Monmouth**, a little museum village, with eight typical buildings from a nineteenth-century town assembled to recreate the ambience of rural Maine. Gen. Henry Dearborn was U.S. marshal for the area in the 1790s, and Monmouth was named for the New Jersey town where he won a critical victory in the Revolutionary War.

Augusta was something of an exception among Maine cities in that it grew up along both banks of a river. Early settlers generally established twin towns on either side, since they found it too difficult to administer both halves of such separated communities. That was the situation along the Androscoggin River, which divides the towns of Lewiston and Auburn, next on your route. Put together, they would be the biggest city in Maine. As it is, **Lewiston** is the second-largest in the state, a city that continues to thrive on textiles. The mills attracted many French-Canadians, and Lewiston celebrates a well-attended Franco-American Festival in the last week of July. New high-tech installations diversify the local economy, and the *Farmer's Almanac* compiles its collection of folk wisdom here.

The campus of Bates College is just east of the road, along Campus Avenue. The college chapel is worth a visit, and the Edmund Muskie Archives are in the college library. That U.S. senator and 1968 Democratic vice-presidential candidate was a Bates graduate. The school is famed for the quality of its debating teams, good training ground for any politician. The campus beauty spot is Mount David, reached by a footpath, which commands a panorama of the area all the way to the White Mountains.

Auburn, built upon hills, became more of a residential community than Lewiston. How hilly is it? Well, there are ski slopes right in town at Lost Valley (which has become known for its night skiing). The factory system was first applied to shoe production in Auburn in 1835 and made it the country's top producer of footwear. That is still an important segment of the economy, and Quoddy Moccasins are made here.

The highway bypasses Portland on the west, running through a succession of outlying towns surrounded by berry farms and rolling land that gently shades into suburbia. The Parson Smith House, on River Road in **South Windham**, was built in 1764 and remained in the same family's hands for 190 years. It is highly regarded by architectural historians for its unaltered exterior structure and well-preserved kitchen.

A little girl named Katie Smith spent many of her summers around Buxton and Hollis in the years after the Civil War. Much later in life, she drew upon those experiences to write some of America's best-loved children's books as Kate Douglas Wiggin.

Her classic *Rebecca of Sunnybrook Farm* became an immediate success when published in 1903, and remains a staple of juvenile literature. Another of her books, *The Old Peabody Pew,* is enacted every August at the Tory Hill Meeting House, near the town of Buxton. Wiggin is buried there, in the family plot.

Alfred is named for the Olde English monarch and it is a pretty little place, with lots of colonial homes along its streets. Sanford was the home of Goodall Mills for eighty-seven years, and this is where its Palm Beach suits were made. (Odd to think of the epitome of light summerwear being made in the Maine climate.) The company closed down in 1954, but Sanford managed to hold on and diversify its economy afterward.

Now U.S. 202 crosses the Salmon Falls River into New Hampshire, skirts the manufacturing town of Rochester and angles southwest through pleasant hill and lake country, past Ayers Lake and the Isinglass River. It joins U.S. 4 at Northwood, and the roads run together into Concord (see U.S. 3). Then U.S. 202 splits off to the west as Hopkinton Road.

The country begins to roll perceptibly, as the old road passes ski areas around Henniker. New Hampshire developed more slowly than some of its New England neighbors because of complications arising from conflicting land grants. The grants awarded to John Mason in 1629 were tied up in colonial courts for generations and the titles weren't finally cleared until the eve of nationhood, in 1787. With no clear title to the land, settlers came slowly and with trepidation.

That's probably why Col. John Hill was so eager to see his settlers multiply. Hill, for whom the town of **Hillsboro** is named, offered to give 100 acres to the first boy and girl born in the settlement if they agreed to marry. They did and he did.

Another early resident of the area was Gov. Benjamin Pierce, who built his dignified home in Hillsboro in 1804. In that same year his son, Franklin, the country's future fourteenth president, was born. The furnishings of the house are not original but are those of an affluent home of the period. Pierce's presidency was undistinguished and his home life unhappy, but he had a nice place to grow up.

The highway crosses the Contoocook River on a stone arched bridge south of Hillsboro and runs alongside the river into Bennington. This is the location of the Monadnock Paper Mill, and the name indicates that you are nearing the portion of the state dominated by that mountain. By New Hampshire standards, Monadnock is not an especially lofty peak. Its summit is 3,165 feet above sea level, only half the height of the tallest of the White Mountains. But its solitary position, apart from any other mountain of comparable size, made it a place of religious awe to the Indians and to many literary figures who came later. It is one of the country's most frequently climbed mountains, the round-trip hike to the summit taking only about 3 hours. With nothing to get in the way of the view, climbers are rewarded on clear days with a panorama that extends all the way to the Atlantic and the city of Boston. Monadnock's beauty was celebrated in poetry by Ralph Waldo Emerson and in prose by Henry David Thoreau, both of whom made the climb. Although the mountain is not directly on this route, it is visible to the west along this stretch of road and its spirit dominates the landscape.

Because of its literary associations, the area around Monadnock became known as a retreat for figures from the intellectual community. This is where composer Edward MacDowell came in 1907 to try to recuperate from a collapse brought on by overwork. MacDowell is best remembered for his *Woodland Sketches,* which contain the perennially popular piano recital piece "To a Wild Rose." He never regained his health and died a year later. His widow, Marian Nevins MacDowell, herself a concert artist, then decided to turn their retreat near **Peterborough** into a place where artists and writers could come for reflection and work. She founded the MacDowell Colony and traveled the country tirelessly to raise funds for it. Over the years some of the country's most distinguished artistic figures have lived and worked here, their privacy rigorously guarded and their solitude undisturbed. The best known of these residents was probably Thornton Wilder, who used Peterborough as his model while writing *Our Town.* Only the main building, Colony Hall, and the MacDowell grave site are open to visitors. There is a small historical museum of the town on Grove Street with a collection of antique toys and ceramics. Before the MacDowells, the most warmly received visitor to the area was probably Brigham Young. The Mormon leader converted 136 local citizens, most of whom followed him to Utah.

Jaffrey is the closest town to the base of Monadnock and is a thriving resort. This is where Emerson wrote his poem "Monadnoc" after the inspiration of his climb, omitting the final *k* in his haste. The town's old meetinghouse, built in 1825, is in the center of Jaffrey, and here the Amos Fortune lectures are held each year. Fortune was a freed slave who prospered as a farmer, and in his will of 1801 he established a fund to be used by the district school. The school closed in 1927, and the bequest was transferred to a series of Friday night lectures held every summer and named for the long-departed Fortune.

For a final look at Monadnock, turn off on eastbound N.H. 119 at **West Rindge** and follow the signs to the Cathedral of the Pines. This is an outdoor shrine to the nation's war dead in an area of natural beauty at the edge of Annett State Forest. The altar is made up of stones from each of the states, and chapels for various denominations are surrounded by gardens. The cathedral was established by Dr. and Mrs. Douglas Sloane as a memorial to their son who was killed in World War II.

U.S. 202 enters Massachusetts along the shore of Lake Monomonac, then passes through Winchendon and into more parkland along Lake Dennison, an Army Corps of Engineers project on the Otter River. After a short run as a freeway with Mass. 2, the road turns south again past Athol and becomes the Daniel Shays Highway. Between here and Holyoke, the road passes through the heartland of a farmers' rebellion that almost led the state to civil war in 1786 and convinced the propertied classes throughout the thirteen former colonies that a strong federal government and constitution were needed.

After the Revolutionary War, the Articles of Confederation were signed. This created a loose alliance among the former British colonies, who were reluctant to surrender any of their rights to a central authority. But a severe postwar depression rocked the country and the thirteen separate governments were powerless to fight it individually. In response, the merchants of Massachusetts, who controlled the legislature, pressed for immediate repayment of debts and taxes by the colony's western farmers.

Unable to pay and threatened with the loss of their land, the farmers, many of them veterans of the war, banded together under the leadership of Captain Shays. They forcefully broke up several courts that were hearing dispossession cases, threatened the arsenal at Springfield and planned to march on Worcester. The state militia was called out in Boston and easily dispersed the loosely organized bands. But the uprising sent a shiver of fear through the colonies. "I am mortified beyond expression when I view the clouds that have spread over the brightest morn to dawn in any country," wrote George Washington from his Virginia home when he heard the news.

Fourteen rebel leaders were tried and sentenced to death, but all were later pardoned. Within months, though, Congress had approved the Annapolis Report, calling for a Constitutional Convention. Captain Shays' uprising may have failed, but it led to far greater things. That's reason enough to have a highway named for you.

The road runs through heavily wooded country along the western edge of the gigantic Quabbin Reservoir, a main source of Boston's drinking water. Several towns in the area were inundated when it was built, and much of the land beneath its surface once belonged to Shays' rebels. Pelham was Captain Shays' home base. From there he managed to gather 1,900 men to march down this road to the Springfield Arsenal. The miltia eventually dispersed his ragged army near the town of Petersham, which now lies on the far side of the reservoir. After his pardon, Shays moved to New York and passed out of history.

You will find access to the reservoir for hiking and fishing just east of **Belchertown**. No swimming is permitted, much to the relief of the people of Boston. The Stone House in Belchertown was built in 1827 and contains a collection of period furniture and domestic decorations. Attached to it is a carriage museum, funded by a Henry Ford donation.

As the road swings west past the St. Hyacinth Franciscan Seminary and the town of Granby, the outline of Mount Tom rises on the western horizon. It is the principal landmark of this part of the

Connecticut River Valley. Across the river is **Holyoke**, another New England milltown that has discovered the rich legacy of its past. It was a planned community, with an intricate, triple-tiered series of canals harnessing the power of nearby Hadley Falls after 1848. Holyoke Heritage State Park has been assembled on 5 acres behind city hall on Appleton Street. The park offers a visitor's center and guided walks along the canals and through the red-brick mills whose turbines were powered by their waters.

This area was quite a sports laboratory in the 1890s. Springfield, to the south, was the birthplace of basketball in 1891 (see U.S. 20) at its YMCA. Not to be outdone, the Holyoke YMCA went out and invented its own game four years later, volleyball. It was called minonette at first, but after a while everyone realized it simply wouldn't do to have a sport that sounded like a small steak. So it became volleyball, and the sport's hall of fame is adjacent to the state park. If you are traveling with kids, you may want to visit the unusually well-designed childrens' museum in the area.

Many of the New England milltowns were heavily French-Canadian in character, but Holyoke is thoroughly Irish. Its St. Patrick's Day Parade, on the Sunday following March 17, is one of the country's largest, and a Celtic Festival is held the third weekend of every August.

The Skinner Silk Mills were one of Holyoke's biggest industries, and Wistariahurst, the mansion built by its owner, remains a civic showplace. It is a monument to turn-of-the-century sensibilities, with lots of Tiffany glass and leather wall coverings and rich parquet floors. There is also a museum of natural history on the property. It is located on the highway just west of downtown.

The road now dips sharply south again, passing through Westfield and into the narrow wedge of Massachusetts that jabs into Connecticut. This uneven boundary is the result of a pioneer surveyor's error. He placed the border 8 miles too far south. As compensation, Massachusetts gave Connecticut title to lands it owned in New Hampshire. Connecticut then sold these lands and used the proceeds to help establish Yale College. This did not mollify the towns along the border, most of which did not want to belong to Massachusetts. So a compromise was reached in 1804 with most of the towns reverting to Connecticut. The section traversed by U.S. 202 was the lone Bay State holdout.

The highway runs along the western edge of Talcott Mountain, the ridge that closes in Hartford and the Connecticut Valley from the west. The initial prosperity of **Simsbury**, the next town on your route, was based on copper smelting. The metal was discovered here as early as 1705 but had to be processed secretly to get around British prohibitions on such activity. When the first copper coins in the colonies were minted here by John Higley in 1737, the secret was out. Some of these coins are displayed at Massacoh Plantation, a complex of historic structures on Hopmeadow Street, one of the state's loveliest thoroughfares. It was named for the hops once grown there for local brewers. Now fine old homes line the way. Massacoh is built around an eighteenth-century mansion and includes a one-room schoolhouse, a tavern, a reproduction of the town's first meetinghouse and exhibits on a former local industry, making safety fuses.

At Weatogue, take a little side trip east on Conn. 185 to Talcott Mountain Park. From the crest, a lookout tower affords views across four states from the former estate of the Heublein family. The tower and estate were originally built by Richard Hoe, whose high-speed press revolutionized the newspaper industry. By permitting more papers to be printed in a shorter time, the Hoe rotary significantly narrowed the gap between the time an event occurred and when it could be reported to a mass readership.

Return to U.S. 202, which joins U.S. 44 at Avon and runs with it through Canton, then cuts away to pass the Nepaug Reservoir on the way to **Torrington**. Many Connecticut towns became identified with a particular metal and the products made from it. In Simsbury, as we have seen, it was copper. In Berlin, tin. In Meriden and Wallingford, silver. And in Torrington, it was brass. Israel Coe began making brass teakettles here in 1835, and the town soon became the country's leading producer of brassware. Needles were also an important part of the local economy. The Hotchkiss-Fyler House is Torrington's stateliest. Built in 1900, it contains original furnishings and is noted for its mahogany paneling and hand-painted walls and ceilings. The Hotchkiss fortune was not made in brass, however, but in munitions.

FOCUS

* * *

When you drive into **Litchfield**, you first think you have arrived in another of those museum villages that speckle New England. It looks so perfect, with broad streets and towering elms and fine homes and a spacious Green. It's as if a Disney planner had been signed up to create a new attraction—Connecticutland.

But Litchfield is quite real as well as extraordinarily beautiful. Some say it is the paradigm of the New England town, the place that comes closest to the image that rushes into our heads when someone says New England. Maybe it's all those famous names that give it a museum feeling. Ethan Allen was born here and so was Harriet Beecher Stowe. Aaron Burr studied law here and so did John Calhoun. Oliver Wolcott was a leading citizen and King George III . . . well, this is where he was melted. Or at least his statue was. On the other hand, maybe it was just planned this way. Litchfield's first settlers had to be approved on the basis of character before they were allowed to move in. That would elicit a perfect frenzy of Constitutional challenges today, but back in 1721 it seemed to work out satisfactorily. I don't know what became of those who were turned away. Went to Manhattan, probably.

The first school in the country devoted entirely to the study of law was started here by Tapping Reeve in 1784. He was Aaron Burr's brother-in-law, and through his doors trouped an astonishing assortment of more than a hundred future congressmen, fifteen governors, six cabinet members and three justices of the U.S. Supreme Court. The school was next door to Reeve's home, and both buildings still stand on South Street, one block from the Green. They are furnished in a style consistent with the period.

Right across the street is Oliver Wolcott's home. Built in 1753, it is one of the oldest in town. Wolcott was one of the signers of the Declaration of Independence, but an even more direct declaration was made in the yard of his house. After ecstatic patriots tore down the statue of George III that stood at New York City's Bowling Green, it was transported here. The lead was melted down and molded into some 40,000 bullets, which were soon returned to the king's loyal subjects.

Wolcott's son was a teenager when his home was turned into an impromptu munitions plant. Later in life, Oliver Wolcott, Jr., built his house just south of the law school. He succeeded Alexander Hamilton (his mentor and close friend) as secretary of the treasury, holding the post in the John Adams cabinet. Wolcott, while ostensibly serving Adams, did everything he could to undermine him. His release of confidential information enabled Hamilton to destroy Adams's bid for reelection in 1800. That vote wound up deadlocked between Thomas Jefferson and Aaron Burr in the Electoral College and was thrown into the House of Representatives. Hamilton disliked Jefferson on political principles but hated Burr personally. He threw Federalist Party support to Jefferson, securing Jefferson's election; an action that led to his fatal duel with Vice President Burr the following year. So the two former neighbors on South Street—Burr, the law student, and Wolcott, the son of the leading citizen—played major roles in this tragic drama. Wolcott later switched parties and was elected governor of Connecticut several times as a Jefferson Democrat.

Portraits of these early notables make up one of the permanent exhibits at the Litchfield Historical Society, at South Street and the Green. Here are the leading citizens of the eighteenth-century town—Wolcotts, Talmadges, Canfields—posed for the formal portraits that validated their importance. Most portraits carry the subject's dates of birth and death on the identifying plaque. In a portrait of a woman born in the 1760s, though, the date of death is blank. How strange that someone born into this sort of prominence should have dropped from sight so completely that no one would know the date of her passing.

Litchfield, after all, was in the forefront of the struggle for womens' rights. Judge Reeve was outspoken on their behalf. The country's first private academy for girls, Miss Pierce's, opened on North Street in 1792. One of the most illustrious women of her time, Harriet Beecher Stowe, was born just a few yards from the school in 1811. Her father, the Rev. Lyman Beecher, was pastor of the Congregational Church here from 1810 to 1826. The church still stands upon its eminence at the head of the Green. The Stowe house, however, has been replaced by an even older home, the Painter House, built in 1685 and moved there in 1959 after the Stowe residence was razed.

Most of Litchfield's old houses have the date of construction proudly displayed in front, and most of them seem to come with a good story or two attached. Col. Benjamin Talmadge's house, for example, is named for the man who was the head of colonial intelligence during the Revolution. He made the first positive identification of British spy Maj. John André after his capture, which led to André's execution shortly afterward. It must have been a poignant moment, because Talmadge had been a close friend of Nathan Hale, hanged as a spy by the British years before.

Anyplace you walk in Litchfield is a delight. All the best theme parks are built that way. Even the real ones.

* * *

Bantam is a Javanese word that has come to mean small or miniature in English. Which does not do much to explain why Connecticut's largest inland body of water is named Bantam Lake. The White Memorial Foundation, west of Litchfield along U.S. 202, occupies almost half the lake's shoreline as a wildlife conservation area. There are hiking trails, fishing and boating facilities and a visitor's center with displays on park wildlife.

Beyond the town of Bantam is Mount Tom State Park (not to be confused with Mount Tom back in Massachusetts), with a road to its summit and a lookout tower too. This is one of the few areas in Connecticut where wine grapes are cultivated. The oldest winery in the state, Haight Vineyards, is in the vicinity, but the most pleasantly situated is the Hopkins Vineyard, just north of **New Preston**, on Hopkins Road along Lake Waramaus. The vineyard boasts a tasting room, picnic area and gallery with arts and crafts exhibits.

Past New Preston, the road follows the Aspetuck River into **New Milford** through splendid hill country. This was the home of Roger Sherman, the only man to sign all four basic documents of America's foundation—the Articles of Association, Declaration of Independence, Articles of Confederation and Constitution. There, go win some trivia contests with that one. Apprenticed as a cobbler, his trade when he arrived in New Milford in 1743, Sherman studied law to improve his station. He eventually moved on to New Haven, where he was elected mayor. He played a critical role at the Constitutional Convention as a frequent speaker and advocate of the rights of the smaller states. His arguments helped win approval of the Connecticut Compromise, the formula that created a bicameral federal legislature with an upper house in which all states were represented equally. Years later, Jefferson pointed him out to a visitor with the comment, "There is Mr. Sherman of Connecticut, who never said a foolish thing in his life." Considering the source, it is hard to conceive of higher praise.

The New Milford Historical Society is located in the Knapp House, built on the Green in 1770. The exhibits celebrate local history. The Green is surrounded by an unusual number of fine brick homes, for which building materials were imported from England.

U.S. 202 joins U.S. 7 west of town and they run together into Danbury, where 202 turns west and links up with U.S. 6. They cross the New York state line in tandem and separate just east of Brewster.

Now the road weaves around the New York City reservoir system, along the perimeter of Amawalk Reservoir and past Franklin D. Roosevelt State Park, near Yorktown. As I mentioned, the route of U.S. 202 was put together with the intent of avoiding the large cities along the coast. That was also its original purpose in New York, although the reason was not so much speed as prudence. Occupation of New York City by the British during the Revolution made communication difficult between New England and the main body of the Continental Army. This was the road used to bypass Manhattan, crossing the Hudson in an area beyond effective British control, then filtering down to New Jersey through the passes of the Ramapo Mountains.

U.S. 202 makes the Hudson crossing at the Bear Mountain Bridge, north of Peekskill. It then runs south with U.S. 9W down the flank of Bear Mountain, overlooking the river (see U.S. 9). At Haverstraw, it turns southwest to run along the base of the Ramapos and snakes its way past the sprawling outposts of New York City suburbia just as travelers on this old road once crept stealthily past the outposts of the watchful British.

VISITING HOURS

MAINE

Lewiston: Bates College Museum, (207) 786-6158. East, off U.S. 202, on College St. Tuesday–Sunday, 1–4, all year. Free.

Monmouth: Village Museum, (207) 933-4444. South of U.S. 202, on Maine 132. Tuesday–Sunday, 1–4, July–Labor Day. Donation.

South Windham: Parson Smith House, (207) 227-3956. North, off U.S. 202, on River Rd. Tuesday, Thursday, and weekends, noon–5, July–Labor Day. Admission.

NEW HAMPSHIRE

Hillsboro: Pierce Homestead, (603) 495-3678. West of U.S. 202, on New Hampshire 9. Friday–Saturday, 10–5; Sunday, noon–5, Memorial Day–Labor Day. Admission.

Peterborough: Historical Museum, (603) 924-3235. West of U.S. 202, on Grove at Main St. Monday–Friday, 10–4, all year. Free.

West Rindge: Cathedral of the Pines, (603) 899-3300. East of U.S. 202, on New Hampshire 119. Daily, 9–4, May–October. Free.

MASSACHUSETTS

Belchertown: Stone House, (413) 323-7502. On U.S. 202, at 20 Maple St. Wednesday and Saturday, 2–5, mid-May–mid-October. Admission.

Holyoke: Heritage State Park, (413) 534-1723. South of U.S. 202, on Dwight St., behind City Hall. Tuesday–Sunday, 9–4:30, all year. Free.

Volleyball Hall of Fame and Children's Museum, (413) 536-5437. Adjacent to Heritage State Park, at 444 Dwight St. Tuesday–Saturday, 10–5; Sunday, noon–5, all year. Admission.

Wistariahurst, (413) 534-2216. On U.S. 202 (Beech St.) at Cabot St. Thursday–Saturday, 1–5. Closed last two weeks of August. Donation.

CONNECTICUT

Litchfield: Tapping Reeve Law School and Home, (203) 567-5862. South of the Green, on South St. Thursday–Monday, noon–4, mid-May–mid-October. Admission.

Historical Society, (203) 567-5862. On the Green. Tuesday–Saturday, 10–4, mid-April–mid-November. Donation.

New Milford: Knapp House, (203) 354-3069. Off U.S. 202, on Connecticut 67, at 6 Aspetuck Ave. Tuesday–Saturday, 1–4, April–October. Donation.

New Preston: Hopkins Vineyard, (203) 868-7954. North from U.S. 202 on Connecticut 45, on Lake Wamaus. Daily, May–December, 11–5; weekends only, at other times. Free.

Simsbury: Massacoh Plantation, (203) 628-2500. On U.S. 202 (Hopmeadow St.). Daily, 1–4, May–October. Admission.

Torrington: Hotchkiss-Fyler House, (203) 482-8260. Off U.S. 202, at 192 Main St. Monday–Friday, 9–4; Saturday, 10–3, all year. Free.

U. S. ROUTE 209

MAINE

VERMONT

NEW HAMPSHIRE

NEW YORK

MASSACHUSETTS

Hurley · Kingston
Ellenville · CONNECTICUT
Port Jervis · RHODE ISLAND

Ronan

Delaware-Hudson Canal

U.S. 209

Kingston to Port Jervis, N.Y.
*   *55 miles*

This is the overland link between three of the great rivers of the East. It starts at the Hudson, runs along the canal that once connected that river to the Delaware, then cuts across Pennsylvania to end up at the Susquehanna. The portion that concerns us runs only a few miles, through lovely scenery along the edge of the Catskills.

* MILEPOSTS *

For two months in 1777, history came to **Hurley**. The British had swarmed up the Hudson from Manhattan in the fall and by October were ready to move on the temporary state capital at Kingston. When Kingston went up in flames, the government quickly retreated inland from the river, and tiny Hurley was temporarily the capital of New York—long enough for the senate to meet a few times and for a British spy to be captured and hanged. The government then departed for Poughkeepsie, leaving Hurley pretty much as it found it.

The town started life as Nieuw Dorp, a Dutch name for a very Dutch village. It was settled by families from Kingston in 1661 and changed its name shortly afterward to honor the new British governor, Francis Lovelace, Baron Hurley, of Ireland. For the next century, the town's leading families—Van Dusens, Elmendorfs, Houghtalings—built their stone houses along the main street. They were joined by some Huguenot families, the Beviers and DuMonds. The names of the occupants have changed, but their houses are still there, the largest concentration of stone houses in the country. Most of them open on Stone House Day, the second Saturday in July.

Every one of these old stone houses comes with a story attached. The state government set up its offices in the Van Dusen House, the biggest in town, built in 1723. The Elmendorf House up the street was in operation then as the Half Moon Tavern. It's the oldest building in Hurley, dating from the late seventeenth century. The Polly Crispell House, across the way, has an iron spike in its chimney to fend off witches. The DuMond House is now called the Guard House, because it was here that the spy Lt. Daniel Taylor was imprisoned before being hanged on an apple tree nearby. Many of the owners whose names identify the homes lie in the old graveyard, at the end of the footpath between the Guard House and the Crispell Cottage.

There are even more old houses on the outlying roads. At the Mattys Ten Eyck House, the owner saluted George Washington with an endless welcoming address as the poor general stood in a downpour and Ten Eyck stood dry in the shelter of his front porch. It is believed that the antislavery crusader Sojourner Truth lived for a time in the Gerardus Hardenberg House when she was a child and herself a slave.

There are convenient walking maps of Hurley in the town library, in the middle of the stone house district. A short ride away is Hurley Patentee Manor, a mid-eighteenth-century English country mansion grafted onto a Dutch cottage from 1696. Many furnishings and decorations are original.

Like the other towns along this route, Hurley enjoyed a brief spurt of prosperity when the Delaware and Hudson Canal opened in 1828. Bluestone was quarried in the area and taken by barge to Kingston, then a leading cement manufacturer. Around the turn of the century, this variety was supplanted by the faster-drying Portland cement, and the canal was shut down permanently in 1899.

The canal and U.S. 209 pass through a natural gap between the Catskills on the west and the Shawangunk Mountains to the east. This is the closest the Delaware River comes to the Hudson. A pair of brothers from Philadelphia, William and Maurice Wurts, came up with the idea of building a canal through this gap to carry anthracite coal inexpensively from the mines of northeastern Pennsylvania to the markets of New York and New England.

The road is two-lane all the way, a bit slow in summer when traffic to the big Catskill resorts is at its peak. At other times, though, it is a delight to drive, with perspectives on the ridges that enclose the valley changing with the miles and time of day.

Accord is a town whose name was imposed on it by the U.S. Post Office. The residents couldn't agree on a name so they suggested Discord. That didn't sound right to postal authorities, so they amended it to this more amiable sentiment.

Ellenville is a major resort crossroads. Many of the biggest hotel complexes lie west of here, but along this road is the Nevele, a typically sprawling facility, which aspires to be all things to all vacationers. The Catskills have long been celebrated in books and movies (such as *Dirty Dancing*) as a playground for the Jewish population of New York City. Many of the big names in show business got their starts here in "the Borscht Belt." (Some of the towns along this route have substantial Jewish populations year-round. Before World War II this was the only significant rural Jewish population in the country.) Many of the big resorts have gone the condominium route, but some of the old standbys survive, looking just like a set from *Marjorie Morningstar*. Ellenville has more recently become noted as a center for the sport of hang gliding, since the valley creates nearly perfect wind conditions for engineless flight. The town really takes off in June and October when glider enthusiasts hold some of the best-attended fly-ins in the country.

Wurtsboro, named after the brothers who built the canal, has preserved a portion of the old town adjacent to the waterway. Canal Towne Emporium, east of the highway, is a restored country store with many antiques for sale.

The town of Cuddibacksville turned a surviving portion of the original canal into a historical park with a museum and waterside demonstrations. Drive through town to the Neversink River bridge and turn right before crossing on Hoag Road to reach the area.

At Port Jervis, named for the canal's chief engineer, the road reaches the Delaware and crosses into Pennsylvania and out of our reach.

VISITING HOURS

NEW YORK

Cuddibacksville: Delaware and Hudson Canal Museum, (914) 754-8870. West on Hoag Road, from the north end of the Neversink River bridge. Wednesday–Sunday, 10–4, all year. Admission.

Hurley: Patentee Manor, (914) 331-5414. Off U.S. 209, on county road 29. Tuesday–Sunday, July–Labor Day, 11–5. Donation.

U. S. ROUTE 219

MAINE

Ronan

VERMONT

NEW
HAMPSHIRE

NEW YORK

MASSACHUSETTS

Hamburg

Ellicottville
Salamanca

CONNECTICUT

RHODE ISLAND

Into the Alleghenies

U.S. 219

Hamburg to Salamanca, N.Y.
* 63 miles

This becomes one of the great mountain roads in the East, running through the heart of the Appalachians in Pennsylvania, Maryland and West Virginia. But in this brief introduction, U.S. 219 never gets much higher than hill level. It begins in the southern outskirts of Buffalo and makes its way past the Seneca Indian Reservation and Allegany State Park before darting into Pennsylvania.

* MILEPOSTS *

In its current incarnation, U.S. 219 begins its journey as a freeway, carrying traffic from central Buffalo to its rapidly growing southern suburbs. It wasn't always that way. On its original route, the road started in the town of Hamburg, and that's where we'll start now. This former route is now numbered N.Y. 391. Take it east from the middle of town, past the interchange with the present U.S. 219 and then along a parallel course with the freeway, south toward North Boston.

The area is called the Boston Valley, and one tavern in the vicinity calls itself Boston Gardens, after the sports arena in the Massachusetts city. It makes you wonder which hockey team the patrons root for when the Buffalo Sabres play the Boston Bruins. The back road cuts through pleasantly scenic countryside. At Springville, The Heart of Rural America according to the sign, it bends back west to link up with current U.S. 219, free at last of its freeway shackles.

At Ashford Hollow, several Buffalo-area artists have combined to create the Griffis Sculpture Park, a 400-acre facility displaying an assortment of abstract steel, aluminum and bronze figures.

Ellicottville is, somewhat surprisingly, a ski resort, with lifts right in town and arcaded sidewalks along the main street. The slopes of Holiday Valley resort are just outside of town. The collection of nicely preserved nineteenth-century buildings here includes a town hall listed on the National Register of Historic Places.

The town was named for Joseph E. Ellicott, head surveyor of the Holland Land Company, which controlled most of the area in the early nineteenth century. The company, based in The Netherlands, gained control of the land from Philadelphia financier Robert Morris. He bought the property after the Revolution, when loans he had made to the colonial cause were repaid.

In extinguishing the last Indian claims to the territory in the Big Tree Treaty of 1797, Morris was dealing with the Seneca, the last remaining members of the old Iroquois Confederacy. The Iroquois' long-standing enmity toward France had driven them into an alliance with Britain, an arrangement that continued into the Revolution. The tribes looked to Britain as a bulwark to stop the white tide of settlement advancing on their western lands. Instead, the alliance destroyed them. Enraged by Tory raids on eastern New York and Pennsylvania, the colonials sent out the Sullivan-Clinton expedition to the Iroquois heartland in the summer of 1779. It was a deliberate campaign of destruction and devastation; the colonials torched the villages they captured and scorched the earth when they left. At war's end, most of the remaining Iroquois joined the British withdrawal into Ontario.

Worse than defeat, though, was the onrush of new settlers who had seen the rich land as soldiers and came back for it at war's end. By the time of the Big Tree Treaty, the Seneca had no recourse but to sign the land away and make the best possible deal.

They were the strongest member of the Iroquois, the Keepers of the Western Door. From their original home around Lake Seneca and the Genesee Valley, they had expanded to take control of southwestern New York. They could put 1,000 warriors into the field, as many as the rest of the Iroquois combined. They also suffered the greatest losses in the Sullivan campaign. Big Tree reduced their holdings to a dozen reservations. The Holland Company sold off preemption rights to the reservation lands in 1810 and the new owner, David A. Ogden, moved immediately to seize them. The twelve reservations were cut down to four. The same number exist today. The largest is the Allegany, surrounding the town of Salamanca. By 1838, even this land was lost, as corrupt chiefs readily accepted payoffs from speculators. But the tribe managed to win a renegotiation four years later in court and reclaimed title to the Allegany tract. Disgusted with the actions of their chiefs, the Seneca discarded the traditional tribal government in 1848 and formed an elective republic. They have maintained that form of government and now have a population of about 6,000.

Because of all the land switches, **Salamanca** wound up as the only American town located within an Indian reservation. The Seneca-Iroquois Museum, on the western edge of Salamanca along N.Y. 17, gives you a small glimpse of the rich history and artistic legacy of this people. There is a traditional bark longhouse here, as well as contemporary artwork by residents of the reservation. Across the road, at American Indian Crafts, visitors can see beadwork being made and purchase samples.

The road now follows the outline of the reservation around the great bend of the Allegheny River as it flows past Allegany State Park. This 65,000-acre area of rolling hills and streams is a complete recreation grounds. There are scenic drives within the park, ski trails, hunting and fishing, boating and campgrounds. It is exceeded in size in New York only by the vast Adirondack and Catskill preserves.

The town of Limestone was part of the oil boom that spread north from the Pennsylvania fields after the Civil War, and the first commercial well in the state was sunk nearby. From here the road dips south into Pennsylvania and out of this book.

VISITING HOURS

NEW YORK

Salamanca. Iroquois Nation Museum, (716) 945-1738. West of U.S. 219, on New York 17 at Broad St. Extension. Monday–Saturday, 10–5; Sunday, noon–5, May–September. Closed Monday, at other times. Donation.

American Indian Crafts, (716) 945-1225. West of U.S. 219, at 719 Broad St. Daily, 10–5, all year. Free.

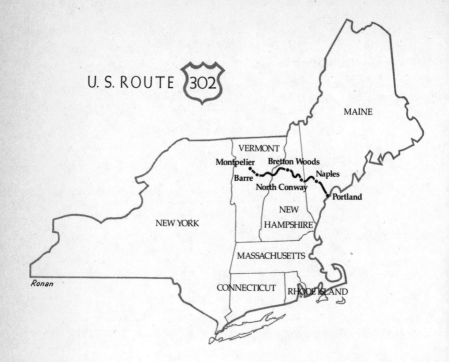

U. S. ROUTE 302

MAINE

VERMONT

Montpelier   Bretton Woods
                                    Naples
Barre   North Conway
                                    Portland

NEW YORK   NEW
                   HAMPSHIRE

                MASSACHUSETTS

Ronan   CONNECTICUT   RHODE ISLAND

To the Roof of New England

U.S. 302

Portland, Maine, to Barre, Vt.
*   *172 miles*

The White Mountains had been glimpsed from afar since the earliest explorations of the northern New England coast. The Cabots saw them on their voyage of 1497, and Samuel de Champlain reported spying high peaks in the distance as he sailed Casco Bay in 1604. But another forty years went by before someone managed to reach Mount Washington, and not until 1771 was Crawford Notch, the pass that opened a new route to the north, discovered.

U.S. 302 is the direct road from the sea to the mountains, the overland route from Portland through Crawford Notch, along the path of the Tenth New Hampshire Turnpike. It passes through magnificent resort areas in Maine and New Hampshire, winds around the base of the highest mountain in the East, then makes its way into the heart of Vermont's granite country. The road can be a bit congested during the peak summer and autumn travel seasons, but it is filled with enough scenery to hold your attention.

* **MILEPOSTS** *

Begin at Forest Avenue, near the Back Cove district of Portland.
The road runs past pleasant residential areas and Baxter Woods
park and quickly makes its way into the countryside near the
mouth of Highland Lake. Once past North Windham, it enters
the Sebago Lake resort area. At 46 square miles, this is the
second-largest inland body of water in Maine, and its proximity
to Portland makes it a popular vacation ground. Its hill-rimmed
surroundings, opening out on occasional glimpses of the White
Mountains, which rise like distant dreams, make the lake a
worthwhile goal.

Nathaniel Hawthorne was brought to Raymond, on the lake's
eastern shore, as a child. His uncle owned a store in Raymond and
built a home for his widowed sister and her eight-year-old son in
1812. It's easy to see how Hawthorne's lifelong fascination with
the White Mountains began here, for the views of the peaks from
Raymond are full of mystery and delight. He later wrote that it
was here "I first got my cursed habit of solitude."

Just past South Casco is the turnoff to Songo Lock and Sebago
Lake State Park. The lock, built in 1830, was part of the old
Cumberland and Oxford Canal, which permitted boat passage
from Portland, through Sebago Lake, all the way up to the head
of Long Lake. Steamboats once made regularly scheduled calls
along this route, and the lock gave them access between the two
lakes. The state park is at the mouth of the Songo River as it
empties into Sebago Lake. It includes 1,300 acres of recreational
facilities, including excellent beaches.

U.S. 302 becomes a causeway as it enters **Naples**, running between Brandy Pond and Long Lake. To the romantics of the early
nineteenth century, Italy's Bay of Naples was the epitome of
scenic splendor. So it took a bit of nerve for this little town in
Maine to call the water it perched upon the Bay of Naples and set
itself up for invidious comparisons. But few have been made. This
Naples, in fact, doesn't come off too badly. The *Songo River Queen*
offers scenic boat rides, which leave from the causeway area, and
rides aboard float planes are available as well.

For an exceptional view of the entire area, continue through the town of Bridgton to Pleasant Mountain. This is a ski resort, and the chairlift here ascends to the 2,000-foot level for a look across the lakes, extending to the peaks to the north.

Young Hawthorne wasn't the only one the sight of those ever-closer mountains set dreaming. They also had their effect on Clarence Mulford, who lived in Fryeburg. But his thoughts turned toward the mountains of the West and led him to create the character who became television's first cowboy hero, Hopalong Cassidy. The local library has an exhibit on Hoppy's author, including his gun collection. Fryeburg was also home for a while to Daniel Webster, who served as a tutor at the local academy in 1802. You'll find an old covered bridge across the Saco River, just off the highway here. The road then passes the local landmark of Jockey Cap, a distinctively shaped hill above the river valley, which has pleasant hiking trails to its crest.

Webster is most closely associated with New Hampshire, and that neighboring state is practically out Fryeburg's back door. Here the road becomes the Theodore Roosevelt Highway (not to be confused with Vermont's Theodore Roosevelt Highway, which is U.S. 2) to honor the conservationist president, whose policies helped preserve the country's natural wonders at a time when economic pressures were threatening to destroy them. The road swings up through Redstone, named for its old granite deposits, and in **North Conway** it comes to one of the scenic areas that so moved the wilderness-lovers of Roosevelt's time.

When Benjamin Champney arrived in North Conway in the 1850s, the story goes, he was so taken with the bang-on view of Mount Washington that he set up his easel right in the middle of the street and started to paint. Reproductions of the works of Champney, and a score of imitators, hung in homes throughout the country in the late nineteenth century. Those chromo prints made the views of the mountains from North Conway among the best-known landscapes in the country and helped mobilize public sentiment behind the conservationists. Champney later boasted that he had made this region as famous as the Barbizon School of France had made Fontainbleu. Some of Champney's works even hung for a time in Windsor Castle, where they were taken by one of his admirers, King Edward VII.

One of the beauty spots in the area is White Horse Cliff in Echo Lake State Park. Hopeful young women began coming here in Victorian times in the belief that if they gazed at the ledge, shut their eyes and counted to 100, the first man they saw when they opened up again would be their husband. I only mention this out of historical interest. No contemporary woman would keep her eyes closed that long. You can ride the ski lift to Mount Cranmore for some grand views and take a pleasant train ride through the Saco Valley aboard the Conway Scenic Railroad. These trips leave from the depot on Main Street.

This is a picturesque area with a large concentration of Victorian inns and dining places, but it is also highly developed commercially, especially around the town of Glen, one of the major intersections in the White Mountains area. N.H. 16 continues north from here through Pinkham Notch, while U.S. 302 swings off to the west to approach Crawford Notch along the gap cut by the Saco River. Once past Bartlett, which is entirely surrounded by mountains, the road begins to enter the notch itself.

Credit for the discovery of Crawford Notch is given to a hunter, Timothy Nash, who saw it after climbing a tree while chasing a moose. A permanent road wasn't built for another thirty years, but Nash was promised a land grant if he could get a horse through the pass he'd found. He did it, but only by transporting the poor animal up and down the cliffsides with ropes. Discovery of this notch at the southern edge of the Presidential Range opened up the New Hampshire north by making it more accessible from the coast. But it isn't known as Nash Notch, because the Crawford family, who opened the first hostelries in the area around 1820, became the best-known local figures to early travelers along this road (then called the Tenth New Hampshire Turnpike).

The road is filled with stories. As it swings north near Harts Location, the wooded slopes of Mount Nancy dominate the western view. The 3,810-foot peak is named, so they say, for a young woman who froze to death in 1778 while pursuing a false lover through the notch. (Maybe she had opened her eyes too soon back at White Horse Ledge.)

A few miles farther on is the Willey House, the best-known place in the notch. Like another local landmark, the Old Man of the Mountains, the Willey House was the subject of a Hawthorne short story. The story tells about the night of August 29, 1826, when the side of the adjacent mountain gave way in a heavy rainstorm and came tumbling into the valley. The seven members of the Samuel Willey family and their two hired hands rushed out of the house to get away. At the last moment, the great rocks divided and missed the house entirely, but they buried the people who had left it. Hawthorne told the story in "The Ambitious Guest," and it remains one of the most haunting tales of the mountains.

Just beyond the Willey House on the highway are two waterfalls: Silver Cascade, which tumbles 1,000 feet down the side of Webster Mountain, and the Flume, which falls 250 feet.

FOCUS
* * *

Mount Washington isn't even half as high as many of the peaks in the Rockies and the Sierra Nevadas. It is less than one-third the elevation of Alaska's Mount McKinley, the highest mountain in the country. Mount Mitchell in North Carolina outstrips it among the peaks east of the Mississippi. An auto road reaches its summit, and so does a railroad.

But Mount Washington stands alone as a place of rugged solitude. The country's western peaks begin their ascent from much higher above sea level, so in the sheer uplift of mass from the surface, Washington is their match. It is also about 260 million years older. The highest winds ever measured on this planet were clocked on its peak. On April 12, 1934, they reached 231 miles an hour, or more than 100 miles an hour harder than the worst hurricanes. So severe is the climate near its 6,288-foot summit that the timberline stops at 4,000 feet above sea level—about 6,000 feet lower than in most of the Rockies. Its climate is Arctic.

It snows there every month of the year, and the temperature at its summit has never registered as high as 75 degrees. According to one local legend, a weather observer stepping outside the summit's weather station during a windstorm was flattened against the wall of the building and had to be dragged inside and pounded back into shape with mallets. That only sounds far-fetched to people who have never felt that wind.

It is less than 100 miles from the sea, and the first North American explorers caught glimpses of it from the coast. Darby Field, of Exeter, New Hampshire, is credited with being the first man crazy enough to climb it, back in 1642. But even after being reached, explored, climbed and, after a fashion, tamed, it continues to exert a strong attraction. Visitors are drawn by its natural beauty, the facilities that have been built around it, the sheer force of its legend and history. By the time of the Civil War, the first crude inns founded by the Crawford family had been replaced by expansive resort hotels. In those years, as the railroad came through and made this once remote area accessible to everyone, as many as fifty trains a day stopped at the local station. The two most vivid reminders of that era are the Mount Washington Hotel at the mountain's base and the Cog Railroad that makes the trip to its summit.

Seen from U.S. 302, the hotel looks like a huge, white ocean liner. Opened in 1902, with the outline of the mountain rising directly behind it, the Mount Washington Hotel is a tourist attraction in its own right. Visitors are charged an entry fee to make the curving, 1-mile drive from the gate at the highway to its portals and to walk inside. This is the largest wooden building in New England, the culmination of the age of grand hotels.

In the excitement that followed the discovery of Crawford Notch, New Hampshire's governor, Benning Wentworth, decided to name the area at its northern end after his own ancestral home, Bretton Hall, in Yorkshire. The local post office is still known as **Bretton Woods**. Industrialist Joseph Stickney bought the site then occupied by an older hotel called the Mount Pleasant, tore it down and, two years and one million dollars later, completed this one. An entire wall just off the hotel's main lobby is devoted to blown-up photographs of the hotel's construction and development.

The best-known part of the hotel is the Gold Room. This is where meetings were held during the 1944 monetary conference that for a time turned Bretton Woods into an international dateline. This conclave made plans for the rebuilding of the world economy after World War II, establishing the gold standard and the U.S. dollar as the foundation of the new era. The room is maintained as a museum. The same cannot be said of the hotel. It may be a bit stuffy in its dress code, jackets at dinner and the like, but it has kept pace with changing demands in resort facilities, while operating within the structure of its Edwardian home.

A few miles west of the hotel is the turnoff to the Mount Washington Cog Railway. The indomitable Crawfords blazed the first hiking trail to the mountain's summit, and Ethan Allen Crawford, the son of the hotel's founder, located a shorter route in 1821. Accompanied by two young ladies and his father, who walked with the aid of a cane, they all traipsed to the top. This eventually became a bridle trail and is essentially the route followed by the cog railroad. (A carriage trail to the peak from the eastern approach was opened in 1861, and this developed into an automobile road, but access is from N.H. 16 on the far side of the mountain and is outside the range of this book.)

The developer of the railway was Sylvester Marsh, who had made a fortune as a Chicago meatpacker but was born a New Hampshireman and frequently visited his home state. On a trip in 1852 he hiked to Mount Washington's summit and was trapped at the top by a sudden change in the weather. He didn't like that a bit, and decided there had to be a better way. It's hard to say no to a Chicago meatpacker. When he determined to build a railroad to the top, the idea was met with the appropriate ridicule. When he applied for a charter from the state legislature, it was suggested that he also be given a charter to build a railroad to the moon.

Everyone thought that gravity alone would defeat him—the run was simply too steep, and any train trying the ascent should slide backward. But Marsh geared the railroad to the mountain by developing a cogged wheel for the locomotive that fitted into the rails, enabling the train to pull itself along. When a demonstration of this principle was given, officials of the Boston, Concord and Montreal Railroad gave it the needed financial boost, and on July 3, 1869, the first run to the top was made. It remains the world's steepest rail line—at the Jacob's Ladder trestle it climbs a 37 percent grade—and it probably runs through the world's worst weather. Even in midsummer, winds of 70 miles an hour and ice along the tracks have closed it down briefly. The round trip in the coal-powered train takes about 3 hours.

The Sherman Adams Summit Building offers a refuge from the elements at the peak and views that can sometimes extend for 130 miles. There is also a museum containing exhibits on the strange phenomena associated with the summit. A hotel that once operated here was torn down several years ago, so once you take a look around, the only thing left to do is board the train for the ride back down.

* * *

The road heads west through Twin Mountain to the little town of Bethlehem, which became a resort under the most serendipitous of circumstances. A group of travelers were injured in a coaching accident nearby and came to this town to recuperate. The experience was so enjoyable that the resulting word of mouth turned Bethlehem into a major White Mountain retreat. It was also known as a refuge from hay fever. Henry Ward Beecher, the famed Brooklyn minister of the nineteenth century, spent his summers here and helped popularize the place. The town is on the slope of Mount Agassiz.

Littleton, on the falls of the Ammonoosuc River, has a pleasant outlook on the nearby mountains, which seems to have given it a corresponding outlook on life. In the late nineteenth century, it was the center of the booming stereoptican industry. That staple of home entertainment was a standard feature in most American parlors before the time of movies and the mass media. The Kilburn Brothers did their best to keep the country supplied with the device's double-imaged photographs from their factory here. The town was also the birthplace of Eleanor H. Porter, who wrote the

Pollyanna books. The happy heroine of those tales became the very synonym for a sunny disposition. The town is still a cheery enough place, as a resort base for nearby Moore Reservoir on the Connecticut River.

The road now bends south to run along with the Ammonoosuc. A short-lived gold boom once enlivened the Lisbon area. The strike was made in 1864 and about fifty thousand dollars worth of gold was taken out of the ground, but more than a million dollars was invested in the mines and you'll never get rich with that sort of return. Bath is another pleasant old town, laid out on terraces above the river, with many colonial-era houses and one of the longest covered bridges in the state, at 392 feet.

At Woodsville, the highway crosses the Connecticut River into Vermont. The highway picks up the Wells River at the town of the same name and begins following it west. Wells River was the head of navigation on the Connecticut into the 1830s, and the route of U.S. 302, over the old Hazen-Bayley Military Road to Canada, was the primary path for overland travelers headed to northern Vermont.

Here the road is known as the William Scott Memorial Highway. Scott was the Union Army sentry who fell asleep at his post, was sentenced to death and was personally pardoned by President Lincoln. He died gallantly at the Battle of Lee's Mills in April 1862. The road is named for him because the nearby town of Groton was his birthplace. There is a monument to him just past West Groton.

U.S. 302 now dips south, around the base of Signal Mountain and Butterfield Mountain and the Groton State Forest, through a sparsely settled, very scenic part of the state.

Barre is called the Granite Capital, and this area produces some of the world's most highly prized monumental stone. Barre's Hope Cemetery, on Merchant Street north of downtown, is a showplace for the craftspeople who work with the local stone, and many of the memorials here were designed as tributes to deceased granite workers by their peers. The area attracted many workers of Scottish descent, and the granite statue of Robert Burns on the lawn of the high school, above City Park, is another local treasure. It was designed by J. Massey Rhind, who died before he could cut the stone. *Youth Triumphant,* an Armistice Day memorial erected in City Park in 1924, is another fine local monument.

Granite was first discovered here on Millstone Hill shortly after the War of 1812. Stone for the statehouse in nearby Montpelier was quarried here. But when the railroad reached the area, it touched off Barre's biggest growth spurt and the city tripled in size from 1880 to 1890. Many of the buildings along North Main Street (noted for the use of granite in their detail) are part of a historic district. There is a lovely restored opera house in the City Hall, and on the second floor of the Aldrich Public Library you'll find the Barre Museum, with exhibits on local history.

The world's largest granite quarry, Rock of Ages, is south of Barre by way of Vt. 14, in **Graniteville**. There are train tours of the sprawling 27-acre site, and craftsworkers demonstrate their techniques.

From the center of Barre, the highway continues northwest for a few miles to its end at the junction with U.S. 2 on the outskirts of Montpelier.

VISITING HOURS

MAINE

Bridgton: Pleasant Mountain Ski Lift, (207) 647-8444. West on U.S. 302. Call for hours and rates.

Fryeburg: Clarence Mulford Exhibit, (207) 935-2731. On U.S. 302, in Public Library, at 98 Main St. Tuesday–Thursday and Saturday, 10–5; Friday, 5–8, all year. Free.

Naples: Sebago Lake Cruises, (207) 693-6861. South, on U.S. 302, from the causeway. Call for schedule and fares.

NEW HAMPSHIRE

Bretton Woods: Mt. Washington Cog Railway, (603) 846-5404. West on U.S. 302. Daily, mid-May–mid-October. Call for schedule and rates.

North Conway: Scenic Railroad, (603) 356-5251. Leave from depot on Main St. Daily, mid-June–late October; weekends only, May and early June. Call for schedule and rates.
   Mt. Cranmore Tramway, (603) 356-5544. North, on U.S. 302. Daily, 9–5:30, late June–mid-October; weekends only, after Memorial Day. Admission.

VERMONT

Barre: Museum, (802) 476-7550. On U.S. 302, in Aldrich Public Library. Thursday and Friday, noon–6; Saturday, 10–1, all year. Free.

Graniteville: Rock of Ages Quarry, (807) 476-3115. South of U.S. 302, on Vermont 14. Daily, 8:30–5, May–October. Free. Train tour, Monday–Friday, 9:30–3:30, June–mid-October. Fare charged.

Index